To
Megan
Enjoy this
Youthful Tale
Dorothy Ralphs
8/27/2016

My Africa

SUNSHINE *and* HAILSTONES

Coming of Age in 1950s South Africa

Dorothy Ralphs

Edited by Martha Fuller
Layout and design by Sharon E Rawlins

Cover Photo:
Checking out the Zulu Basket Sellers
(Center Row) Dorothy and Jane (Back Row) Sheila and Sally

d.ralphs@me.com
sunshineandhailstones.com

ISBN 978-0-692-73321-9

Printed in the United States of America

❖

❖

❖ CONTENTS ❖

❖

ACKNOWLEDGEMENT

Seven years ago in 2009 I decided to take a writing class. I found Martha Fuller at the University of California, Irvine. Over the years I wrote vignettes and stories of my childhood memories. Gradually I learned more and more about the craft of writing and came to develop an enormous appreciation for the sessions with Martha every Thursday. She encouraged me to create a coming of age memoir and weave in vintage photographs to bring my experiences in South Africa to life. Not only did I have her enthusiasm for my stories, but her creativity, sharp editing skills and continuous guidance to see it to completion. I cannot thank her enough.

❖

❖ FORWARD ❖

In 1913, the Union of South Africa government legislated the Native Land Act, which earmarked 10% of the land available to blacks, or natives, as they became commonly known, and 90% for whites. This Act formed the cornerstone for legal separation of the races.

By the time I was born in 1938, South Africa was fully segregated. As a child I only saw natives living in rural areas, usually in primitive thatched huts. When they began seeking work in the cities, as domestic help and gardeners, their employers provided housing for them in segregated quarters. They were separated in every way, on the buses, trains and even shopping.

In 1940, my father went away to fight against the Germans in World War ll. 334,000 South Africans volunteered for full time military service. In 1942, Field Marshal Rommel captured 10,000 South African prisoners during the fall of Tobruk in Libya. Luckily my father was not captured as he got tick bite fever and was sent to a hospital in Cairo to recover.

When the war ended, South Africa held an election. General Smuts, the wartime Prime Minister of South Africa and the only non-British advisor to Winston Churchill, represented the United Party. The Afrikaners National Party ran against him. Afraid of losing control, many English speaking citizens and the majority of Afrikaners who were against blacks having any voting rights, as they outnumbered the white population 20:1, voted for the Nationalist Party.

In 1948, the Nationalist Party won an overwhelming victory. Smuts was out and D.F. Malan became Prime Minister. Serious implementation of Apartheid began. Stringent pass laws severely restricting the movement of non-whites were enforced. Drinking rules and curfews were established and job discrimination laws were enacted. Only whites or Indians could drive buses and taxis, and protest gatherings were limited to small numbers. The government built townships far out of town for the growing native population in cities, making it more difficult for them to get to and from work. They began striking for better transportation and to be allowed to drive taxis.

In the 1950s, my mother (and some whites) became active against the rise of enforced segregation. She regularly stood on the steps of the Town Hall with other women wearing a black sash across their chests. They were often booed by passing whites. When I left South Africa in 1958, only about 250,000 of approximately five million whites were actively protesting government actions.

❖ PROLOGUE ❖

Darkness descends quickly in the South African bush. We spend the last hour of light in the midst of a pride of nine female lions. Spread out in small groups they lie in wait as an impala buck, unaware of impending danger, crosses their path. Opportunists at heart, the lions lay immobile and patient. Every now and then they creep along the ground inch by inch, never taking their eyes off the prey. Six of us sit in the Land Rover, the engine stilled, watching. In the twenty years I lived in Africa, I never witnessed a lion kill. I'm not sure I want to now.

Up ahead the agile young buck trots directly in the lions' view. The buck has broken from the herd of young males hoping to take over a female herd nearby. With his desire triggered by the rut or mating season, he focuses on taking over another male guarding his female herd. I hold my breath as three lions move closer to the buck. Two stalk away to cut off his escape. With such a large pride, the buck doesn't stand much of a chance. I hardly breathe. The kill looks inevitable. I clutch the safety bar as our guide whispers what is about to happen. I dread the moment.

We hear the dominant male impala uttering an array of noisy grunts as he aggressively protects his female herd. The young buck intent on stealing the small female herd appears unaware of the danger. Secretly, I hope he will get away. The lions inch closer and closer, ready to spring. The piercing screech of a vervet monkey breaks the silence. Spotting the lions, the monkey swings from branch to branch shrieking his warning. The impala stiffens, his head erect, ears standing on end. He springs to life, leaps ten feet into the air and sprints away into the Mopani trees, barely escaping death.

"Oh, wow that was tense!" I let go of the cross bar. "I'm glad he got away."

"No man, we've come a long way to see this," says the tourist in the back. "I wish we could have seen the kill." For many, to see a kill is the ultimate reward for a visit to the South African bush.

"I think it's time to head back to camp," says the ranger. He turns the key, the engine roars to life and we turn around towards the road. I watch the Mopani trees silhouetted stark and black against the bright red sky just as the sun sets behind the Drakensberg Mountains. We trundle along swinging and swaying, our spotter lighting the way ahead. Narrower than most of the roads leading to camp, we rock along on the unfamiliar trail. I can't see where we are going. The last four nights when the sun went down and nighttime enveloped the land, we headed back to camp the same way. "Are we on the right road back to camp? It doesn't feel the same." The Land Rover bumps along tossing us about. I grip the safety bar tightly.

Our ranger concentrates on the driving. He points to an owl in the trees and the various sounds of the hot African night.

"I see lights in the bushes," I say. "What's happening?" He doesn't answer. Danger? I cling to Boris as there have been a lot of elephants around that day and they are hard to see in the dark.

As we get nearer to the lights I can make out a large square box dangling by a rope from the trees. Our ranger pulls up next to the box, the surrounding trees lit with hurricane lamps.

Everyone screams at once. "Happy 56th Anniversary!" The spotter jumps off the truck, opens a flap and shines his light inside the container to reveal six glasses and a cold bottle of champagne in a silver ice bucket. Astounded, Boris and I stand together in the balmy night air and watch as the champagne flows. "Cheers!" Everyone holds up their glasses in the twinkling light and takes a long sip.

After all these years we are back in the place of my birth, in the land we both love so much, celebrating our long happy life together. With our new friends we clink our glasses and kiss sweetly. We have come full circle.

❖

My grandmother Lillian Crawford, Granny, went out to Kenya in 1909 to marry Mr. Lindsay. They lived in Mombasa until one day Mr. Lindsay disappeared and never returned. After a year Granny, Mom (Connie age fifteen) and her sister, Aunt Dorothy, left Kenya and moved to South Africa. Granny met Mr. Lewis, a local businessman in Durban, and married him.

Granny, Aunt Dorothy, Mom

Mr. Lewis with Granny when she first came to South Africa

Mr. Lewis and Granny (Lillian Crawford)
Aunt Dorothy

My father David Greenland was born in Lucknow, India where his father was stationed with the British Army. My Dad was only ten years old when a horse kicked his father in the head and they had to return to England, where his father died from the injury. Dad came to South Africa with his mother and two sisters Vida and Dorothy (Aunt Dolly) to stay with their aunt who ran a boarding house in Durban.

Mom and Dad met on a holiday to Tweedie in Natal. Mom was with a crowd of her friends chaperoned by one of the mothers. Dad had come to Tweedie with two of his best friends.

The three of them, Life Guards on Durban Beach, looked very handsome in their full length striped bathing suits.

The first time Dad went to Granny's house to meet Mom, he told Mom the meal was so dainty he had to go out and buy a couple of meat pies afterwards to fill him up.

❖

In 1935, Mom and Dad were married in St. Paul's Church in Durban.

Mom (Connie Lindsay) escorted into
St. Paul's Church, Durban, by Mr. Lewis

Mom and Dad

The Wedding Party

Article published in **The Natal Mercury**, Durban, January 12, 1935

WEDDING AT ST. PAUL'S

MISS C. LINDSAY MARRIED

Roses and other delicately shaded flowers in pink and white formed a charming background for the wedding of Miss Connie Lindsay, the elder daughter of Mr. and Mrs. L. Lewis, when she was married this afternoon at St. Paul's Church to Mr. Dave Greenland, the only son of Mrs. D. Greenland and the late Mr. Greenland of Red Hill. The bride and her parents live at Dudley House. Archdeacon Heywood Harris officiated, and Mr. W. Deane was the organist. The soloist during the signing of the register was a young chorister from the church choir.

Given away by her father, Miss Lindsay made a dainty bride in her gown of sheer white satin, with rich pearl embroidery on the raglan shoulder-line and yoking. The corsage of satin was gathered softly into the yoke, and the sleeves puffed out at the elbows in rich, supple folds, and were tight from there to the wrists. The skirt was plain and shaped to the figure with a long satin train. Miss Lindsay wore a veil of Brussels lace fitted into a silver caplet falling in a point over one side and trimmed with orange blossoms. She carried a sheaf of white roses and wore silver shoes.

THE BRIDESMAIDS

The two bridesmaids were the Misses Dorothy Lindsay (her sister) and Sheila Gooding, whose picture frocks were of deep parma pink rose-patterned lace, made tight-fitting to the knees and trimmed with deep godets of self-toned faille. Ruchings of faille also trimmed the frocks, and the frilly epaulettes were arranged as puff sleeves, with yokes of pink net appliqued with lace.

Both bridesmaids wore picture hats of pink straw in fancy crinoline, trimmed with pink bows and flowers, and pink open-work shoes, and carried bouquets of pink roses. Their necklets were gifts from the bridegroom.

Little Miss Vida Daan Swan, a niece of the bridegroom, looked charming in her frock of pink taffeta with two deep frills on the ankle-length skirt, and a fischu effect on the corsage of three deep frills of taffeta. A sash completed the effect, and she wore a Dolly Varden hat of pink flowers and carried a posy of pink flowers to tone. Her gift from the bridegroom was a gold bracelet.

Mr. Edgar Kidd was best man and Mr. "Tickey" Fulcher was the groomsman.

THE RECEPTION

A reception was held at the Federal Hotel, where guests enjoyed dancing. Mr. and Mrs. Lewis and Mrs. Greenland received them.

A gown of beige georgette and lace with a long three-quarter coat was worn by Mrs. Lewis with puff sleeves and ruched trimming. Her hat in beige straw was trimmed to tone and she carried matching bag and gloves. A spray of roses was pinned on one shoulder.

Mrs. Greenland favoured deep brown lace and georgette for her ensemble, worn with a long lace coat. A spray of pink roses was worn and her brown hat toned with her gloves and bag.

Among those present were: Mrs. C. V. Swan and Mrs. D. Snashall (sisters of the bridegroom) Mr. and Mrs. Adam Anderson, Mr. and Mrs. J. T. Hall, Mr. and Mrs. S. Sanderson, Mr. and Mrs. J. Smith, Mr. and Mrs. Brass and Major and Mrs. Raftery.

Many beautiful presents were received. The bride received a cheque from Tomango, Ltd., where she was employed and the bridegroom received a gift from the Durban Borough Police, of which he is a member.

Later, Mr. and Mrs. Dave Greenland left on their honeymoon, which is to be spent in the Natal Midlands. For travelling Mrs. Greenland chose a white silk marocain frock figured all over with red and blue half moons, and the long swagger coat to match in deep blue was trimmed with red and white half-moons. She wore a beige straw pancake hat with beige shoes and carried a bag and gloves to match.

On their return, Mr. and Mrs. Dave Greenland will live at Durban North.

Dad, Mom, Granny and Mr. Lewis

Dad and his Mother

Granny at Mom's Wedding

Albert Falls
1938

Mom and Dad

On a hot sultry night in April 1938, Mom struggled through labor. She soon forgot the misery when she held me in her arms.

A skinny baby, I weighed in at six pounds two ounces. She stayed for two weeks in the sanatorium relaxing luxuriously while learning how to care for me. A greedy little thing, I sucked hungrily on her small breasts. At two months, one of Mom's friends gave me the once over and held up my arm. "Isn't she thin?" she exclaimed. Mom took a good look and decided to give me a bottle. I guzzled it down and fell right to sleep. She realized she no longer had enough milk to satisfy me. "You poor thing. No wonder you're always so desperate when I feed you. I never thought I might be starving you." Years later she told me, "I tucked my bosoms into my bra and never looked back."

Dad was a young policeman then. They lived near the police station in a small house provided for them, located in the tiny country village of Albert Falls, South Africa. The house stood on one side of the falls and a dusty dirt road connected them to the nearest town of Pietermaritzburg. They lived there contentedly. Dad did his rounds on a black horse and had two native police assistants whose jobs were to take care of the horses, the grounds and the station. He learned to speak Zulu, which helped him many times in later life. A small general store kept basic supplies for local residents both black and white. The only bridge crossing the falls was built for the train going to Greytown sixty miles north of Maritzburg.

I loved to hear Mom's stories about those days. "When we lay in bed at night we could hear the falls cascading over the

Dad in his police uniform

rocks, the tree beetles and the endless chirping of crickets. Your Dad fell in love with horses when we were there. He looked so smart in his uniform with his helmet and polished boots as he mounted his black horse and rode off on patrol."

As a small child playing, I followed the old native assistant around the yard, copying whatever he did. He swept the area, kept the stables clean and raked. Mom never worried about the dirt or danger because the old native kept a sharp eye on me at all times.

When Mom and Dad got married, they had an old Harley Davidson motorbike. When I came on the scene they traded it for a two-seater Ford with a dickey seat that opened out at the back. Whenever they went anywhere they popped me in the back with their little Fox Terrier and a nice warm blanket. The dog loved the ride. He barked at the natives walking beside the road as we bounced along leaving a trail of dust behind.

Dad with his Harley

Helping sweep at the police station

Riding Dad's horse

In my baby bath with Dad

❖ 2 ❖

Granny's House, Durban 1941

Cousin Tony and me

When I grew older we would go to see Granny in Durban, a larger town sixty miles away. Granny lived in a big house on a hill with her friendly husband Mr. Lewis, Aunty Dorothy and Uncle Edgar, and my cousin Tony born a year after me. Mr. Lewis was not our real Grandpa, but he let us sit on his lap when we visited and he bought us nice presents for Christmas. Sometimes I was allowed to stay with Granny for a few days. I loved that because I could play with Tony.

He did naughty things like sliding down the stairs on his blackboard. Once he opened a tin of paint and we painted the outside of the garage. He told me Granny said we could, but when Aunt Dorothy came outside and found us, we both got a jolly good hiding. Another time I stayed for several days. When Mommy came to pick me up she brought me a new baby sister we named Sheila. Small and cuddly, she made us all laugh when she smiled.

❖

One afternoon I overheard Granny and Mr. Lewis talking about Hitler and Germany.

"You know Dave, you and Edgar may have to go to war one of these days," Granny said.

"Don't be ridiculous Mother, you always think the worst. I'm sure they will find a way to stop that man, besides we are so far away, what does it have to do with us?" Mommy did not like talking about the war in front of us. I didn't hear war talk again until one day I came in from playing outside with our native boy to see Mommy sitting at the kitchen table with Dad. She held a letter open in her hand, tears streaming down her face. I had never seen Mommy cry before. "Oh Dave, what am I going to do without you, with two small children? My God we don't know how long you'll be gone. Now we won't be able to stay in Albert Falls."

Cousin Tony with me at Granny's house

The next thing I knew we were moving into Granny's house. "Daddy is going to have to go away for a while and become a soldier," Mom explained, "so we can't live at the police station anymore. You must behave nicely while we are living here." I didn't mind moving because it meant I could play with Tony.

That Christmas Granny gave Sheila and me each the most beautiful china dolls. Their china faces, hands and legs were attached to soft rag bodies. I loved my doll with her soft golden curls and flashing eyes that flopped shut when I lay her down. One day when I was playing outside with Tony building a fort, Sheila got my doll. She tried to stuff her into the toy pram with hers, but as she shoved her, my doll fell to the floor and smashed to pieces. I hated my little sister that day. Mommy carefully glued all the pieces together, but my china doll never looked the same with yellow glue lines across her soft pink cheeks.

With my china doll

We were quite happy living with Granny, but then Mr. Lewis died. Granny was so upset and we couldn't stay there anymore because the house had to be sold.

❖ 3 ❖

Camperdown Hotel
1942

Wearing a pink dress and bow

When Granny, Mom and Aunt Dorothy moved to the Camperdown Hotel (also known as Maizelands) I was four years old. The owners helped out with families of soldiers going away to war, allowing them to stay quite cheaply. Rooms were filled with mothers and their children. We shared the bathroom halfway down the hallway with people we did not know. Every night Mom bathed my younger sister Sheila and I together in a big, deep enamel tub. The water was always a dirty red color when we finished. "I don't know how you kids get so dirty," Mom complained, but we knew. Our world was a buzz of war games and plans to fight off Hitler. We had been digging a fort for weeks out behind the pigsty. The hole we made got deeper and deeper and one of the boys told us we could hide in it if the Germans came. We gathered old planks and branches and stacked them ready beside the hole so we could jump in and cover us if we heard them coming. We could never play in the bath for very long like we used to at Granny's house. "Hurry up, there are other people waiting," said Mom as we stood dripping on the plank mat. She rubbed a scratchy towel hastily over us, then gave us a push out the door and down the hallway.

We made friends easily and were allowed to roam all over the farmyard and often visited the pigs. Small and pink, they were very smelly and messy, but they didn't seem to mind us poking them with a stick. They would squeal and run away as we giggled at their funny shaped bottoms, but then come right back to the fence and look up at us with their round flat snouts. They'd snort and snuffle standing in the muck of vegetable peelings and old food from the kitchen.

Every day an old native girl scrubbed the wooden table in the center of the verandah and polished the hard cement stoop with black polish. She would get down on her hands and knees to rub, brush and polish with a big cloth until it shone. We'd

Camperdown Hotel "Maizelands" 1942
Aunt Dorothy seated on verandah, Mom standing to the right,
front row Tony and I, 4th and 5th from left

beg her to let us sit on her wide back as she crawled around the
floor. Most of the time she put up with us hopping on and off.
She'd laugh a low gruff giggle, wiggle about, then get sick of it
and chase us all away, *"Hamba, hamba mena sabenza!"*

In the afternoons, the mothers gathered on the verandah
for tea. A white tablecloth covered the long wooden table where
the native girl laid out the afternoon tea and cakes. The children
sat in rows on the steps while they had their tea or we could
have a glass of Milo, a thick chocolate drink with brown froth
on top. I liked to scoop the froth off with a teaspoon and lick
it slowly.

In my flower costume

One Sunday, we visited Dad for the first time in the tent city outside Pietermaritzburg where he'd been training to be a soldier. He was supposed to go away to the war but broke his leg playing rugby for the army and couldn't go until he was better, so we were able to visit him quite often.

Every Sunday we drove along the main road from Camperdown up the hill towards Maritzburg. As soon as we came over the crest we could see the tent city, a hillside covered with rows and rows of canvas tents. As soon as I spied those tents, I knew I was getting closer to Dad.

The car bounced over the bumpy entrance and I clung to the bar in the dickey seat. A nice soldier greeted Mom at the gate and showed us where to park. The grass was squashed flat from the cars driving in and out. Rows of dingy green army trucks stood unused near the parking lot. Sweaty, grubby soldiers in their khaki shorts and shirts wandered everywhere. When we got out of the car we could feel the heat rise up from the Maritzburg valley below. As we walked between the tents looking for Dad, soldiers waved and greeted us. "You looking for Dave, he's down that way." Everyone knew our Dad because of his broken leg. The cast covered his foot and half his leg. He showed us how they bound a piece of metal into the cast under his heel that allowed him to walk about.

The faded khaki green tents each had a large flap held up by two wooden poles stuck in the ground to shade the opening. They were very neat inside with four army cots made up with a folded blanket on the end. Dad's kit bag stood tightly packed beside his cot. Mom and Dad would sit close on a bench near Dad's tent. "Buzz off and play you kids," Mom would wave us away. Two years younger than me, Sheila was too small to play, so we'd dig holes behind the tent in the rain trenches, gather rocks, and make a dam so the water would run another way.

Sometimes Dad came to stay at the hotel for a few days. He often played the fool. He would stick Sheila in a pillowcase and hang her on a hook on the back of the bedroom door because she was so small. She'd wave her fat little arms, smiling and cooing and we all laughed happily. I liked having Dad around because he loved to swim. Even though the hotel swimming pool was full of green murky water, we didn't care because it cooled us off. I could ride on Dad's back clinging to his neck, while he swam where it was too deep for me to stand. "Don't hang on so tight Doff, you're choking me!" he'd gurgle, pretending he was sinking so I'd hold on even tighter. One day I let go of the side of the pool and went under, scrambling and kicking about as the murky water swirled in front of my eyes. I thought I was going to drown, but Dad swooped me up and out just in time.

We often went to the beachfront in Durban before Dad left. I loved the excitement of it all. Bright striped umbrellas and deck chairs, Indian women in their saris selling popcorn and peanuts, and Indian waiters running around with trays of

At the beach

cold frothy drinks for sale. Aloe plants grew in abundance in the gardens and Dad would break off a chunk and rub the bitter liquid on my two fingers that I had a habit of popping into my mouth. Mom and Dad were constantly trying to find a way to stop me sucking my fingers.

The day finally came when Dad's leg healed and he had to go off to war. I still did not understand about the war, but Mommy said Dad was going to fight Hitler and the Germans

Dad in front of bitter aloe

far away and all the Dads had to go. We drove into Durban Harbor and parked near three large grey ships waiting to take the soldiers away. I looked at the chimney-stacks puffing smoke and the huge guns front and back pointing out ready to kill Hitler if he sailed by.

I stood on the dockside and looked up at Mommy crying. She had her arms wrapped around Dad's shoulders. All around, mothers hugged soldiers and sobbed. Some of Dad's friends were leaving on the same ship. The natives hooked giant nets filled with wooden boxes onto cranes, which swung out over our heads onto the ship and dropped down on the deck. Then the crane swung back again and the natives shouted in Zulu as they grabbed the big hook and fixed it to another net filled with more crates and boxes. I wondered what they were taking in the boxes, but just as I was about to ask, Dad waved me away with his hand, his other arm wrapped around Mom's waist. "I'm thirsty," I whined, trying to get attention. Dad bought me a mineral, a sweet, red drink in a glass bottle shaped like a bowling pin. "Now go and play with the other kids," he said, "I want to talk to your Mother alone before I have to leave."

Mom and Dad always chased us away when they wanted to talk. The mineral gave me bubbles in my stomach and I belched with relief. I spotted a heap of what looked like fine black sand and decided to mix it with the rest of the mineral to make little cakes. A couple of other children, equally bored with their parents, joined in the cake making fun. It kept us busy for quite a while mixing and patting our nice round cakes, then placing them in rows on a scrap of cardboard. Feeling quite pleased with myself, I marched over to show Mom. She took one look at me. "What on earth have you been playing in?" she screeched, wiping the tears from her eyes. I looked down at my filthy blackened dress. She reached over, grabbed me by the arm, and gave me a good slap on the bum for making such a mess and getting all dirty just when Daddy was going away. I slunk back to the little black cakes and continued patting them, getting dirtier and blacker. "I hate you Mommy. I was only making nice chocolate cakes," I mumbled to myself as I slapped the cakes harder. They looked real to me and I didn't want my Dad to go away either. If he's going, I thought, why couldn't he see the nice cakes I made before he left? Just then Mom shouted, "Hey kids, come over and give your Dad a big hug before he leaves." We ran over and clasped our arms around his legs. He scooped Sheila up and spun her around her high over his head.

Dad with me on his lap

"My baby girl is going to be all grown up when I get back!" Then he hugged and kissed me as Mommy tried to wipe my hands clean with a bit of spit on the corner of Dad's hankie. He squeezed Mommy tight one more time, pecked me on the cheek, then picked up his kitbag and ran up the gangplank.

"Come on," Mommy said, forgetting all about the black cakes. She grabbed my hand, tears streaming down her cheeks. "Wave to Daddy. There he is at the top of the gangplank." I stared up at the hundreds of soldiers standing at the railings waving. The ship was so big and high I couldn't see Dad. A band played a marching song as the natives wheeled the gangplank away from the side of the ship and it slowly pulled away from the dock. All the grown-ups held colored streamers. I watched as they broke and fluttered down into the water, their red, white and blue ends sinking into the bay. I tried to peer over the side to see, but Mommy tugged on me roughly. "Get away from the edge, the last thing I need is for you to fall in." I knew I wasn't going to fall but I stepped back next to Mom. We watched the soldiers wave and blow kisses as they got smaller and smaller and the ship went over the side of the earth and disappeared from sight. Mommy looked so sad, blowing her nose and rubbing her eyes. She picked Sheila up and took my hand. "Come on, lets get away from here and go home, you're an absolute disgrace," she said and marched us off towards the car.

Holding Dad's hand before
he left for North Africa

❖ 4 ❖

The Octagonal House
1942 – 1943

The Octagonal House

Shortly after Dad left, Granny bought another house and Aunty Dorothy and Tony moved in with her. Mom and her friend Aunty Todge rented a weird octagonal house leaving all the hotel friends behind. The living room sat in the middle of the house, and the bedrooms, bathroom and kitchen were off to the side in the angles. Surrounded by a big garden, the house came with an old, grey speckled horse that grazed on the lawn and kept it short.

23

Mom, Sheila and I

I never knew Aunty Todge's real name, but we were allowed to call her aunty because she and Mommy were old friends. Aunty Todge said her husband had gone to the Suez Canal in Egypt near the pyramids. He was going to escort ships through the canal so they didn't get blown up. She had two little girls, Jane the eldest, older than me, and Sally. Jane thought she knew everything. Sally was a wimpy girl with curls, who whined and complained all the time.

We settled into the funny shaped house all crowded together. Mom painted the glass on the headlamps of the car with black paint, and then she and Aunty Todge hung long black curtains across all the windows that had to be closed at night. "If the Germans invade, they won't be able to find us, our house will be so dark outside." I lay in bed at night terrified of the darkness, staring hard at the ceiling with beads of light flashing in my

Checking out the Zulu Basket Sellers
(Center Row) Dorothy and Jane (Back Row) Sheila and Sally

eyes. I imagined soldiers with guns running into the house and capturing us. The sirens went off every day with a loud piercing whine. "They're practicing to make sure they work, just in case. But don't worry. There will be lots of warning if anything really does happen."

After a while, Mom and Aunty Todge decided Jane and I should to go to school, so every morning Mommy took us to the train station. Jane, my friend Maureen and I, would climb up the two big steps onto the train, ride past two stations and then get off where we were met by Miss McFee. She ran a small school in her old house not far from the station. Miss McFee

Sheila and I by the Ford

Tony and I with Nanny holding Sheila

was very thin and flat with white hair and a pasty pale face. She didn't wear rouge or lipstick. Her dresses were plain and straight, a belt pulled her dress tight around her skinny waist. We liked her because she was always there and never shouted at us. She listened to all our stories and our worries about the war.

We could tell when we reached the station where we had to get off because we could see an enormous billboard high overhead with a picture of a native child covered in oozing sores. His watery eyes and lumpy swollen lips made him look very sick. "There's a smallpox epidemic and this billboard is to remind people to get their vaccination," Miss McFee explained to us.

I didn't have to worry because I had already been vaccinated. I proudly showed Miss McPhee my scar. "They cut a cross on your arm with a sharp pointy knife and drop some smallpox into the cut," I said. I found the process most interesting. While standing in line, I watched the other kids get their vaccination and howl loudly over the little cut. I made up my mind I was not going to make any fuss when they got to me. I felt quite sick for a couple of days. The cut turned into a bubble, then into a big sore with yellow puss oozing out and finally a brown scab. Miss McFee listened intently to my story and muttered in astonishment at the details, as she studied the scar.

At Miss McFee's school we learned the alphabet and numbers and learned to read. Miss McFee believed children should learn about money too. She had paper notes and real looking cardboard coins. She lined up the small green school chairs in a long row and we boarded "the train". We sat on the chairs while she played train sounds on her wind-up gramophone and we pretended to arrive at a station to go shopping. We marched up to a table where she had placed a box of sand, a set of scales and different size brown paper bags. One girl played shopkeeper and weighed out a pound of pretend sugar or flour from the sand and scooped it into a paper bag. We paid with our cardboard money and then hopped back onto the train. I loved the train game. I told Mommy the school had a real electric train that went to the shops and wound around the garden. It seemed very real to me. One morning Mom told me she was coming to visit the school, so I hastily informed her that the train was broken.

Lucky Packets were a novel item but rare for us. Occasionally our Granny came to visit with a packet for each of us. I tore it open in excitement and found a small celluloid doll as big as my finger inside. Celluloid, a thin plastic material was easy to squash so you had to handle it carefully and not allow your little sister to touch it.

A couple of the girls in school had the kind of relatives who knit and crocheted dainty clothes that fit their doll just like a real baby. They would bring the doll to school all nicely dressed to share. They were so beautiful. They fascinated me. Mom made my doll a dress. She took a small piece of material, cut two holes in it for the arms to go through and tied it onto the doll with a thin piece of ribbon. The dress looked much too homemade so I decided not to take it to school. Instead, I began conjuring up wonderful pictures in my mind. How lovely my doll would look in a pale pink knitted dress with a frilly little bonnet. In my imagination, my doll began to acquire lots of beautifully made dresses, crocheted with fine white or pink cotton. I described the clothes to Miss McFee in great detail. She always listened sweetly. "I can hardly wait to see your doll all dressed up," she said, as I added another outfit in my mind. My vivid creations never got me into trouble because even though Miss McFee showed such enthusiasm, she never pressed too hard for me to bring the doll in.

Portrait of Mom with Sheila (R) and Me (L) which she sent to Dad

It was strange living with another family. Our mothers were often away doing volunteer work or packing and sending parcels to soldiers' families in England. Mom said because of food rationing they had no sugar, so the parcels were full of good things to eat and a bag of sugar. They wrapped the parcels in old flour sacks and Mom would sew them up tight with a long sharp needle and string. She wrote the name and address with an indelible purple pencil. If you spit on the pencil, it would write nice and dark so the postman could read it. Once, I licked the pencil and tried to write with it. My tongue turned purple and it tasted bitter. Mom took one look at me. "Have you been using my indelible pencil again, your mouth is all purple?" I had to run to the bathroom, spit out the bitter taste and drink a big gulp of water. I had purple lips for two days.

Jane bossed all of us around a lot, but our first Zulu nanny would stick up for whiny Sally if Jane got too annoying. We called her Nanny. I never knew her by any other name. She seemed old and was quite fat. She always wore a pink uniform and a white apron, stiffly starched and shiny from repeated ironing. She had a merry smile, a deep gruff laugh and twinkling brown eyes. I loved Nanny's shiny brown skin scrubbed clean and her smell of soap. She completely devoted herself to us. She gave us a light smack if we were naughty, laughed and teased, played ball with us and put up with our games of nonsense. She gave us lots of loving care and bathed us every night before Mom came home from helping with the war.

We were never invited into Nanny's *kia* situated at the lower end of the garden. I thought since she was brown maybe all her things would be brown too. One afternoon, I peeked into her *kia* surprised to see her bed covered in white linens with a beautifully embroidered pillowcase on her pillow. It too was stiff and starched. Next to her bed stood a small table covered with another pretty piece of embroidery and a big alarm clock ticking away loudly. In the corner sat an old polished chair with a lace cushion on it. All her clothes hung on a piece of rope strung across the corner of the room. She had a small shower and toilet but no washbasin. I wondered how she could clean her teeth. This peak into the private world of our native servant was my first realization they were people too, just like us.

I'm to the left of Nanny with Sheila and Sally

We had been taught to place our knife and fork together straight on the plate when we finished our meal. If we forgot and left them sticking out sideways, Jane would tell us all about it. "Only Hitler had such bad manners that he doesn't put his knife and fork together," she would remind us smugly. I often wondered how she knew Hitler since he was far away across the sea.

My friend Maureen and I thought we were quite grown up catching a train to school and back every day. We often saw ladies on the train clutching their strapless handbags under their arms. We thought they looked very smart, so we decided to ask our mothers for a handbag we could carry too. Mom gave me a big blue one with dimples all over that looked like ostrich skin with a brown bone clasp across the top. I felt really grown up. We marched into the station, our handbags tucked under our arms. As we sat on the train seat we noticed people looking at us. Maureen and I thought they must be admiring our bags. It never occurred to us we looked completely ridiculous clutching a grown up handbag.

The day of my fifth birthday when I arrived at Miss McFee's, I proudly announced, "I'm five today!" Miss McFee made a pretty cake with five candles on it for me to blow out. Granny gave me a gold ring with a D engraved on it and I showed off the ring to all the other children. One of the children asked if she could try it on so I slipped it off and handed it over to her happily. She hadn't even put the ring on when she dropped it. It rolled across the wooden floor of the verandah and vanished in the crack between the floorboards. I dashed to the floor putting one eye against the narrow opening to try to spot the ring. Dark, dirty and full of spider webs, I couldn't see a thing. Miss McFee said she couldn't go underneath because nobody had ever been down there. "You shouldn't have taken it off and let some other child try it on," she told me without sympathy. I never saw my ring again.

While Dad was away we always spent Christmas day at Granny's house. Christmas was always a lavish affair. William the cook who worked for her for many years made the most delicious bread and cooked extravagant breakfasts and dinners. His little finger was thin and shriveled and had no nail. We were most fascinated by it. We'd ask him to show it to us and tell the story over and over of how it was poisoned and swelled up and finally rotted away. Half of it fell off leaving the funny little finger stump. Always a good sport, he let us feel and touch it.

❖ 5 ❖

Redhill
1943 – 1944

Nanny and her friend with Sheila and me

When Aunty Todge announced she had to return to England with Jane and Sally, that was the end of the octagonal house with the big garden. We had to move to a small house closer to my aunt's in a town called Red Hill because of the red dirt. Nanny didn't like living in town. She told Mom she was going home to be near her family. The last thing I saw of Nanny was when a small buck came running down the road. The native gardeners rushed out into the street, killed the terrified creature and cut it up to share. Nanny got the stomach lining and entrails for making sausages. She washed the stomach lining in the sink over and over until it was pale and white and I could see the tiny bumps all over it. "It makes the best stew in the world," she said. I didn't think I wanted to try it but Nanny insisted. It was tough and chewy but tasty, especially smothered in lots of thick potato gravy. The next day Nanny hugged and kissed us goodbye. We felt very sad when she went off to catch the bus to her home.

After Nanny left, Mom decided to get a housekeeper, as she had a job and had to go off to work every day. The first one, Miss Voster, a colored lady (a person of mixed race) arrived with a small suitcase. She placed a picture of her son, who was away in the war, on her dressing table. We weren't allowed to go in her room but we could peek because she never shut the door during the day. She arrived wearing a doek tied over her hair and under her chin. She folded it up, placed it on the dressing table and never moved it again. Next to her bed, she kept a bible with a pair of thin glasses I never saw her wear. She didn't do much. Most of the time she was out on the street talking to other housekeepers or sitting in the kitchen reading. Mommy wanted to come home to a nice cooked dinner after work, but it was always boiled vegetables. Miss Voster didn't know how to cook anything else so Mommy said she had to go.

The next housekeeper, Miss van der Merwe had a dark, sallow face with sunken eyes and wore a brown hat perched on her head. She assured Mom she could handle us and that she would do the housework too. This sounded good to Mom and she arrived the next day in the same clothes with a suitcase and a big box. She never left her bedroom door open though so we couldn't see inside her room. Two days later, we noticed a bad smell all over the house. Mom consulted with Miss van der Merwe and she explained to Mommy that she did not believe in bathing. Water was very bad for her skin and she rubbed cream over her body daily. Mommy tried to tell her tactfully that was not acceptable and she would have to bathe if she wanted to stay. Miss van der Merwe marched out of the house, down the front steps and departed within half an hour. That was the last time Mom hired a housekeeper.

Once we settled into Redhill, Mom said I had to go off to kindergarten. I would be going to the Convent High School in Durban because my cousin Vida went there and I could ride on the bus to school with her. "She'll keep an eye on you so you will be safe," Mom said. The school went all the way from kindergarten up to twelfth grade.

Mom bought me two white long sleeve shirts, a red and black striped tie, a black gym tunic with box pleats, black bloomers and new black shoes. Aunt Vida (Dad's sister) gave me two pairs of pretty white hand knitted socks. As soon as we got on the double decker bus Vida forgot all about me. "Sit there," she said pointing to an empty seat. She was thirteen and had loads of friends. They ran up the stairs of the bus, shrieking, laughing and teasing each other the whole way to school. I was so scared I didn't move from the first seat near the door on the lower deck of the bus. Fortunately when it was time to get off, Vida bounced down the stairs and yelled for me to follow her.

Vida showed me to my classroom and then disappeared. I stood near the door staring around the big room. Most children knew each other because they had been together for a while but I was joining the class in the middle of a term. No one spoke a word to me. The walls were full of pictures they had drawn. Each of them stood beside a wooden desk waiting for the teacher to arrive. Minutes later, a stern nun wearing a long black habit and white veil swished briskly passed me into the room. The girls cried out in unison, "Good morning Sister Regina," as they scrambled into their seats. It surprised me to have a nun for a teacher. She did not smile when the class greeted her. "Good morning class," she announced and then turned towards me. Squinting through her gold-rimmed glasses she looked me over. "So, you are the new girl. What's your name?" Sister Regina pointed to a desk in the front row. "You may sit in this empty desk here."

I inched towards it with all eyes on me, clutching my new brown school suitcase, with nothing but a pencil and my sandwich in it. Everyone watched as I placed the suitcase under the desk. I hated the first day. Since I had on my new uniform I looked like I fit, but there it ended. I wished someone would speak to me, but the whole class just stared and ignored me the rest of the day. When the bell rang to go outside for lunch, they rushed out and I stood there wondering what I should do.

I walked outside trying to be invisible and sat on a bench by myself. I opened my lunch and looked at my jam sandwich. There was a brown biscuit next to it, wrapped in wax paper and a banana. I glanced around anxiously, hoping to see a familiar face, maybe cousin Vida, while I picked and fiddled with my lunch. When the bell rang, I was glad to throw it in the rubbish bin and rush back to the safety of my desk.

After school Vida met me outside. We walked to the bus with her noisy friends. I tagged along wishing I had lots of friends like her. Once on the bus, I sat alone on the lower deck. Vida bounced up the stairs. "I'll tell you when we get off," she yelled, laughing and chatting. At least I was on the bus, she had seen to that.

The school held a fundraising festival with all sorts of things for sale like cakes, biscuits and homemade doll clothes. You could guess how many beans in the bottle and win a decorated cake, or try to drop a penny through a bucket of water and get it to land on a two shilling piece, or maybe even half-a-crown. I only had sixpence to spend so I bought a raffle ticket. Two of the prizes I desperately wanted to win were a big doll dressed in beautifully sewn clothes and a small bed with handmade sheets and pillows. Later in the afternoon they began drawing tickets out of a hat. Slowly all the best prizes were given away and a smug young girl won the big doll. All the girls flocked around admiring it. I was so envious. As I stood on the sidelines watching I heard my name called out. I rushed up to the table to find I had won the little doll bed. I sat down on a bench to examine the sheets and found myself surrounded by the other jealous girls who had not won anything. For the first time in my life I had something everyone wanted. I enjoyed the attention and shared the doll bed. I loved the way they admired it and wished they could have the set too. I went home happy, bursting with excitement to show it off to Mom and Sheila.

The next day I wanted to take the bed to school, but Mom said school was not for playing. A couple of kids asked me if I brought the bed so they could play with it. Once they knew I had left it home no one bothered with me anymore and I was as lonely as ever. I found it difficult to make friends at Convent High. We had to be quiet in the classroom and line up to go out for PE. When break time came I didn't know how to be invited to play with the other kids and I would stand there hoping someone would ask me. When we were lining up for PE a girl accused me of pushing her out of the line.

"I didn't push you, you pushed me," I said.

"No I didn't. You're just a brat and no one likes you." She had such a mean voice and made an ugly face.

"I hate you," I said back, "I hope you die." She pushed me again, glaring at me and stuck out her tongue. A week later she was run over by a bus while waiting at the bus stop. The whole school prayed for her family and everyone cried and said how nice she was. All I could think about was how I had wished she'd die and now God had got her killed because of me. I couldn't tell anybody. I just kept it inside and I never wished a bad thing on anybody ever again. I dreamed about her standing in line and pictured her squashed by the bus. I felt horrible. When Mommy said prayers with me at night I thought of what I had done. At the end we always said God bless Mommy and Daddy, my aunties and uncles and cousins and my sisters. After Mommy left I asked God to bless the girl who died too.

I was seven and a half when the telegram arrived at the front door. Telegrams always made Mom nervous. She ripped open the envelope and I stood waiting while she scanned the paper. ARRIVING MONDAY AT SNELL PARADE BARRACKS, DURBAN, it read in simple block letters. "Oh my God! Dad's coming home next week." She rushed into the house, picked up the phone and began ringing everyone. It seemed such a long time since Dad went away to war. I couldn't even remember what he looked like. Sheila was so young when he left, she didn't remember him at all. That week Mom cleaned and tidied the house. We couldn't make a mess or play with our things. "Don't leave stuff lying about, your father's coming home," she fussed. She moved the lounge furniture around every few days trying to make it look just right.

The day finally came to go and pick up Dad. We got up early and put on our best dresses. Mom had a new perm and her curly shining hair made her look very pretty. I watched her sitting at her dressing table carefully powdering her face and dabbing rouge on her cheeks. She brushed her lips with pale lipstick, checked herself in the mirror, licked her fingers and smoothed them over her eyebrows. The day before Mom washed our hair so it was nice and clean. She brushed mine up on one side and tied it with a big bow. She clipped Sheila's hair out of her eyes with a bobby pin because it was too short for a bow like mine.

We got into the car, the air warm and sticky. Mom chucked an umbrella in the back. "We might need this. Doff you can sit on the front seat with Sheila now, but you'll have to get in the dickey seat when we drive home." We piled into the old Ford and drove from Redhill into Durban.

Mom found a parking spot in the sports grounds near the barracks. She grabbed the umbrella, "You never know when we'll see your father, and it might rain this afternoon so we better be prepared." We followed her down the street onto the Snell Parade, a long wide street lined with enormous jacaranda trees. I could hear the waves pounding on the sand from the ocean on the one side and see the tall fence of the barracks on the other. Crowds of women and children stood or sat on the grass along both sides of the road. "By golly I had no idea there'd be such a crowd. We'll go over to the entrance and find out when Dad is due to arrive." Mom marched up to a soldier standing at attention by a wooden sentry box. The gate was closed, but we could see trucks and soldiers milling about inside. Mom waved the telegram, "Are you able to tell me when my husband will be arriving?"

"No Ma'am." He relaxed his stance and spread his feet apart. "He'll be coming off one of the ships. Two arrive today, one tomorrow and one the next day. They'll be bringing them here all day by lorry until everyone is off-loaded." Just then a huge, dusty green lorry pulled up to the gate filled with soldiers. They shouted and waved at the crowds on the roadside. Women shrieked and ran up to the truck as soldiers jumped over the sides yelling names. Mom, Sheila and I stood there in the chaos staring. "I think we'll have to park ourselves on the side of the road like everyone else." Mom took our hands in hers and marched us away from the lorry to a vacant bit of grass along the pavement. While we lay on the grass waiting for Dad to come from the ship Mom nagged me about my finger sucking. "Dorothy, here's a chance to stop that and show Dad what a big girl you are now." I wanted to stop too but I just couldn't. All the waiting made me more excited than ever. Every time a lorry drove along the road towards the entrance, women screamed and sobbed when they saw their man. Soldiers jumped from the lorries and ran towards them hugging and laughing with joy.

Mom didn't pack sandwiches or drinks so she bought us a meat pie and a mineral. We sat around in the heat, rolling on the grass and nagging. "When's Daddy coming?" We asked her at least a hundred times. Eventually the gate soldier told everyone no more lorries would be coming. "Maybe tomorrow will be your day." Hot and tired, we dragged ourselves back to the car and home.

The second day, Mom packed a picnic of sandwiches, biscuits and mangos. She mixed a bottle of orange squash and wrapped it in a wet towel. "I'll be able to clean up your faces after you've eaten the mangos." She tied the bow in my hair, but my posh dress was too dirty to wear again so I had to put on one of my church dresses. We took a blanket to sit on this time and Mom brought a book. She never opened the book though because she began talking to other waiting mothers. They went on about how long the war lasted, about wounds and the state of affairs during the time the men were gone. Mom said Dad had been fighting in North Africa against Rommel. She told them how Dad had escaped being taken prisoner when Rommel defeated the Eighth Army at Tobruk. At the time, Dad had tick-bite fever and lay in a hospital in Cairo, Egypt. Every time a lorry passed, Mom jumped up and ran with the others hoping to see Dad and then sat back down on the grass with a sigh of disappointment. I played with some of the kids waiting. We climbed trees and swung from the branches. Dad did not arrive that day.

On the third day, we didn't dress up. "There's no use you putting on good clothes, you just dirty everything." Mom packed another picnic and we climbed into the car feeling quite miserable.

"Is Daddy ever going to come?"

"I don't know, I'm just as anxious as you. I don't know what to tell you. I hope he'll show up today." We parked the car again and dragged all our stuff to the side of the road. There weren't as many people waiting. A couple of lorries passed by, but we didn't see Dad.

"Maybe he's already here and we missed him, and he thinks we aren't going to pick him up?" Mom didn't answer me but looked towards the gate again. The excitement we felt the first day had faded away to disappointment and anxiety.

I stretched out on my back on the blanket and looked at the big fluffy clouds forming in the sky, imagining jeep and truck shapes and funny pictures, daydreaming. All of a sudden Mom flew out into the road, "Dave, Dave!" she yelled at the top of her lungs. She didn't stop screaming his name as she ran by the side of the lorry. Sheila and I jumped up and ran behind her. When I saw Dad hanging over the side, brown and tanned, I knew his face after all. He jumped out onto the road with his arms outspread like a soaring angel and landed on his two feet. He picked Mom up, hugged and kissed her and spun her around. The he put her down, bent low and took Sheila and me in each arm. "How's my girls?" he said, as if he'd never been away. He squatted in the middle of the road holding us. I smelled his army uniform, his thick woolly socks and dusty boots. Mommy started bawling so Dad stood up and took her in his arms again. They clung to each other for a long time and then he pulled himself away. "I've got to sign out and pick up my kitbag before we can go." He took Mom's hand and we skipped along beside him to the gate. We watched him disappear inside the barracks. "It won't be long now," Mom sniffled. It didn't matter, Daddy was home and soon we'd all be happy, together again.

Mom and Dad decided to take us to the Bulwer Hotel in the foothills of the Drakensberg Mountains for a short holiday before Dad got settled back into our life. Mom bought me a pair of grey flannel dungarees as winter was coming and there would be heavy frost up there. I loved those pants and wore them every day with a grey tie that came with them. It was so cold we wore gloves and hats and I could only suck my fingers when I was tucked into bed smothered with heavy warm blankets.

I didn't really know how long Dad had been gone but it was different having him home. We would sneak a peek at them kissing and we could see how happy Mom was. Dad began telling us what to do and Mom started cooking real dinners every night. Before Dad came home we often ate "easy dinners" – a meat pie from the bakery or lovely heavy chunks of bread broken up into a bowl, smothered with milk and loads of sugar. Now we had to eat peas and beans and sometimes pumpkin. I didn't understand why we had to eat such horrid food. We had managed just fine before.

Driving the calves on holiday at the Bulwer Hotel

Wearing my dungarees and tie

Dad went off to work at the plant owned by our grandmother. When Mr. Lewis died she inherited his business so she gave Dad a job. *The Durban Saw Hospital* sharpened saws of all shapes and sizes. Mr. Lewis had invented a machine that rolled wire in large bundles and the company made a lot of money. Now Granny was rich.

❖ 6 ❖

Pinetown
1945 – 1947

Sheila and I

One evening Mommy sat Sheila and me down on their bed and told us she had very exciting news. She had another baby growing in her tummy and we would soon have a new baby in the house, a little brother if we were lucky. With Daddy home and our house so small, they were going to look for a bigger house. "Does that mean I have to change schools?" I asked. I had become used to Convent High and could find my way around without Vida's help, so I wasn't too sure I would like the move. "We don't know yet, depends where we find the right house," Mom answered, avoiding the question.

They found an old house in Pinetown about ten miles outside Durban and Redhill. The white house stood in the middle of three acres of land, so I felt quite happy. It had a red corrugated iron roof with a verandah across the front and enormous mango trees grew in the garden. Molly, a black cow came with the property. She grazed peacefully in the field fenced with barbed wire. Since Pinetown was ten miles from Convent High, I realized I would have to change schools and start all over again.

There was no toilet inside the house so we had to walk down the garden to go. I hated it. I imagined all sorts of things lurking in the shadows. When I looked down inside I saw the bucket under the seat full of horrid stuff, and light coming in through the flap at the back where the bucket was changed. Twice a week a lorry drove along the street and a native would run down the driveway with a large sack folded on his head like a hood. He carried a fresh bucket on his shoulder that smelled of disinfectant. He'd pull out the full bucket and shove in the clean one, then run back up the driveway, put it on the truck and they'd move on to the next house. "Mom, the lavatory bucket man just came," I'd shout when I saw them.

Even though by day, pretty creepers with bright orange flowers covered the lavatory, I was scared stiff to go there in the dark. What if a spider or a snake bit my bottom? I had seen spiders crawling around under the seat in the daytime and I didn't want to take any chances. "Never fear when I am near," Dad would say, "I'll take you anytime and you will be perfectly safe." He had to take us last thing every night before we went to bed.

Soon after we moved Mom went off to hospital and came home with a new baby sister they named Patricia. We called her Trisha or Trish. Cuddly and warm, she smelled of milk and Johnsons baby powder and I loved her right away even though she was a girl.

Our days were quite different now. We loved the big old house with its wild garden full of trees to climb and places to play. Molly the cow didn't mind us at all and we could watch our new garden boy milking her. Mom bought thirty baby ducklings and a lot of fluffy yellow chicks. Dad built a wire chicken run and we took turns feeding them and holding their fuzzy little bodies in our hands.

Once we settled in I had to face going to a new school. I walked across a field each day to meet two other girls and our mothers shared taking us to school. We had to drive a few miles up a windy road to get to St. Mary's. Mom took me to buy a new blue uniform. It had a funny lace up neckline with a black shoelace threaded through six holes and tied in a bow just under my chin. It itched and tickled all day. The first day my neck was all red from scratching.

Our teacher Miss Clarence had grey hair tied back in a bun and looked a hundred years old. She wore a blue smock every day over her real clothes so she didn't get dirty or slop paint on her dress. She introduced me to the class and asked the girls to be friendly. A couple of girls asked me to eat lunch with them and gradually life settled down at the new school. I always had a jam and cheese sandwich, a cookie or a bit of leftover cake for lunch and the school allowed us to keep a tin of Ovaltine in the tuck shop. On cold days we could ask for our tin and get a big spoonful in a mug which matron filled with hot water to warm us up.

Miss Clarence could paint beautiful flowers. She picked a Strelitzia from the garden and stood it in a vase of water. She showed us how to draw it lightly with a pencil and then paint in the colors with a soft brush in watercolor. I had never been shown how to draw and paint before and it came easily to me. Miss Clarence said my efforts were very good and I felt so proud. I couldn't wait for the next drawing class so I could show off again. Miss Clarence also taught us how to write in cursive. We practiced each letter over and over in a hardbound exercise book until we could write them perfectly. Then she allowed us to join the letters and write a whole sentence. She insisted on perfect writing all the time no matter what we were studying so I learned to have very neat handwriting. I was happy at St. Mary's.

When I got home from school Sheila would run up the driveway to greet me and we'd play with our new baby sister on the bed, bouncing her about. Sheila and I also made a playroom under the water tank that filled with rainwater from the gutters and sat on top of a cement support. We had a play stove, a doll's

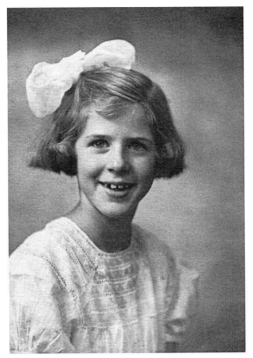

Me with a bow in my hair taken by famous
Durban photographer, Bernard Mills

bed and a couple of children's wicker chairs. One afternoon, I went out to play in our playroom and saw a long black mamba curled up on my chair. I rushed up the back steps into the house to call Dad. He came running out with his shotgun.

"Where? Where?" he shouted, pointing the gun into the playroom.

"On the chair," I screeched, terrified.

Boom! He blasted three shots into the chair and blew that snake to smithereens. All I could see were bits and pieces and a huge hole in the middle of my favorite chair.

Each night Mom tucked me into bed after Dad had taken us down the garden to go one last time in the lavatory bucket. I would kneel by the bed and Mom and I said our prayers. I prayed for Mommy and Daddy and all my aunties, uncles and cousins, ending with, "Now I lay me down to sleep, I pray the Lord, my soul to keep, If I should die before I wake, I pray the Lord my soul to take. Amen." I sometimes wondered if I was going to die but I always woke up in the morning, so I didn't worry about it too much. I repeated those words with sincerity and belief in my heart. After prayers I hopped into bed under my warm army blanket and Mommy kissed me goodnight.

Every night after Mommy left the room I stared at a dark mark on the wall right near my head. I pictured a pretty high heel shoe and I often fell asleep seeing this beautiful shoe as I sucked my fingers contentedly. I don't know how many nights I pondered it but eventually I took a pencil and drew around the mark to complete the shoe as I imagined it. It didn't come out looking at all like I pictured in my mind. The next night when Mommy tucked me in she saw my drawing. She stopped hugging me and took a good look.

"Dorothy, have you been drawing on the wall?" she asked, horrified that I would do such a thing.

"Yes, I couldn't help it. It looked like a shoe so I just drew it." I could tell she didn't see that pretty shoe in my head. She yanked the blankets back and spanked me hard on my bottom. "Don't you ever draw on the walls again, do you understand me?" she shouted. "Now, go to sleep and you can wash the wall tomorrow." She stormed out of the room. I lay there crying, looking at the stupid ugly shoe. It didn't look like a shoe at all, just a scribble. When I tried to wash the wall the paint came off too. Dad couldn't believe I would do such a thing. The whole world seemed to hate me that day.

I often went to the post office to collect the mail for Mom because we didn't have mail delivery. It was quite a long walk through fields of grass and down the main street to the post office at the bottom of the road near the train station. One afternoon I wandered home thumbing through the letters carelessly. I spotted one with Doris on the front, so I opened the envelope thinking the letter was for me. Inside was a letter written in Zulu to our current nanny, Doris. Since my name was Dorothy she had been told to choose another name. She chose Mavis so I always thought of her as Mavis. Mom called her "a cheeky city girl". Not warm and cuddly like Nanny, but quite defiant and not prone to taking any instruction. She did not like us kids at all and showed it when Mom was away from the house. I hastily shoved the letter back inside the envelope and tried to stick it shut with a bit of spit. When I got home I handed the letter to Mavis. "The post office gave it to me like that, all torn open," I said. I was really quite scared of her.

Mommy was furious. "The postman said they were sorry they opened it by mistake." She examined the letter. I could tell she suspected something was up.

"The postman gave it to me like that," I lied.

"Well I'll just have to go and tell the postman off," she replied.

I did not know how to get out of the lie and felt miserable. Mavis made a big scene about white kids snooping and looking into her personal things. I knew I wasn't really snooping. I wished a bolt of lightning or a big clap of thunder would strike and take away that lie, but God did not come to my rescue. Mavis carried on and I burst into tears and poured out the whole truth. I could tell by the look on Mom's face she knew I had been fibbing all along and she gave me a lengthy lecture about telling the truth.

Mavis quit the next day so she could go back to being Doris. "I don't want white people telling me what name to use." She stuck her tongue out at me as she walked up the driveway into the road. I had learned my first lesson about being truthful and respectful regardless of the color of a person's skin.

A colored family lived next door to us. Their mixed blood made their skin lighter brown than natives. We were not supposed to have anything to do with the four children who were around our age, but we always wanted to play with them. The garden stretched a long way down below the house and big trees hid us from view. We loved to go to the bottom of the garden to play and laugh. I couldn't see any reason why we shouldn't have fun with colored kids. We thought our parents were silly and made a pact not to tell.

A lot of Indian families also lived in Pinetown. They had darker skin than coloreds and straight black hair. Their ancestors emigrated from India to work in the sugar cane fields. One afternoon we were sitting in a mango tree eating mangos. Several Indian children walking home from school passed under the branches that hung over the road unaware of our presence. We thought it hilarious to toss the mango pips down on top of them. We laughed and giggled as they ran away. We didn't realize how horrid we were, but we were lucky our mother didn't catch us.

Another time on my way home from school, one of the next-door colored boys called out. "Come over here under the tree so I can tell you a secret." I loved secrets so I obliged. When I joined him under the tree, his big brother who was hiding high up in the branches poured a whole bag of sand down on me. It got into my hair, my eyes, my mouth and my clothes. I screamed and ran home as fast as I could to tell on the colored kid. Mom just said, "kids will be kids."

I had joined a Brownie Troop, a pre-Girl Scout group. I loved my smart brown pleated uniform with all the badges sewn on the sleeve and my brand new pair of brown lace up shoes that matched. I only had one pair of shoes. Walking home one hot, sultry day after the brownie meeting, I took a short cut across a tall grassy field. Heavy rain had fallen about an hour before and I couldn't resist the puddles scattered along the path. I whipped off my shoes and tramped happily through every puddle, mud squelching between my toes, splashing about, not a care in the world. When I got home speckled with mud, I flung my school bag down on the kitchen floor and realized I only had one shoe. I rifled frantically through my bag for the other shoe, my thoughts racing. I rushed out the door to go back and search along the path. I had only just walked the path minutes before, surely I'd find the shoe lying somewhere. I reached the other side of the field where I'd sat on the grass to take my shoes off. I frantically looked for it and then retraced my steps, searching in the thick long grass all the way back home. I didn't know what I was going to tell Mom, I couldn't find the shoe anywhere. A feeling of panic swept over me.

I crept into the house and down the hall into my bedroom, hoping I could avoid any confrontation. I wasn't ready to face the truth. I lay on the bed thinking what to do. Mom was sure to find out. I decided to get it over with and tiptoed into the kitchen hovering silently behind Mom, not saying a word. She turned and frowned at me. "What have you done now Dorothy? I can tell by the look on your face something's wrong." I hated the way Mom could read me like a book. Relieved, I confessed to losing one shoe.

That evening when Dad came home, Mom told him what I'd done. He called me aside and suggested we go walk along the path again and see if he could find it. We searched and searched. It seemed to have disappeared completely. I never found the shoe but I kept the other one for a long time, just in case. That lone shoe sat on my dresser staring at me.

I didn't have a pair of shoes for school the next day. I did have an old pair, but the soles had worn loose and Dad had wired them together with little bits of wire quite a few times.

The wire kept breaking and I would have to walk along flapping my foot forward so the sole didn't fold back. Dad wired up the old shoes one more time as there was no money for another pair. I would have to wait until the next payday before I could get new ones.

During the heat of the summer we often played outside with the hose. One day Dad announced that he would build us a swimming pool. We watched Dad and our native digging away for weeks. I imagined a beautiful blue pool like I had seen in pictures. The hole didn't look like it was big enough to me, but Dad assured us we'd love the pool. After a few weeks Dad began mixing cement with sand and water in the garden wheelbarrow. Slowly he plastered the sides and the bottom of the hole and we waited for it to dry. Then he used the hose to fill it with

The new swimming pool!

water. It didn't look one bit like the pool I imagined. We had to crawl around on our hands and knees to stay under the water, but Dad seemed very pleased with the pool. He hopped in with us and sat on the bottom with his head still above the water. We splashed around and jumped in and out. In spite of the size we ended up having lots of fun.

Soon after, Dad bought a horse and named him Tommy. He was tall, black and beautiful. We learned how to brush his coat and his tail and polish his hooves, but we were never allowed to ride him alone. Dad would lead us around the garden for a few minutes before he went out for a ride. One morning Dad went down to feed him as usual. When he walked back into the kitchen while we were eating our porridge his face told us something was terribly wrong.

"Tommy's cut his hoof. He is in a bad way. I'm going to have to call the vet."

"Can we go and see Dad?"

"No, you can't. It doesn't look good and he's in a very dangerous state." When the vet arrived they went right to the stable to check Tommy out. The minute they walked back into the house we could see it was bad news. "It's no use Con, it looks like his hoof is almost severed and he will never walk properly again. We'll have to put him down." Everyone began to cry. We had grown very fond of Tommy. That afternoon the gardener came and dug a big hole in the middle of the field. The next day we sat on the bed with Mom in her bedroom while Dad and the vet went to put Tommy out of his misery. "Let's all cover our ears with our hands so we can't hear Dad shoot. He has to fire into Tommy's brain so he won't feel any pain." I stuck my fingers in my ears as tight as I could but I still heard the bang of the gun.

Later that day after Tommy was buried in the hole, Dad nailed two pieces of wood together to make a cross and we painted "Tommy" on it with the date. We all stood on the mound of dirt. "God bless our Tommy and look after him in heaven." Dad crossed his chest and I could tell he was all choked up. We stuck the cross into the ground so it could stay there forever.

A few weeks later, a friend gave Mom and Dad a white terrier we named Tessie. She quickly learned how to follow us all over the yard. She would bark and greet us everyday when we walked down the driveway. I grew to love the little white dog and looked forward to her rushing up to me whenever I came home. She slept on my bed at night. She played and romped in the evenings, and never left our side. One morning, when Mom got up to make the tea, Tessie was lying on the kitchen floor. She didn't run up to Mom when she walked in. "What's the matter Tess, tired out from your busy day yesterday?" Mom bent down to pat her. Tessie wagged her tail pathetically when Mom felt her body, but she didn't get up. "Dave, there's something wrong with this dog." We all rushed into the kitchen to check out our little Tessie. She just lay there. She could barely lift her head and gave her tail a sad wag. When I got home from school that afternoon, I rushed into the kitchen to see Tessie, missing her usual happy greeting. Mom pointed to a cardboard box on the kitchen floor. "There she is. The vet says she's very sick. She has distemper and he's done all he can for her. He gave her some medicine, but he can't promise she will get better." I sat down on the floor beside her. She felt very warm and whimpered softly when I patted her. Eventually Mommy made us go to bed and promised she would stay up all night with her. In the morning I jumped out of bed the minute I woke up and ran into the kitchen.

"How's Tessie?" I could see the tears in Mom's eyes and I knew I didn't have to ask anymore.

"She died in the night, poor thing. She was so sick she couldn't fight the disease."

"Where is she? I want to hug her one more time."

Mom took us into her bedroom and we looked at poor little Tessie lying there on the bed as if she were asleep. It was so hard to believe she would never jump up again, or lick us or bark. I put my head against her cold, white fluffy body, held her to me and cried. Mom let us miss school that day because we were too upset to go. Later on, the garden boy dug a small hole and we placed her gently into it wrapped in her tiny blanket. We covered her up as our tears dripped onto the dirt. When Dad came home, he made another cross. We stood around her as we said a prayer and she went up to heaven. After a few months Dad came home with a lovely brown Rhodesian ridgeback puppy. We named him Jock.

Shortly after Tessie died Mom told us she was going to have another baby. "We're hoping you'll get a baby brother and we'll name him David after his grandpa and father," she said. When I came home from school one afternoon Mommy was gone and Aunt Dolly greeted us at the door. "Mom's gone off to get your new brother, so I'll be staying for a couple of weeks." We loved having her around. She was great fun and sang loudly as she worked around the house. At last Mom came home with the new baby, another girl, but she was so cuddly and round we loved her anyway and named her Elizabeth.

After I had been at St. Mary's for a year, the headmistress made an announcement in Assembly. A girl I did not know had died of polio. The senior girls were crying and I could hear sniffing and blowing noses in the Assembly Hall. The teachers were sad all day and the whole school mourned her death. I didn't know what mourning was. The fear of polio took over. It was catching, but no one knew how. We were told to wash our hands all the time and try not to breathe on anybody. We felt as if a strange beast lurked in the shadow of a cough, a sneeze or the touch of a friend. Girls would simply disappear without explanation and no one told us what happened to them. One girl came back to school after an absence of a few weeks walking on crutches. Her one leg dragged. She had had polio but they said she was lucky. She didn't look lucky to me. The polio scare waned as summer ended and winter came. The disease preferred hot days. I relaxed a little, thinking maybe I wouldn't catch it after all. We prayed for polio victims at church and when I said my prayers at night. "Please God, make them better and don't let me and my sisters get polio."

I began taking piano lessons at St. Mary's. I received one lesson a week with the piano teacher and we could practice every day on the school pianos. They had three small rooms next to each other and each room had an old upright piano and a Bentwood chair. Girls were able to learn to play the piano even if they did not have a piano at home. I was scheduled to use the practice room from 3:30 to 4:30 p.m. every afternoon. The schedule was tight and although no teacher checked us, we knew someone kept an eye on the rooms to make sure each girl did her practicing. One afternoon, about three quarters of the way through my practice time, I needed to have a wee. I squirmed and crossed my legs. I tried to carry on playing, but as the minutes ticked by the urge grew stronger. I checked the round clock on the wall. I still had five minutes to go. I squeezed my legs tighter and clutched my crotch desperately trying not to let go. I could not hold on another minute. I wet my pants right on the Bentwood chair. It ran though the holes and puddled onto the wood floor, slowly soaking into the worn old planks. I packed up my music books, stuffed them into my satchel and walked out.

Many months later, there was a big fuss going around the school. A girl had drawn a naughty picture and written on the wall of the bathrooms. This was considered the most terrible of deeds. Nice girls did not do such things. The whole school was called into the Assembly Hall and we were told the culprit had twenty four hours to own up or everyone would be punished. I couldn't imagine what they would do to us but I was sure it would be awful. The following day, a girl named Ann marched up to me. I often wished I could be her friend. She seemed so confident, not scared of anything. Her thick blonde braid swung about as she approached me. Her face covered in fine blond hairs looked pink and blotchy. The laces at the neck of her uniform were tied so tight it scrunched up and pulled the whole front all crooked around her pink flesh. "I saw Lucy Brown drawing on the lavatory wall," she said in a raspy voice. "Why don't you go and tell the head prefect?" I thought if I did she would like me and become my friend. So I went to the prefects' office and said I saw Lucy Brown drawing on the lavatory walls. Lucy was called into the office and questioned. She told the head prefect it was me who had drawn on the walls. While we were sitting in the classroom quietly practicing our cursive, a fat girl knocked on the door. "Miss Clarence, could Dorothy G. come to the head-mistress's office right away please?" I felt my face turn red and my heart pounding in my chest. All eyes were on me as I slunk out of the classroom following the fat girl. No one got called to her office for nothing. What could she want me for? When we walked in she pointed to a chair. The head prefect glared at me, hands on her hips, her ponytail swinging from side to side.

"Why did you say you saw Lucy Brown drawing on the wall when it was you?" she screeched.

"Me? It wasn't me." I stammered. I told them what Ann told me. No one believed me. I couldn't figure out why they believed Lucy Brown. How could I explain why I said I saw Lucy? They didn't know I did what Ann said because I wanted her to like me. I started to cry. "Somebody is lying," the prefect screamed. "I will give you until tomorrow morning to tell the truth." After lunch, I went up to Ann. "Why did you tell me you saw Lucy drawing on the walls?" She turned away, her face cold and unfriendly. "You're a liar," she said, as she trounced off, her yellow pigtail bouncing at the back of her head. I had already learned my lesson. I would never have drawn on the walls. Why wouldn't they believe me? I walked up to another girl who had been quite friendly to me.

"You believe me don't you?"

"There's a lie in belief," she said.

I spelled b-e-l-i-e-f out in my head. Oh no! I started to cry again. The whole school thought I was a liar and had drawn on the walls. Girls I didn't even know approached me, "Why did you do it?" they asked. My pathetic denials fell on deaf ears. I did not have any idea how to deal with it, how to change people's minds or how to defend myself. Terrified, I wondered what sort of punishment they were considering for me. A few days later, I told the teacher I felt sick. She let me go home with the kindergarten children's carpool. I overheard one of the mothers telling another mom she thought I was faking. I was but I just had to escape the agony of being ostracized.

The day I pretended to be sick, I finally told Mom what happened. Bawling and sobbing, I spilled out the whole story. I didn't know why I had done what Ann asked but I had. I was in so much trouble and so unhappy. It all felt a lot better when Mom believed me and I had told someone at last. She tried to analyze how I became such a stupid kid and told me once again, how important it was to tell the truth. The next day we went to see the headmistress. She sat and talked with me. Even she could not understand why I had done it, but with Mom by my side she believed me. A few weeks later the term came to an end and school closed for the holidays. What a relief. I learned a painful lesson that has stayed with me for the rest of my life.

❖ 7 ❖

Merryfield Farm
1947 – 1951

Merryfield Farm when we first arrived

Dad had dreamed of owning a farm for a long time. He was not happy working in town for Granny in a hot dirty factory. Even though we lived on our three acres in Pinetown with a horse, a cow and lots of ducks and chickens, Dad wanted to own a real farm. We drove all over Natal with Mom and Dad looking at places for sale. Some of the farms were run down and some too expensive, while others had picturesque homes and gardens as well as large farming acreage. I imagined living in some of the prettiest places, although I knew we could never really afford any of them. Mom and Dad kept on looking, hoping to find just the right place at an affordable price.

At last they found a three hundred acre farm near Greytown. It had an old wattle and daub house painted white with a green corrugated iron roof, surrounded by a eucalyptus plantation. The fruit orchards and fields could produce a living for us. We had fun watching Mom and Dad picture and plan our new life on the farm. They signed the papers and made an agreement to buy everything. "The place comes lock, stock and barrel," Dad said. "That means we're buying all their animals too, pigs, cows, chickens and ducks, the whole kit and caboodle. We'll all be very busy learning how to cope from the minute we get there." We could hardly wait.

Dad's best friend worked at Massey Harris Tractors, a farm equipment company. He promised to get Dad a new tractor. In addition, because it was late in the season, they would lend him a second tractor so he could get the fields ploughed in time. The company agreed to publish an article about him sitting on a Massey Harris tractor in *The Farmer's Weekly*. The tractors would arrive a week after we got there.

At last we were all packed and loaded. Dad hired a skinny Indian man with a big lorry to move our furniture to the farm. I looked at it piled high with all our stuff, the sofa and the old kitchen table where we had eaten so many breakfasts. The chair legs stuck out in between the ropes the Indian had strung back and forth across the top. "I think it tied velly secure," he assured my Dad, standing back to survey his work.

"Everyone go to the lav one last time, I don't want to stop every five minutes for you kids to wee," Dad shouted. "Hurry up and let's get on our way." Mom was already sitting in the car with the cat tied up in a pillowcase wiggling and meowing on her lap. We piled into the back seat, my three sisters and I, with Jock our new Rhodesian Ridgeback dog, and a basket full of sandwiches and bananas to eat on the long drive. The Indian pulled the lorry out of our driveway in front of us, the high precarious load swaying as he turned up the road and headed for the farm.

We left Pinetown, the familiar streets and places we knew fading in the distance. The heat made me feel carsick. Jock panted and drooled on my lap, so just after we passed through Pietermaritzburg and up the hill out of the valley we had to stop so I wouldn't be sick. It was a relief for all of us when we pulled over on the side of the road to get out, stretch our legs and enjoy the fresh air. Mom passed out sandwiches and gave us all a drink of water. She opened the thermos and poured a cup of tea for Dad and herself. "We'll have to hurry along Dave, we can't leave the cat in the pillow case too much longer." Dad whistled for Jock who bounded out of a bush he'd been sniffing, and hopped back into the car, leaping all over us and scratching my legs. We squealed and complained about him as he flopped on us panting, unaware of how annoying he was. As we headed towards Greytown, the road wound in and out amongst plantations for miles so we couldn't see anything except row after row of wattle trees.

Dad looked out the window. "I think we're getting close to Greytown now." We could barely hear him. We had the windows rolled all the way down with the air blowing into the back to cool us off and help me not to feel carsick. Just as we drove over a hill out of the wattle plantations, the town lying in a valley below came into sight. We drove along the main street past a few shops and the general store. Tools, ploughs and all sorts of farm contraptions I had never seen before were out front.

The middle of the street was tarred but we had to pull off onto the dirt at the side to park. There weren't many cars about but the town was teaming with natives walking along the road. Many women carried huge bags of meal or bundles of wood balanced on their heads. Most of the men sat around on the roadside or on boxes talking in Zulu and laughing. Mom made me wait in the car holding the cat while they went in to buy milk, bread and things they thought we might need. By now the frightened cat had wet the pillowcase. He yowled and meowed while I clutched him tight and Jock sniffed at the squirming wet bundle.

The sign over the store, painted in green lettering and outlined with gold, read *Ross's Dry Goods and Haberdashery — Feeds and Seeds for All Your Needs.* I liked the way it rhymed and I sang it over and over in my head. Mom and Dad came out of the store both carrying boxes, which they piled into the back on top of us.

"Only six more miles to go kids," Dad said as he climbed back into the front of the old Ford. We trundled out of town and crossed over the bridge where the tarmac ended. Then Dad sped along the wide dirt road towards our new farm. I looked back out the window, but I couldn't see Greytown for the dust clouds blocking the view behind us. We drove up another hill passing more natives walking in all directions. The wattle plantations ended and most of the hills on either side were planted with rows of sprouting green corn, their leaves waving gently in the breeze. "That's what we are going to grow as soon as the tractors arrive and we get the fields ploughed and planted," Dad shouted into the wind. All I could think about was getting out of the stinking car.

Mom saw a sign *Umvosana* stamped in black metal letters on a small square of rusty white tin. "There's our turn off." She pointed left and Dad turned the steering wheel sharply, swerving onto the narrow dirt road. We lurched and fell over each other screeching as the boxes flew about the car. Jock scrambled all over us. Mom hung onto the door handle. "Slow down Dave," she screeched as we straightened ourselves out. I craned my neck to see if I could help find our new farm, but the grass was so tall on either side I couldn't see anything.

"We're looking for a sign that says *Merryfield Farm*," Mom said looking at the piece of paper in her hands, trying to read the simple map she had drawn in pencil. Dad inched along the road looking left and right. We came up to a railroad track and saw to our left the grass was cleared away. Another very large sign that read *Umvosana* was nailed onto two rough thick poles. "I think that's our train station." It didn't look like much like a station to me. There were no buildings, just the sign, a few wooden crates piled up on the raised platform and a couple of natives in raggedy clothes standing talking.

We came across an African woman on the side of the narrow road, a baby tied on her back with a pink blanket. She was barefoot with her head covered in a bright red doek, fastened in a knot at the back of her neck. She stepped into the grass and turned to look at us.

Dad pulled up next to her. She stared at us with her big brown eyes and smiled pleasantly when Dad spoke to her in Zulu. The baby on her back seemed to be fast asleep. We didn't know what they were saying but she pointed down the road in the direction we were going. She carried a long bundle of wood on her head that swung around as she talked. Dad thanked her and the baby slept on soundly, its head flopping about as she waddled off down the road. We inched along, then Dad spotted a grey wooden plank nailed to a wattle pole, with the words *Merryfield Farm* and an arrow painted on it. The sign pointed left along the railroad track.

I knew we were getting close then. We turned another corner and came to a long driveway lined on both sides with tall thick bushes covered in red berries. The road turned into two worn dirt tracks the width of the car wheels. We still couldn't see the house but a hundred yards further on we came to a gate attached to two white square pillars about four feet high. The car vibrated and bounced as Dad drove over a cattle grid between the posts. At last we could see the house.

"Here we are safe and sound," Dad said merrily as he pressed the brakes and stopped the car in front of the house. He opened the door and put his feet on the firm dirt driveway. "Watch out for the cat," Mom yelled as we scrambled out. Jock barked and jumped over us. He ran right over to a fruit tree in the middle of the lawn and did the longest dog pee I had ever seen. He was just as happy as we were to get out of the hot car. He ran about wagging his tail, sniffing and marking every bush and tree. I stood quietly, breathing in the smell of cows and grass and wet dirt. I stretched my arms and legs taking it all in.

A beautiful green lawn dotted with fruit trees spread out in front of the house. A verandah wrapped around two sides and the green corrugated tin roof glinted in the late afternoon sun. After we had a good stretch we looked around. Dad opened the front door with a big key and we went inside to check out the new house. By this time it was getting late and there was no sign of the lorry and our things. The old pine floors creaked as we peered into the two rooms on either side of the passageway. One would be a bedroom for Mom and Dad and the other for my three sisters. I would have my own room at the back near the kitchen. It was an old storage room, but Mom said even though small it would make a cozy room for me. I was so glad

I would not have to share with my three sisters. The passage opened into a large living room with a high stone fireplace and a dining room off to the right. The bathroom was down the hall. "There's a real flushing toilet," Mom said, "and we won't have to go outside anymore." A big kitchen stretched across the back of the house with a black stove filling the corner. Hot water pipes went out of the stove up into the ceiling and a fat chimney pipe reached up through the roof. We followed Dad out the back door onto the verandah surprised to find the two native families who lived on the farm waiting to greet us. They had lived on the farm for a long time and simply stayed on with whoever owned the farm.

They all stood in a row. A handsome young Zulu man with short curly hair stepped forward extending both hands, his muscular, dark brown body bare and shiny. He wore no clothes except for a traditional *beshu*. "*How. Baas, Gunjani wena?*" he greeted us as Dad grabbed his hands and spoke to him in Zulu. He told us his name, *Begiswe*. As he spoke to Dad, his bright brown eyes and wide smile made us feel at ease. Large white wooden circles about two inches across stuck in his ear lobes and flapped around as he turned to introduce his family. His wife stepped forward shyly and put out her hand. She greeted us with a half curtsy as if we were important, and told us her name, *Jabulile*. She wore a dark cloth wrapped around the lower part of her body, covering a large round stomach, her top bare. We stared at her. "I think she's having a baby," I whispered to Sheila. Her breasts hung down like two big mangos, brown and shiny. Two young boys stepped forward following their mother. Giggling, they covered their mouths with their calloused hands. They were wearing tatty, boys shorts and nothing else, their feet bare and dusty. Only Dad could speak Zulu so we just stood looking at each other there, each of us not knowing what the other was thinking.

Bigiswe smiled warmly and shook Mom's hands. We were too busy staring at the *beshu*. I knew the word but had never seen one. It consists of a big square of cowhide hanging at the back and lots of fronds in front made of circles of hide threaded onto a strip of leather. The fronds dangled and wobbled in front of his "you know what's" as Mom called them. He didn't even have any pants on that I could tell.

The other family was colored. The boss of the family introduced himself as Mkovo. He wore a dirty khaki shirt and pants frayed at the bottom. His feet were bare. He had a wide smile, big ears and a crop of wooly hair sprinkled with sawdust and fluff. I wondered what he had been doing when we drove up. A skinny wrinkled old lady stepped forward. She greeted us with a crooked smile, which showed gummy gaps between her stained uneven teeth. Her grey curly hair stuck out of her flowered doek, so it looked like a wrapped brillo pad. I could see her floppy bosoms dangling inside her dress, which was buttoned all they way down the front. Her little toe stuck out of a hole in her old bedroom slippers revealing a gnarly yellow toenail. Mkovo called her Granny, but her name was Minnie. Mkovo could speak English and so could his pretty slender wife

Miriam, who would be helping Mom in the house. Lastly an old dark colored man ambled awkwardly up and shook hands with Dad. Shy and hesitant he seemed unsure how we would react to him. His clothes were torn and shabby and he had scars all over his body. His scruffy grey beard was sparse and patchy, the whites of his eyes a yellowish brown. But he had a nice smile and spoke softly in English. Later we found out he suffered from epilepsy. His name was Sipufwe.

The lorry finally arrived. Everyone gathered around and began unpacking our worldly belongings. They spread the furniture out on the front lawn so Mom could direct where everything would go as Dad translated feverishly. We couldn't wait to see where we would sleep that night. While they were moving the furniture into the house we kids decided to do a bit of exploring. Around the back of the house we spotted a huge tank for our water supply. Later we learned there were three dams up on top of the hill filled with sweet spring water, which bubbled out of the ground and was pumped into the tank.

A high chicken wire fence housed lots of brown and black speckled chickens, clucking and scratching the dirt. Sipufwe carried a bucket of ground corn and tossed it amongst the chickens creating a mad scramble for their evening meal.

Mkovo's wife came in and lit a fire inside the stove. She fished out some candles and lit them too. "Don't we have electric lights Dad?" I realized it was getting dark and there were no lights anywhere except for the candles. I took a candlestick and walked through the kitchen into the center room of the house with the stone fireplace. Shadows stretched across the room. In the semi-darkness I saw our familiar old sofa and Dad's favorite chair placed right next to the fireplace. Dad opened a box and pulled out a funny looking lantern. "Bring that candle closer Doff, I can't see a darn thing and Mom can't find the bloody instructions." He fiddled with a tiny mesh bag he called a mantle, his big fingers having trouble threading a string onto the center of the lamp. "Is this all the light we have Dad?" I asked, thinking that they must have known there was no electricity but just hadn't mentioned it. Dad got the string tied finally and the lantern flared up bringing the room to life. The table where he put his cigarettes stood next to his familiar worn chair and our Granny's beautiful, old, stinkwood table had been placed in the center of the room. Later the rose bowl always filled with the Royal Dalton china roses, made the room feel like home.

I decided to check out the bathroom. "Take the candle with you Doff, it'll be dark down that passage." The first door appeared to be a room with nothing but shelves. As I opened the second door slowly, the hinges creaked. I held up the candle and saw a long ancient bathtub with curved sides and claw feet. It had small patches of chipped enamel here and there. The claws had been painted white once but looked worn and banged up. Two brass taps stuck out of the wall over the bathtub and an old rubber plug dangled on a rusty chain. A washbasin hung on the wall nearby. I turned on the cold tap, cupped my hands and drank the sweet spring water thirstily. No sign of a toilet. Dad had told us it was inside, so I walked further along the passage. The candle cast an eerie light and my shadow stretched all the way down the passage. Then I saw it. A real flushing toilet with a water tank attached to the wall high above and a long chain waiting to be pulled. I put the candle down on the floor and yanked it right away. The water swished down the pipe and spun around in the bowl washing everything away. I wouldn't have to go to an outhouse anymore.

The beds were finally in place. Mom couldn't find the sheets but we didn't care, we were so tired after our long day of travel and discovery we lay down on the bare mattresses. I covered myself with an old army blanket and fell asleep as soon as my head hit the pillow. I could hardly wait for the next day to explore our new home.

Sheila and I awoke early the next morning to the smell of bacon and eggs cooking on the stove. Miriam had made a large pot of hot tea and Dad went outside to survey the fields with Begizwe and Mkovo. We gulped down our breakfast, drank our tea and dashed outside to investigate. We wandered out of the gate down a dirt road and came across an old cowshed with thirty cows munching away on some hay. Behind the shed, three big fat pink pigs and a snorting old black one, all sniffing and rummaging about in the mud, occupied a fenced pigpen. It smelled terrible and looked disgusting to us. Normally Mkovo milked the cows very early and fed the pigs right after, but since he had gone out with Dad to show him around the farm they were still waiting to be milked.

In the daylight we saw how badly the fields were overgrown with tall green weeds. I overheard Dad telling Mom we would have to plough soon and plant the corn seeds or it would be too late in the season to get a decent crop. Every day Dad met the evening train to see if the tractors had arrived, but they did not come. As the days wore on, they became very anxious, even though there was so much to do and learn.

We met our first neighbor when he came over to introduce himself to Dad and offered to help with ploughing the weeds. Mr. Lourens, a middle aged Afrikaner, with scraggy brown hair splattered with grey, bushy eyebrows, deep blue eyes and a big red nose with lumps on it, had a big smile. He spoke with a thick Afrikaans accent. "Ag, man. I've been watching these weeds grow like mad hoping someone would buy this farm and fix it up. I'm bloody glad to welcome you here," he shook Dad's hand vigorously.

"I want you to meet the missus soon, so bring your wife over when you have a minute." Their children were all grown up so we were disappointed to learn they didn't have any kids for us to play with. After Dad told him the story about the tractor delay, he offered to lend us an old tractor he had. This turned our to be a lifesaver for us even though it was the most ancient tractor I had ever seen. It was large and rusty and the wheels had no tires, but it had big steel spokes so it did not get stuck in the muddy fields. The noisy engine coughed and spluttered, belching and smoking but it could pull the plough.

My cousin Dave, a tall handsome but gangly sixteen-year old who we all looked up to, had come to the farm to help Mom and Dad. It was Michaelmas school holidays and he could drive. He quickly learned how to handle the beat up old tractor and plowed all day, back and forth until dark. It took a long time to plough the weedy fields with a one-track plough, but Dave worked hard and the smell of fresh plowed dirt filled the evening air.

Early one morning Sheila and I asked to ride on the back of the tractor so Dave let us climb up behind him. We were wearing dresses so we seated ourselves carefully on a bar behind Dave clutching onto the edge of his metal seat. As he let out the

Dave on the tractor in front, with Dad on the tractor behind

clutch, the tractor jerked and Sheila fell off right in between the tractor wheels and the plough. I screamed and jumped off shouting for Dad. Sheila started yelling and crying. Her dress caught in the wheel of the plough so she couldn't escape. She reached her arms out to me in terror, her distorted face begging me to save her as the wheels clutched her dress. We were on the edge of the field close to the house. Dad was having breakfast and a cup of tea in the kitchen with Mom when he heard me screaming. He came flying out, leaping like a springbuck across the yard in his khaki shorts and big old army boots, his face stricken with fear from the sounds. He saw Sheila trapped under the wheel of the plough. He lunged forward and snatched her away from the approaching blade just as Dave let out the clutch. The tractor lurched forward, plowing the torn remains of Sheila's dress into the ground. Later Dave told Dad that he could not have held the clutch in much longer, his calf muscles were bursting with pain and the clutch was too strong for him.

A few days after this incident two tractors arrived on a huge truck and were offloaded onto the front lawn. Since they were delivered so late, the company sent a second tractor on loan to help get the fields plowed more quickly. The tractors looked small next to the big old clunker we had borrowed, but they were new shiny red with real tires and the man from Massey Harris assured us they would do the job. Now two people could plow the fields. Mr. Laurens lent Dad another plough and said he thought the corn would be planted just in time to get us a decent crop if the rains came soon. Mom and Dad posed next to the tractors out in the field and they took a lot of pictures for the *Farmers Weekly* article. Later we proudly showed off the advertisement with Dad's signature on the bottom attesting to the wonder of a Massey Harris tractor. "It's a bloody miracle we got the fields plowed," Dad said to Mom, "they were so damn late with the delivery." He didn't say anything to his friend Ernie, but he didn't seem all that happy about the pictures and the ad.

When we finally settled into the farmhouse Dad asked if I wanted to go for a walk up the hill to visit the *kraals* of our two families, to see where they lived and become better acquainted. The farm was mostly flat except for a steep round hill on the northwest boundary, which was still part of the farm.

(Left) Massey Harris, Salesman   (Right) Dad on his tractor

Both families had built their *kraals* on the hillside, close to the three dams that stored our water. We trudged up the steep hill on a primitive road, more like a worn track, with a scary slope cut into the hillside. At the top of the hill there was a cattle dip — a long narrow furrow filled with water. They added disinfectant to the water and dipped the cattle to prevent diseases caused by ticks. On dipping day, Mkovo would herd the cattle into the pen to the opening and push them into the water. They swam through the dip and came out smelling of disinfectant and shook themselves off. The cattle trudging up the hill every week had carved the track out. Whenever Dad drove the truck up that road, I was afraid it might tip over and we'd fall out and roll down the hill. I always clung tightly to the sides.

The first *kraal* we came to had only one hut, which appeared to be a large round single room with a thatched roof. Minnie, the old colored Granny was sitting outside on a grass mat crocheting, her light brown, wrinkled hands flicking the crochet needle in and out of the thread like a machine. "I'm making a nice doily for your Ma'am, keep the flies out of the milk and sugar," she cackled and smiled her toothless grin. Her daughter Miriam emerged through the low door opening. Smoke drifted out from the top of the hut and I could smell the aroma of burnt mealie meal. Several chickens scattered and a little girl with porridge all over her face and a handful of the mealie meal rolled into a ball peeked out at us. She wore a torn, grubby dress with the belt ends dangling to the ground untied. The old uncle sat by the fire in the center of the hut. I hoped he wouldn't have one of those fits we had been told about. Later we became very fond of old Granny and visited her regularly. We had doilies to cover everything, large and small, pretty crochet work with heavy multi-colored beadwork fringes.

Dad talked with Miriam about the arrangement that she would work for our family six months of the year. Granny was too old to do much and Mkovo worked with Dad all the time. He had been allocated ten acres of land for many years, which he planted with whatever he wanted. He used the farm tractor to plough and the whole family looked after their crops during the growing season.

We moved on to the next *kraal* with two huts, both simple round rooms made from interwoven wattle branches and mud with thatched roofs, low door openings and no windows. They were situated amongst mango trees that provided shade and a pleasant outdoor area. Begiswe's wife came out to greet us, followed by a small child about two years old and three *umfaans*, young boys of various ages. Two wore *beshus*, the other one had on an old pair of khaki shorts and a tatty shirt. They giggled and spoke to me in Zulu while Dad talked to their mother. "*Wena booga mena?*" one said to me indicating his style of dress. I had no clue what they were saying but wasn't about to let on. I shook my head as if to say "no" and they shrieked with laughter. We giggled and laughed too, even though we didn't have any idea why we were laughing. I later found out they had asked me if I could see what they were wearing!

Begiswe's wife would also work six months of the year in our home, but she was having a baby soon so she would work when she was able. She grew hot green chilies and tomatoes near the hut and she also worked in their fields when needed.

We gradually adjusted to farm life — lots of space, no electricity and no shops. The farm Zulus did not speak any English so Dad and Mkovo were our interpreters. We picked up Zulu a few words at a time and gradually learned to communicate.

Soon after we settled in, I came outside to see Dad measuring and nailing four short pieces of wood together.

"What you making Dad?"

"It's a fridge to keep us going until the new one arrives," he said. It didn't look much like a fridge to me. He continued banging pieces of wood together, covered it inside and out with

With our friends on the tractor, our new dog Trixie on the left

chicken wire and filled the space with bits of charcoal from the stove. He made a door and attached hinges and a catch. When he finished, he hammered a big nail into the tree outside the kitchen door and hung the box on it. He pulled the hose over and tied it to the top. When he gently turned on the tap, it dripped over the charcoal and ran down the tree making a puddle at the bottom. Jock and Trixie wandered over and took a long drink. "There you are Doff," he said, "that'll keep things cool for a while." Mom put the milk and butter inside the new fridge.

The next day Dad found an enormous mushroom the size of a plate and brought it to Mom to put in the fridge. In the morning I heard him say, "We'll have some nice fried mushroom with our breakfast this morning Con." He fished the plate out of the fridge and walked into the kitchen, "Good God Con," he exclaimed in horror, "you won't believe this." Nothing remained but a crawling bed of white maggots devouring the last bits of Dad's prize mushroom.

A week later a real fridge arrived in a big box on the train. Mkove and Bigiswe had to unload it and then load it onto the wagon pulled by the tractor. Dad filled a small tank in the bottom with paraffin and lit it. I couldn't understand how a small flame made a fridge cold but it worked. At last we could have a lovely drink of cold water filled with ice.

After things settled down, Mom opened up the box of pictures and began hanging them around the house. Dad loved rugby and had played a lot so he had several pictures of the

Our family with Mrs. Morton and her three girls

teams he had played with. Dad wanted them hanging in the passage and dining room or anywhere else there was a space. "Dave, we are not having rugby pictures hanging all over the house," Mom announced. "We'll put them all together in one room. How about we make the dining room the rugby picture room?" Dad agreed and Mom hung the pictures. Dad often looked at the pictures of young men sitting in rows with their arms folded and a huge silver trophy at their feet remembering "those good old days." Mom displayed the trophies on the dining room sideboard and Jabulile polished them every week.

During winter rugby season we drove into town on Saturdays so Dad could watch the games. He ran up and down the field calling the players names while Mom sat on a blanket shivering with her thermos of tea. We ran around playing with the other kids. We met a lot of Afrikaans kids and shouted rudely at each other. They called us *rooineks* and we called them *boeties*. The best players were most often Afrikaners so a friendly strange mixture of insults and cheers permeated the afternoon fun.

The orchard on the farm had been there for many years. Lots of plum, peach and nectarine trees produced delicious juicy fruit, and the five enormous old apple trees, which stood like sentries on each corner, were covered in masses of white blossoms when we first arrived. When the blossoms fell, green leaves sparkled in the sunlight and hundreds of delicious green apples loaded the branches so they hung heavy and low, close to the ground. Dad asked our Zulus not to pick the apples, but if they found one fallen they were welcome to take it. Our grandmother had written to say she was coming to visit the farm and would be arriving in a week.

The fields were plowed at last and planted with mealies. The young plants were growing vigorously in the hot South African sun and Mom and Dad were gradually becoming real farmers. Most afternoons, enormous black clouds swirled across the farm and the sky darkened. Loud claps of thunder and lightning followed by a heavy pelting rain lasted fifteen minutes or so before the clouds moved on and the sun came out again.

The old Ford was becoming very useful. Dad had been buying calves to expand our herd but he had to get them home somehow. One morning I saw him taking the back seat out of the car and underneath that old 1938 seat was a sturdy metal frame, quite flat and solid.

"What you doing Dad?" I couldn't imagine why he'd take the seat out.

"Going to pick up a new calf," he said, as if he did it everyday. I watched and tried to imagine a calf standing in the back of the car. He took one of the *umfaans* with him to hold the calf and off they went. I wanted to go too. I always wanted to be in the middle of things, but he told me this time I would only get in the way.

When they arrived back my sister and I dashed out to see the new calf. Dad opened the back door and there stood a poor little black calf, shivering and shaking, her ears pinned against her head stiff with fear. Her big cow eyes bulged and the *umfaan* clung to the rope looped around her neck. All of a sudden the calf lost control and cow dung squirted everywhere. Hot, smelly and slippery, her little hooves splayed about. Cow dung splashed all over the back of the old Ford and the calf went down on her side. Dad grabbed her two front feet, the *umfaan* held onto her back and they heaved the calf out of the car upside down like a hunted trophy buck. They dropped her down on solid ground. She planted her hooves thankfully and scampered about. Bigeswe's son Tegwaan trotted her down to the cowshed where she joined with all her new friends.

❖

There weren't many trees around my school in Greytown, and even though much bigger than my last one, it wasn't very pretty. Long narrow buildings with arched corridors spread around the grounds. I hated having to get used to new teachers. Since we wore every day clothes we stood out like flowers in a desert. I wished just one person would say something to me. At break time I wandered about watching some of the girls gather together playing hand ball, while some played house under a big tree. I felt so envious of their chatter and laughter, climbing an old tree and shouting out from their imaginary second story. I tried to think of something to say that would make them interested in me, but they were in their own make believe world. Sheila and I found each other at lunchtime and ate together huddled in the corner of the playground trying not to look new.

A week after school started, a bolt of bright yellow checked fabric arrived in the postbag and Mom sewed all night to make our new uniforms. I was so pleased to have a uniform at last and look like one of the crowd. One of the popular girls asked me where I came from when she saw me all dressed up. I hoped she would be my friend, but she soon moved on to the games and took no more notice of me.

"I can play handball," I said, as she walked out the next day.

"Ok, let's see."

I ran into the square and the ball came flying. I rushed at it with my fists clutched tight and missed.

"I thought you said you could play?" she laughed.

"I can, I really can, gimme another chance?" This time I caught it and it flew back to the other side of the square.

"Ok," she said slowly. "You're in."

At first Dad drove us the six miles to school but he soon decided we could catch the train back and forth every day. It arrived every morning punctually in Umvozana station at 7:14 a.m. from Kranskop, stopping only briefly to pick up passengers and drop off goods. If we were a few minutes late Dad had to drive us into town. We only missed it a few times as he simply woke us much earlier with a cup of hot tea and would bluff about the time. For breakfast we'd have a big bowl of mealie meal porridge, smothered in butter, brown sugar and milk. After we dressed, we'd braid our long hair. Dad insisted we braid it everyday. He also thought the train was a great way for us to get to school. "You don't have far to walk from the station to the school. Just look after your little sister and don't talk to strangers."

Once we arrived we lined up outside our classrooms. When the bell rang all classes marched into the assembly held in the school hall. We stood in lines like an army, in order by height, slouching carelessly, waiting for the principal to arrive. A beak nosed young teacher played a John Philip Sousa march on the piano. Her new curly perm bounced and her shoulders hunched as she struck the keys with enthusiasm. Her hands pranced up and down on the keyboard while she swayed from side to side to the beat of her own music. With a book clutched under his arm, the principal marched in across the stage and the teachers rose to attention. His ruddy pock marked face looked stern under his mop of grey hair. He stopped in the center and looked us over briefly. "Let us pray," he bellowed. We bowed our heads, but I peeked to see him read the message for the new term. Slow and monotone, he asked God to help us learn to the best of our ability. I hoped God would help me, the new kid, get through the next few weeks.

We all sang "Onward Christian Soldiers". I knew this hymn well because Dad liked it, so I decided this place couldn't be all that bad. After announcements everyone marched out to their classrooms in long lines, shortest kids first, which meant I was at the back of the line as usual. The teacher stood straight and tall beside his desk. He had a smooth olive complexion and his big ears stuck out on either side of his head. Stern eyebrows grew across his brow and his brownish lips didn't smile. His long neck seemed choked by a stiff collar and a striped bow tie. Everyone stood beside his or her desk at attention. I coughed loudly wishing I could stop the tickle in my throat.

"*Wat is jou naam?*" He pointed a ruler at me. "*Is ye sik?*" He addressed me in Afrikaans. Please God, I hope I don't have to speak Afrikaans all day.

"*Nee meneer,*" I said and coughed again. "My *naam* is Dorothy Greenland." I cringed, I hated my surname. Saying it out loud was even more distressing. I knew inside all the kids snickered at the name.

"Greenland," he said laughing. "*Ek sal jou 'Groenland' naam.*" I became Groenland from that day forward.

Mr. Eleker, both our classroom and Afrikaans teacher, only spoke to us in Afrikaans, he never used the English language. The walls were adorned with white cards displaying Afrikaans nouns and verbs. Mr. Eleker read *Beeld*, the Afrikaans newspaper every morning before we arrived. He'd fold it neatly when we marched into the room and place it on the corner of his very tidy desk. On the one corner he had a couple of books piled and on the other a stack of exercise books for marking. He informed us in Afrikaans that he did not read English newspapers. He stuck out a long finger and pointed to a desk near the front. "*Groenland, hier is jou plek.*"

I slunk from the back corner up to the front desk, all eyes on me, probably laughing inwardly about my silly last name he'd just bellowed again. "*Sit klas,*" he ordered. Everyone shuffled behind their desks and sat down. Desk lids opened and banged shut. In the corner of my desk was a small glass inkwell. The ink monitor walked around the class filling them with dark blue ink from a big bottle, stained and blotched from a million refills. Excited, I fished out my pen with its new G Nib from my pencil box. I would show Mr. Eleker how neatly I could write.

The Arithmetic teacher was Irish. He came to South Africa after the war. His face was bright red and he had the bushiest eyebrows I had ever seen. I got a close look at them as he leaned over my desk to help me. I'd stare at his eyebrows while he explained the problem, then wonder what he had told me as he walked away.

Even on hot days, he wore a thick tweed sports coat with grey flannel trousers and had no patience if you didn't understand the problem. Once he whacked me on the shoulders

In front of the farmhouse

with his book. "Dorothy, you blithering idiot," he shouted in his Irish accent, spit flying out between his smoke stained teeth. I just ducked. I never told Mom because I liked him in spite of his quick temper.

I mostly enjoyed school. We studied Math, English, Geography, History, Science and Afrikaans, which was compulsory. Dad told us we had to learn it because the Afrikaners were trying to make it the first language of the land

and wanted everyone to speak it. Our family did not like most Afrikaners because they felt superior to the Africans and did not treat them fairly. Mr. Eleker was quite mad. One day he threw an inkwell at one of the kids. It hit the back of the classroom, glass spattered everywhere and dark blue ink ran slowly down the wall. It horrified me that a teacher could do such a thing. We had to tell a story in Afrikaans once a month. I would try to tell a funny story about life on the farm and distract him from the fact that I was lousy at his beloved language.

At last Granny arrived in her grey chauffer driven Chrysler for a visit. Granny's arrival was always an exciting event for she never came empty handed. I stood watching as she stepped out of the car in all her grandeur. She wore a wide summer hat adorned in flowers, her face beaming as she greeted us all with cuddly hugs. Warm and round, Granny's flowing dress draped and hung in silky folds. Her skin was smooth and soft. I loved the way she colored her cheeks with rouge, powdered her face and smelled of scent.

We could hardly wait to show Granny around the farm and I gave up my small bedroom for her. As Bigiswe carried her suitcase inside, we followed, all talking at once telling her about the new calves, the ducks, chickens and pigs. Miriam made a big pot of tea so Granny could sit down and recover from her long drive. I swigged my tea quickly and pushed the biscuits towards Granny trying to get her attention. Finally she stood up. "Come on, let's go and look around," she said, "I can see you kids are dying to tell me everything."

We had great fun telling her all about the calf transporting, leaving no details out. "Would you like to look inside the car? We can show you where the calf pooped," I said enthusiastically.

"I'm perfectly capable of imagining it from your flamboyant descriptions." The look on her face said everything.

A few days later, Mom and Granny sat outside on the verandah enjoying their third cup of tea. Granny was admiring the apple trees at the back of the garden laden with fruit. "Why don't you try and sell some of those apples Connie?" They got up and wandered out to study the situation. I was sitting on the grass doing nothing so I followed them towards the trees. Showing off a little, I shook a branch and a few apples fell to the ground. Granny picked one up and took a big bite. "You know Con, these apples are really sweet and delicious. I think you should try and sell them and make a few extra bob." They decided they would advertise and see what happened.

"Seven shillings and sixpence for a crate," Granny decided without knowing how many apples fit into the box. The following day Granny departed with her chauffeur in grand style, laden down with apples, fruits and vegetables, and a couple of chickens. As soon as she arrived home she got to work making quite sure we could sell all the apples and make some money. She placed ads in the *Cape Sunday Times, Johannesburg Sunday Times, Rhodesian Sunday Times* and *Natal Sunday Mercury* for three consecutive Sundays. You could buy a crate of the most delicious fresh apples straight off the tree. Simply mail your postal order today with three shillings extra for shipping and your order will be filled.

Farmers received their mail quite differently from the way city people did. We had two large postbags made of thick green canvas with a leather strap for carrying and a drawstring closer padlocked through two grommets. Every day the morning train on its way to Greytown stopped at our station and picked up the empty mailbags left early in the morning by the local farmers. The afternoon return train out of Greytown would throw out the mailbags at each station on the way to Kranskop, its final destination. Our address was P.O. Bag Umvozana, the name of our station. Most of the time Sheila and I came back from school on that train and would carry the mailbag home. Sometimes when it was hot we would argue about whose turn it was to carry the bag and would kick it down the dusty road all the way home, laughing and giggling and imagining what would happen if Mom saw us. We never gave a thought to what might be in it. We'd shake off the dust as we got closer to the house, chuck it down on the verandah, plop down in a chair and guzzle our afternoon tea.

Several days after Granny's departure we found the mailbag pretty full and much heavier.

"I wonder what can be in it?" Mom said as she gave it a shake.

"Well let's go tip it onto the dining room table." She tipped out the mailbag and hundreds of letters scattered all over the table. All orders for apples. There were so many, every one of us had to work late that evening, picking and packing apples into small wooden boxes. Luckily Dad had purchased a few dozen in Greytown, "Just in case your Mother is right and we do get a couple of orders." That night we filled all the orders, Mom made labels and Dad put them on the train in the morning. The next day the mailbag was even fuller and heavier with more orders.

We had more orders than apples. Mom telephoned Granny to cancel the advertising. When she hung up, I could see by the look on her face something terrible was wrong. Granny had just told Mom that she had placed the ad in all the national newspapers for three consecutive Sundays so we could be sure to sell all the apples. Granny had no idea how many apples there were or how many filled a crate.

"That's the trouble with your bloody mother Con, she's always interfering and trying to run everyone's life. She thinks she knows everything!" I could see Dad was mad. A pall came over the whole family. Day after day the mailbag was bursting with apple orders. We'd drag it home despondently and drop it onto the verandah floor.

"More orders today Mom," we'd shout as we walked in the door. First we packed apples enthusiastically, but as they ran out we would come home to find Mom sitting at the dining room table returning money orders and writing apology letters. On top of everything else, the Zulus had been enjoying the apples too. We were reminded Dad had told them it was ok to eat them if they were on the ground. Well, just a little shake of the tree and they had all they wanted. For a few days the bag was so heavy Dad had to drive to the station and fetch it, as it was too heavy to carry home. The initial excitement of so many orders turned to dismay when we picked up the bag and it was stuffed again. The dining room table was covered with letters and money orders. Not only did we not have enough apples, but also we had to return hundreds of unfilled orders. Day after day, late into the night Mom and Dad wrote apologetic letters, stuffing each one into a new envelope with the money order and a new stamp. All the money from the apple sales was going towards returning all the unfilled orders. One letter involved a complaint that they had not received the apples nor had the money order been returned. "Now I'm being accused of stealing!" Mom burst into tears, "I'm sick of the whole darn fiasco. I don't think I'll ever eat another one of those damn apples ever again." She put her head down on her hands on the table and her shoulders shook as she sobbed harder than I'd ever seen. Slowly the number of letters subsided and our house returned to normal. "Don't ever let your Mother help us again Con, we won't last another year with her kind of help."

Several days after the apple fiasco died down, the phone in the passage rang two longs and a short. "It's our number," I shouted to Mom. She rushed to answer and a man on the other end said that a new Chevrolet truck had been ordered and would be delivered the following week. "There has to be a mistake," Dad said, "I didn't order a truck. This farm doesn't make enough money for such a luxury." But sure enough, a

Granny in front of the House of Parliament,
Cape Town

week later a man drove into the driveway in a brand new brown Chevrolet truck. He opened the door and sauntered out with his hat in his hand.

"I'm looking for Dave Greenland."

"Dad," I yelled as I ran around the new truck. "Is this for us?" Dad came running out of the house when he heard all the commotion and his mouth fell open in shock.

"I am delivering the truck courtesy of Mrs. Lewis." Quite overwhelmed, Mom telephoned Granny.

"Connie," she said over the phone, "You can't have those children riding around in a filthy old car and use it for moving cattle as well. It's simply not done."

Mom and Dad sat inside the new truck, running their hands over the smooth dashboard, studying all the dials and breathing in the brand new smell. We jumped into the back and tapped on the window, pressing our lips against the glass and making a face at Mom. Dad gripped the steering wheel and turned the key. The engine roared and we shrieked with anticipation. "We might as well make the most of it kids. Sit down in the back there and hold on tight." Dad put it into gear, let out the clutch and the truck leaped into life. We spun around the driveway and drove all over the farm roads, splashing through puddles and potholes. We kids slid around in the truck bed thinking it was the most fun we had ever had in our whole life.

Some time before Christmas, Bigeswe, Mokovo and Sipufwe, the old guy with epilepsy, started building a rondavel out in the garden. A rondavel is a round room, made with sticks and mud and finished with a beautiful thatched roof. This rondavel provided a place for our Christmas guests to stay. There were two windows on either side and a Dutch door. On hot nights the bottom half could be shut and the top left wide open to let in the air and the evening breezes. They painted the mud finish with whitewash, a mixture of lime and water, which kept the termites away. Mom bought four old beds and a chest of draws with a big basin and a water jug on top so guests could wash their face. She found a cheap wardrobe at the church rummage sale.

One hot sunny afternoon in November, when Mom opened up the postbag she found a notice there was a package arriving on the train the following Saturday. "It has to be something from Granny for Christmas. I can't believe how the days fly, it seems like we just got here."

When the packages arrived at the station Dad had to get Bigeswe and Mkove to help him load them on the truck. He stacked them in a shed outside. "No touching those bloody boxes now you kids. Stay out of them until Christmas," Dad warned. The boxes were huge. When I stood next to them they were bigger than me. Everyday we looked at the boxes and dreamed of what might be in them. I poked a few holes in the sides with a sharp stick to see if I could see anything but everything was wrapped in brown paper and remained mysterious until Christmas Day.

About a week before Christmas Granny arrived. As usual her chauffeur drove her up the long driveway in her grey Chrysler with Aunt Dorothy, Uncle Edgar and cousin Tony. The car was filled with presents and little surprises. Being summer, she wore her big flowered hat and a flowery dress. Her squirrel's foot broach, set in a silver clasp with a big yellow stone that set it off, was pinned to her frock. "I never drive anywhere without this foot, its my good luck broach," she told me. I loved to sit on her lap and stroke the squirrel's foot and run my fingers over the long claws.

A few days later Aunt Dolly and her boys, Dave, Pete and Mike arrived on the train. What fun it was having such a crowd around the house. Mom and the aunts made a Christmas pudding. Everyone took a turn stirring the batter and making a wish. I closed my eyes tight and wished for a bike. The batter smelled so delicious with raisins, fruit, brown sugar and spices. I took a big swipe with my finger and licked it slowly. The next minute Dad marched into the kitchen. "Who wants to help cut the Christmas tree?" We dashed outside following him into the eucalyptus plantation. I pictured a real tree, a fir tree that smelled of pine cones, pointy and dark green. I couldn't imagine where we were going to get one. Dad stopped next to an enormous eucalyptus tree and hacked off a branch. He held it straight up. "What do you think kids?" We looked at him in disbelief. Were we going to have a branch for a Christmas tree?

"Well this will have to do. There aren't any fir trees around here and we can't afford to buy one so you just have to use your imagination this year." He propped it up in the corner of the lounge. I looked at its drooping leaves sadly trying to picture a real Christmas tree. Dad walked into the lounge and put it in a bucket and packed sand around it so it stood up straight. We tossed cotton balls at it, which stuck here and there, made paper chains out of newspaper and painted them. Mom had some pretty glass balls from Granny's old collection and eventually our branch started to look quite pretty. We laid out the Nativity scene underneath to finish it off. On Christmas Eve we left a carrot for Rudolph and a cookie for Father Christmas.

We went to bed happily, filled with anticipation of what might be in the box.

Our first Christmas on the farm, we woke to the sound of the old rooster crowing. We crept out at the crack of dawn, dumbfounded by the sight of so many presents around the tree. A bike for me and one for Sheila, a wicker doll's pram for Trish and our little sister Ebie, with a doll and blanket inside. For Mom, a lovely warm coat and loads of cans of tinned peaches, pears, apricots, chicken and condensed milk. And for Dad, a hat to keep the sun off. Everyone had a present. Aunty Dolly gave knitted booties and a coat for our newest African baby we named Bongi. Her Zulu name was *Sibongile*. Mom gave Begiswe and Mkovo some canned peaches for each family as well as small toys for all their children.

About twenty turkeys wandered around our farm. Begiswe killed three of them the day before so every family had a turkey to eat with lots of new potatoes. We popped Christmas crackers and put on the silly paper hats. It struck me that I had a small head because the paper hat always fell down over my eyes, whereas they stayed on top of everyone else's head. After the delicious dinner Mom came into the dining room with the Christmas pudding all a-flame. It looked so beautiful and smelled rich and fruity. The sight held me spellbound. Slowly it burned out and Mom served a thick slice to each one of us. Even if you hated Christmas pudding you had to eat it, as each slice was full of coins Granny brought. We never knew if we were going to get the piece with a half a crown in it or just a sixpence. Dad would gobble his up, cough, splutter and spit out a five-shilling piece. This made us search all the more in case there was another fiver somewhere.

The day after Christmas we had a great idea. We big kids would ride our new bikes around the long tractor shed out back at breakneck speed. As we rounded the corner the other kids would ram us with the new doll prams and try to knock us off the bikes as we roared past speeding and dodging the prams. Whichever side you were on, the game was great fun. Unexpectedly Mom came out of the house and put a stop to the whole game.

"Aw gee Mom, we were having such fun, we weren't breaking anything." But there stood our little sisters waiting to get their prams back with Mommy on their side. "They're such spoiled sports, always telling and ruining our fun," I complained. The most exciting part of the Christmas season was having our cousins stay for the rest of the school holidays.

Dad had scraped up enough money to buy me a BB gun so I could hunt. Every afternoon around five, Pete and I would go out hunting *duiwe*. Pete had his own BB gun. We crept along the river's edge, searching for a resting dove in the trees, guns ready. When we spotted one, we would both take aim and hope to hit the poor thing. Much of the time we missed, but some evenings we shot two or three and the next day Mom roasted them for us to eat. It surprised me they had such a tiny body and so little meat on them. They didn't look nearly that small with feathers on.

Dad was disappointed he didn't have any sons, so I tried to make up for it by doing anything and everything to show him he had a hardy daughter. On Sunday afternoons Dad cleaned all his guns. He pulled them apart and showed me how to oil them and drag a long rod through the barrel with a bit of cloth on the end. Dad held up the gun.

"See Doff, you look through this barrel and make sure you don't see a speck of dirt. If it's not clean pull the rod through again." I'd peer through to make sure there wasn't a spec. Some afternoons he nailed a tin can to a tree. "Now aim carefully. Line up your sight with the sight at the end of the gun and pull the trigger slowly." The first time I fired, the thrust caught me off guard me and I realized I had to hold on firmly. I didn't want Dad to be disappointed in me because I was a girl. It helped to have all boy cousins. We played rough games on the front lawn, rode the bikes through mud and muck, chased the cows and rode on the wagon with the natives when they drove out into the fields to hoe and weed. Our faces were tanned from the hot African sun and I never wore shoes. The soles of my feet were hardened and calloused. I could tramp over anything without a whimper. I was becoming a really tough kid.

One of the neighbors heard how much Dad loved horses so he offered him an old black horse nobody rode anymore. Dad was thrilled and named him Tommy after his last horse that died.

Come January, all the cousins had to return home to their city life and school. As we waved goodbye, we girls felt empty and lost. We ran along the track following the train as it slowly left the station, waving madly as they disappeared out of sight. Our summer Christmas holiday on the farm was nearing the end.

❖

We had a storeroom in the house where Mom kept bags of mealie meal, rice and sugar. Each week she would measure out a certain amount for Miriam and Bigeswe's wife for the week. We had to share everything equally to survive until we could harvest our first crop. There was very little money around while we waited for those mealies to ripen. All three families, white, black and colored depended on the harvest.

One morning Mkovo came running up to the house shouting for Dad. "Come quick Bass, come. Come!" Daisy, one of our young cows had fallen into an irrigation furrow. She had been struggling to get out all night but had drowned in the shallow water of the furrow. They found her lying on her back with her feet sticking up into the air. First they tied a rope around her belly and then tied her front and back feet together. Everyone pulled until we dragged her out onto the bank. I fell over backwards as she came shooting out and we all laughed with the effort. Poor Daisy. Mkove skinned her, they cut her open and we looked inside at her miles of slippery innards. Dad pointed out her heart and they took out the liver, the kidneys and her full stomach that looked like a big football. Her skin made a nice mat for the floor of Minnie's hut. The innards were kept to make sausages and everybody shared the meat. Bigiswe wanted the feet. He was going to cook them up and enjoy them with his family. Thank goodness I didn't have to eat cow's feet.

Mkovo tried to teach me how to milk a cow. I watched as he deftly pulled the teats, using both hands at the same time, squeezing a long stream of warm milk into the stainless steel bucket. When I pulled awkwardly on the teat, nothing happened. I tried many times to master the art of milking but never did. Besides, I didn't like the look of milk straight from the cow all steamy and frothy. I spotted a few udder hairs floating about on top and I never drank a glass of milk again.

After Bigiswe's wife gave birth to her first baby girl, she continued to work in the house. She tied Bongi on her back with a brand new pink blanket Mommy had bought at Ross's store on tick as my Dad used to say. We bought everything on tick waiting for the big day when the crops would yield their bounty and we'd have cash once again. Whenever the baby fussed, she simply untied her and let her have a suck of her full *numbies*. We white children had never seen anyone feed their baby so openly.

We played with the *umfaans* because they were our only playmates, but there was an undertone present when other white farmers visited. "Do you let your kids play with those little *umfaans?*" they would ask my Dad. Most of the neighboring farmers were Afrikaners who strongly disapproved of white children playing with black children. "Those blacks must keep their place. They must be made aware of their position in society," said old Mr. Havemann. I listened inquisitively to their talk. The elections were coming up in the next year. For the first time I heard political terms such as the Black Question, the Nationalist Party and the United Party and discussions about whether coloreds should be allowed to vote. Evidence of the treatment of blacks and whites instituted by the government was everywhere. In town, the toilets were marked *Whites Only* and *Blacks Only* or *Nie-Blankes*, which meant no whites.

The country trains were mostly goods trains with one carriage for passengers. The carriage was divided into three compartments. The front compartment, paneled with varnished wood had comfortable green leather seats. It was marked *Whites Only* in both English and Afrikaans. The other two compartments marked *Blacks Only* were quite dirty and had hard wooden seats crowded together. They were always full of passengers laughing and calling out to their friends standing on the station platform as the train puffed its way out of town.

I asked Mom why we had soft leather seats and the blacks had to sit on hard wooden ones. She explained it wasn't fair. That was why they were going to vote for the United Party in the upcoming elections. Mom and Dad stood for equality and fair treatment of all races. The Nationalist Party believed they were superior to both the black race and mixed races. They believed in segregation in all walks of life.

Ross's store where we bought our school uniforms, shoes, clothes for grownups and tinned food had a front entrance for whites. They had a separate entrance around the back for natives, Indians and coloreds where they sold blankets, tinned foods, material for saris, skins for *beshus,* boxes of matches and hurricane lamps.

One day we were sitting in the back of the truck giggling and laughing while waiting for Mom and Dad to come out of Ross's. An Indian woman walking by thought we were laughing at her. "Shut up white sausage," she shouted. We had never heard another race dare speak so rudely.

Mom and Dad began to disagree with the Afrikaans farmers and bonded with the English-speaking farmers. On the train we shouted names at the Afrikaans kids and they called us *rooineks* and *kaffir lovers.* Tensions ran high. It was all political talk, in the fields, at church, in the stores. Everyone talked about who would win the election. In the evening my father read the English speaking paper, *The Natal Mercury.* "Those bloody Nats," he would say to my mother, "it looks like they might win this election and Smuts will be out." They were terrified the Nationalist Party might win and enforce even more segregation. They believed that General Smuts would be much fairer to all races and give them a better chance in life. I didn't really know anything about equality. The natives always lived in separate housing and we never ate meals together. Africans worked for us, not we for them, and they called my Dad *Bass.* They treated white people with great deference. As I grew older and had closer relationships with the natives on our farm, I began to think about how they were treated. I heard my parents talking with their friends about the difficulties the natives faced and began to think more seriously about the Native Question as they called it. In town where natives had to use separate bathrooms from whites and go into stores from the back door, the separation was more obvious.

Politics permeated our lives more and more. The United Party encouraged immigration from Britain hoping their English language would align them with our beliefs and offset the growing Afrikaner population.

In the train on the way to school we met the Newmarch boys, who were from England and had British accents. They looked quite scruffy, their bushy red hair always unkempt. Their dad became my dad's best friend and they often talked about the war together, although not when we could hear. Dad said he couldn't tell us all the terrible things he had seen. Mrs. Newmarch was very English and very pale. If she stayed in the sun too long she turned bright pink. Mom liked her and felt sorry for her because she was extremely homesick for England. They had even less money than we did.

The Newmarches had a tall windmill that creaked all night if the wind blew. It pumped water out of a well and filled a big green tank by the side of their house. They didn't have dams like we did so they were dependent on the wind for a good water supply. Poor Mrs. Newmarch hated the heat. She was always complaining and fanning herself with a newspaper.

Mom and Dad called Mrs. Newmarch a war bride. Mr. and Mrs. Newmarch were novice farmers like us trying to make it in the difficult world of farming. She couldn't speak any Zulu and had never had to deal with Africans before but she bore no prejudices. She treated her natives with kindness and love but she felt very lonely. Their primitive house had simple wattle and daub walls with a corrugated tin roof and white-washed walls. Their floors were made of many layers of dried cow dung spread over the hard red dirt, then polished with real floor polish. The floors didn't smell like cow dung, just polish. Their kitchen contained a wood burning stove, a table and a simple cupboard with chicken wire doors. The water in the kitchen sink came from a pump connected to the rusty old windmill outside the house. An old yellow flycatcher hung in the center of the room. It must have been there for ages because it was almost black so many flies had stuck to it and there were still hundreds of flies buzzing about the place. Mrs. Newmarch came from a pretty English world and found African farm life very different. I heard her try to tell her African maid what to do one afternoon. She picked up the folded washing and carried it to the place she wanted it to be. *"Put lo lappa,"* she said. We snickered and giggled at her efforts to communicate, so Mom tried to explain to us how homesick she was. She envied Mom for her four daughters and Mom envied her for her four sons.

Everyone played a sport at the new school. I learned to play tennis, but living out in the country we had nowhere to play after school. There was a dilapidated unused clay tennis court on Mr. Newmarch's farm, which had been neglected for many years.

"Please can we fix it Mr. Newmarch?" we begged.

"If you want to roll it and paint the lines and look after it, you're on your own kids," he said.

We were so excited. It took Sheila and I and the Newmarch boys weeks to get the court ready. Luckily it rained so it was soft enough to roll. A rusty old roller left in the corner of the tennis court had been lying idle for so long that it would not move when pushed. We soaked it with a can of 3-in-1 oil pinched from Dad's workshop and slowly it loosened up.

Dad gave us some string to mark the lines. We mixed up a handful of lime powder with water in a bucket, found an old paintbrush and proceeded to paint the lines. Every time we bent over to paint, the Newmarch boys would tease us and laugh at our bloomers showing. We didn't tell on them though as we'd get kicked off their farm and wouldn't have a tennis court.

When we finally played tennis, the ball would fly in every direction. The surface was so uneven you could never tell which way it would go. We laughed and played, making the most of it, happy to be able to play on the weekends whenever we wanted.

Since we lived out of town we never saw our school friends except at school. We socialized with our neighbors during the weekends. We played lots of tennis or cards and were often invited to afternoon teas with one of the neighboring families. We never got together after dark as no one had electricity.

The Klingenbergs were our nearest neighbors on the south side of the farm. They were German. Mr. Klingenberg's dad lived with them but he couldn't speak any English. He looked about a hundred years old. His thin body couldn't hold his pants up so he hooked them up with a pair of old striped braces. He was a bit deaf and we snickered and whispered when he came out to check on us grousing away in German. He usually wore a pair of tatty bedroom slippers and dragged his feet, shaking up the dust as he shuffled about. Since we knew he couldn't hear what we were saying, we giggled and made fun of him all the more when he wasn't looking.

The four Klingenberg boys were great fun. They taught us how to fish in their dam and how to shoot straight. In the summer after a hailstorm, they showed us how to make ice cream. They mixed hailstones and salt together and set a bowl filled with lots of cream, eggs, vanilla and sugar into the icy mixture. We'd take turns stirring until it got very thick, then sit and eat it scraping the bowl until there was none left.

The Tathams were wonderful neighbors to Mom and Dad. Right from the start they hit it off. Although they had children older than us, we loved going there. Their 10,000-acre farm a mile away was always welcoming. Wide green lawns and a beautiful garden surrounded their large spacious house. They had a real tennis court and always let me play tennis with their family. The house had lovely furniture and flowery chintz covered sofas. When they invited us over for tennis we had to wear white. I wore my white school shirt with the sleeves rolled up as high as they could roll and my only pair of white shorts. I thought I looked quite spiffy.

One summer they arranged a big hunt day on their farm. Farmers gathered from all around the area, bringing their dogs and their own *umfaans* to beat the bushes and the grass. Dad allowed me to come along after a lot of pleading. I was the only girl allowed on the hunt. I wore my khaki shorts, a green shirt and Dad's long socks so I didn't get blisters from walking all day. Our host Mr. Tatham instructed all the men. "We get the *umfaans* in a long row up front of us and they beat the grass to shake out the birds." They handed each *umfaan* a freshly cut leafy branch and we set off in a row behind them. They flushed out partridge and guinea fowl and the farmers shot them from the sky. The dogs rushed to pick up the dead birds and a couple of older natives carried the bounty home. I didn't shoot anything but was thrilled to go along. We slogged through the grass all day, the sun beating down on our heads. We arrived home dusty and dirty, our socks covered in blackjacks, tiny sticky seeds that stuck to everything. My legs were scratched and bleeding and I was so pooped I could barely stand. "Well Doff, you did well today. I'm proud of you." Dad slapped me on the back and I nearly fell over, but I was pleased with myself for getting through the day.

When we arrived back, African women dressed in clean pink uniforms handed out wet towels to the hunters. I flopped down on the lawn, took off my thorny socks and ran the hose over my tired dirty feet. I overheard one of the farmers chatting with my Dad. "By gosh that daughter of yours did well. I never thought she'd make it" I lay back down on the grass and looked up at the clouds smiling to myself, happily exhausted. After the hunt we were invited into their dining room for the biggest feast I had ever seen.

Whether it was for a hunt or tennis, the Tathams' put on an extravagant affair. They served gin for the grown ups and store bought minerals for us. I loved cream sodas. They laid out lavish spreads of cold roast chicken, sliced beef and ham on large platters. Assorted fruits and salads were served in beautiful cut glass bowls. We kids thought it looked so enticing we sneaked back more than once for seconds. "Stop eating like pigs," Mom would whisper, giving us a pinch. "I know you've had more than your share."

The Havemanns' next door also owned a very large farm so although they were our neighbors they did not live close by. Mom said Mrs. Havemann listened in on the party line. She could hear her breathing when she was talking to our Aunt Dolly. We shared our phone with five other neighbors. Each house had a different ring created by turning a handle. Three or four turns for a long and one turn for a short. The switchboard in town reached us by ringing three shorts and a long. The phone hung on a big wooden box screwed to the wall in the passage near the front door, just outside Mommy's bedroom. If you were near the phone you'd know exactly who was receiving the call by the ringing signal. The phone rang constantly so we would listen carefully to see if it was our signal. We didn't get many calls, but Mrs. Havemann did. It annoyed my mother. "That bally woman is always sitting on the phone. You'd think she had better things to do."

If we wanted to place a call to Aunt Dolly we just turned the handle furiously for one long ring and the operator would pick up. When Mom was out we would telephone a neighbor and ask a silly question, then hang up.

"You should have heard Mrs. Havemann shout at me when I asked her what was black and red all over?"

"You naughty children," she'd shout, "I'm going to tell your mother you're playing on the phone line. You can go to jail for this."

One Sunday morning the phone rang very early.

"Hey Mom, the phone's ringing for us. Shall I pick it up?"

"Yes, go on, hurry before they give up."

"Can I speak to your father?" I recognized Mr. Havemann's voice.

When Dad hung up he looked shocked and glared at me, "Old Tommy is dead, but he's on the Havemann's property. I don't know how the hell he got onto their farm. You kids probably left the gate open." We always got the blame for everything. "This is the second Tommy we have lost, man I feel upset." Poor Dad loved his horses so much.

Mom took her apron off, climbed into the truck with Dad and we piled in to go and see where Tommy had died. I had never seen a dead horse close up before. Dad roared up the driveway to the road, dust flying behind us. He turned right at the top, scooted over a cattle grid and we were on our way to the Havemanns.

Mrs. Havemann walked out of the kitchen door when we drove up and came to greet us. She was a big lady, with huge round bosoms, wearing a white apron, speckled with blood and flour and bits of meat stuck all over it. "Sorry, I'm such a mess," she said, dusting herself off. "But do come inside. I'm so sorry about your horse," she smiled warmly. She had smooth skin, pink cheeks and her hair was pulled back into a bun at the nape of her neck. I liked her right away and felt ashamed for having made the prank calls.

"I'm making sausages," she told us. I had never seen sausages being made. I thought they only came in strings of six from the butcher shop. Mrs. Havemann made a pot of tea and we sat politely drinking while the men went to check Tommy. I couldn't wait to get out there, but Mom made us stay in the house and wait. "You can't go just in case things are too gory. We don't know what's happened to him yet."

Mrs. Havemann offered to show Mom how she made sausages so we trooped after Mom into the kitchen. Mrs. Havemann stretched the end of a long piece of washed out sheep intestines onto the sausage machine and pushed the minced up chunks of pork and lots of spices into the top. As she turned the handle round and round the stuffing came shooting out into the skin, filling it up and making a very long sausage. Every six inches, she did a little twist, and there were six sausages. They looked almost as good as the store bought ones.

Just as we were admiring the homemade sausages, Dad walked back into the house with Mr. Havemann. A short skinny man with a wrinkled face, darkly tanned from the sun, he wore old grey slacks and a grubby checked shirt. He took off his hat and held it against his belly. The snakeskin headband on his hat looked sweaty and cracked. I wondered if he had killed that snake just like our Dad did.

"Tommy is dead alright but he looks just like he's sleeping. No injuries that I can see. We're going to have to load him onto the wagon and take him home to bury him."

After much discussion about how to get the horse onto the wagon and home, Mr. Havemann suggested the native boys dig a hole on his farm and push old Tommy the second into it. We rushed out of the farmhouse down to the fields where he lay. After six natives dug the hole, they pushed and shoved and heaved. Tommy fell into the hole making a huge cloud of dust, his legs bent and broken. As he landed, we leaned over and peered down to get a last look at him. It was a good thing to bury him right there because the flies were gathering around his eyes and mouth. "He'll be stinking like hell soon," Dad said. I watched as the first spade of dirt landed on poor old Tommy. We'd had a lot of fun on his back. I was sad to see him in the hole but this time I didn't cry. I simply looked at him with his soft old face being covered up with dirt and the flies buzzing about furiously.

❖

Mom and Dad did everything they could to make some extra money that first year in order to survive. Part of the farm purchases included four enormous fat pigs. One day the biggest, a round hairy pink mamma produced eighteen of the cutest little baby pigs. We were fascinated with them. They scrambled for food, pushing and shoving each other, squealing and squeaking. Mother pig was so clumsy she accidentally lay on one baby and squashed it. After that we had to take turns feeding the little pigs with a baby bottle so they could survive. They were being raised for bacon and at three months of age they would go to the bacon factory. "They will sell for some nice cash," Dad told us. We didn't think too much about it then. The baby pigs snorted and sucked hungrily on their bottle. Some of them could suck from their mother but she only had eight teats and there were so many babies. They scrambled greedily when it was their turn with mother pig. She just lay there grunting happily. Like us kids, she wasn't thinking about the day they would go off to make bacon for cash.

As the weather warmed up, Mom began working on the five-acre field of roses. Row upon row sprouted beautiful dark green leaves and long stemmed buds began popping out all over them. When we arrived home from school dragging the mailbag, I flopped down hot and tired ready for a big cool drink of spring water. We found a note on the kitchen table. "Come down to the rose field and help as soon as you get home." My sister and I moaned and groaned to each other and finally dragged ourselves down the road to find out what we had to do. We found Mom decked out in a full brimmed hat cutting long stems of slightly opened roses. We could already smell the sweet rich scent of the red buds. Mom showed us how to scrape the thorns off the stems and roll one dozen at a time in wet newspaper. We packed them into large shallow cardboard boxes that Mom tied up with string. She made labels and threw the boxes in the back of the truck. As soon as we finished, Dad sped up the road just as the train came into the station. He threw the boxes onto the train and it pulled out towards Greytown and on to Durban. A dozen roses sold for a mere seven shillings. I hated the roses, the thorns and the soggy newspaper. But we did what we had to do for it was clear there was no money in the house. One day when Dad was off to town, I asked for a pencil and he told me I would have to wait until a few checks came in.

Mom and Dad tried making butter to sell. The fifteen brown Jersey cows produced thick, creamy yellow milk. The other fifteen patchy black and white cows produced more milk but with a lower cream content. Every cow had a calf and was milked every day. Mkovo poured the milk into a big stainless steel separator. Thick rich cream emerged from one spout and ran into a stainless steel milk can while runny watery skimmed milk poured out another spout into a bucket on the other side. The pigs loved the skimmed milk mixed in with vegetables and meal. They lapped it up hungrily.

They gave me the job of making the butter. I hated it. The cream was poured into a large jar. Paddles attached to the lid churned inside the jar when I turned the handle on top. My arms ached from the slow, boring job. I whined and complained regularly to Mom. For all this effort we only produced about four to five pounds of butter a week so it seemed like a lot of work for so little money. The alternative to making butter was to sell the cream direct. That was a lot easier and we made about the same meager amount of money.

❖

Living on the farm we seemed to be dirty all the time. On Sundays getting four girls dressed for church, their hair braided, shoes polished and into the car, took a lot of nagging. Mom would scrutinize the parting in our hair and give it a good rub with a facecloth to clean our scalp. She dressed in her one and only church suit, a brown-flecked skirt and matching jacket with a frilly blouse fluffing around her neck. She always powdered her face and rubbed rouge on her cheeks in a pink circle, then smeared her lips with her only lipstick, worn thin from being used on one side. After that she'd run a comb though her wavy hair, smile at herself in the mirror and put on her round brown felt hat with it's small brim and two pheasant feathers, which stuck out like a mast on a ship.

Dad started the truck and got the engine running while we scrambled around gathering ourselves together and finally jumped into the back. Mom would climb into the front of the truck and slam the door as Dad roared up the driveway. "By God Con, you'll be late for your own funeral," he'd say every time. She didn't answer. Her pursed lips said it all.

❖

One hot summer night the rain pour
corrugated tin roof of our old farmhouse. I wa
of the tree branches flicking back and fort
my tiny bedroom. I often lay there imagining the snapes of the
Tokoloshe lurking outside my window or a baboon creeping
across the yard. Sipufwe told us many stories of how Tokoloshe
crept down from the hills and stole a child away, never to be
seen again. When he told us stories his brown eyes bulged out
and his head turned nervously from side to side as if Tokoloshe
was going to jump on him at any moment. "He's a tiny little
man and can make you sick if you disobey your mother." He
shook his finger in my face. "He even scared the baboons back
into the hills." The Zulus were terrified of the Tokoloshe.

A baboon did come down one night and was creeping
around the yard when Jock went after him right outside my
window. I was too scared to get out of bed. I put my head under
the blankets but I could still hear the screeching bark of the
baboon and Jock's fierce growling. Thank goodness he chased
the baboon away and we never saw it around the house again.
Meanwhile Dad rushed outside. "It's a bloody wonder this dog
isn't dead. I've known chaps to lose their dog in a baboon fight.
Good boy Jock!" He carried Jock into the kitchen and laid him
down on the floor. He patted him gently as he searched his body
for wounds, but he only found a few scratches and one nasty
bite on his side.

Another stormy night the rain fell so heavily I couldn't sleep
and I lay watching the rain drip down the windowpanes. I heard

a loud banging on the kitchen door. I didn't know what time it was but I knew it was late because Dad always made us go to bed by nine on school nights and I had been tossing around for quite a while. I jumped out of bed and rushed into the kitchen to see poor old Sipufwe being dragged through the back door, groaning loudly. As Mkovo and Bigiswe laid him on the floor, his head drooped back and spit ran out of the side of his mouth down into the grey curly hairs of his tatty beard. Mom and Dad rushed into the kitchen to see what all the commotion was about. Sipufwe had had a fit while cooking the Putu for the next morning and fallen right into the fire. I secretly wished I could have seen him having a fit because Mom had told me all about it. "You don't want to see it. He shakes and shivers and arches his back. There is nothing you can do, you just have to wait until he wakes up."

Mom leaned over Sipufwe to see how badly he was burned. "Get me the First Aid Kit, Dave. He's got some nasty burns on one of his legs and his arms. It could have been much worse, he's lucky this time." I tried to sneak in closer and get a good look. Sipufwe groaned. Miriam put a pillow under his head. He seemed unconscious except for his groaning. I saw the burn on his leg. The skin was peeling off and I could see brown bubbles on the sides. Muscle and blood oozed from the burnt flesh. I didn't know Zulus were pink underneath their brown skin. I tried to squeeze in between Mom and Dad to get a better look. "Get out of the way Doff, I can't see what I am doing." Mom blocked my view as she wiped the wound clean and patted it with baking soda. She bandaged him up so he looked like a soldier from the war. One leg, his arm and his head were all wrapped in white gauze. He groaned as they carried him off in the pouring rain to his hut. "He'll sleep all day and only feel the pain later when he recovers from the fit." Mom began packing up all the mess and the First Aid Kit. Dad looked at his watch. "Good God Kids, if you don't hurry and get dressed we'll miss the train."

We rushed back to the bedroom to dress and Mom made some tea. "Here eat this, I've made your sandwiches and Dad will drive you to school." Sheila and I piled into the front of the truck with Dad. It was still pouring and the roads were very wet. Dad roared up the driveway, mud spattering all over the windshield and we hit the main road at a good speed. We loved a ride like this, the truck slipping and sliding along the dirt road, which had turned to soggy yellow clay. All of a sudden the truck flipped around and slid into a high bank on the right side. Dad revved the engine furiously and the tires spun like mad, spraying sheets of mud high into the air behind the truck. We didn't move an inch. Dad jumped out of the truck to take a good look. He tried putting the gear in reverse and revved the engine again. "It's no use kids, I'll have to put on the chains. It's the only way to get out of this mess."

It was still pouring with rain. Dad spread the chains in front of the wheels in the mud. His nubby fingers worked skillfully. The rain dripped down his tanned face and off his eyelashes. His shirt was soaking wet by then as he patiently stretched the chains out. He hopped back into the truck and pressed his muddy boots on the accelerator. "Well here goes, kids!" He put the truck into gear and slowly eased forward. The wheels gripped the chains so we were able to move onto them. Dad jumped out again and hooked the chains close around the wheels. We crawled through the mud until we hit the tarmac at the bridge. The chains clattered and clunked on the tarred road all the way up the hill to school. We were only a few minutes late.

❖

I still had the habit of sucking my two middle fingers. I hardly noticed I did it, but Mom and Dad tried everything to get me to stop. "You look like an idiot walking around sucking your fingers and twiddling your nose," Dad said. Mom rubbed aloe on my fingers several times. It was awfully bitter but I soon licked it off. "You know you are going to have buck teeth if you don't stop sucking your fingers." Eventually a solution came up. My friend Nola invited me to come to their house to spend the weekend and I desperately wanted to go. Mr. and Mrs. Monk were real sports and loved to play cards and other games with us children. We never did things like that in our house and I thought it was such fun.

"Shall I tell her I can't come Mom? I can't let them see me sucking my fingers."

"No, I've been thinking about how to get you to stop. I'm going to wrap both your fingers with this thick sticky

Elastoplast." I told Nola I would come for the weekend and worried all week if I could stop. Friday, Mom wrapped my fingers up tight. "Just tell her you cut your fingers." I stuck them in my mouth and it felt horrible and I couldn't get it off. There was no warm comforting feeling and I wondered if I would survive the weekend.

Both Saturday and Sunday we played rummy all afternoon and everyone asked me about my fingers and I lied happily. When we went to bed I stuck my fingers in my mouth. The plaster was scratchy and smelled of medicine and I just could not suck them. That weekend I had to suffer through it. I hardly slept at all but I was cured. I never sucked my fingers again.

❖

We had a black slow combustion stove in the corner of the kitchen that looked like an enormous steam engine winter and summer. The center of life, it served as tea maker, cooker, oven, dryer and water heater. It warmed and dried us on cold nights as we ran from the bathroom to the kitchen wrapped in a towel.

First thing every morning Miriam emptied out the cold grey ashes, polished the black surfaces with a wire brush and shined up the handles. She filled the stove with crumpled old newspapers and fragrant eucalyptus logs. The sound of crackling wood and sparks flying up the chimney woke me most mornings. The heavy iron doors rattled and clinked as the eucalyptus burned rapidly inside heating the water, turning the kitchen into the coziest room in the house. By the time the wood settled into red-hot ashes, the shiny stainless steel handles were too hot to touch. When I heard Miriam plonk a big pot of water on the stove for the mealie meal porridge and fill the kettle for tea, I knew I'd have to get up soon.

Dad usually went out to meet Bigiswe and Mkovo and get the day's activities going before the three of them trooped back in for a cup of hot tea. During the winter, they huddled around the stove, but in summer it was too hot inside and they drank the tea out on the back verandah. They poured it into old, chipped, enamel mugs and sweetened it with two or three spoons of sugar. The Zulus loved sugar. Old Sipufwe would smack his fat scarred lips with pleasure as he added another teaspoon to his cup, stirred it with gusto and slurped noisily.

In the winter the heat from the stove gradually warmed the back of the house. I lay in bed bundled up under three, grey army blankets with only my nose uncovered. When Mom brought me my tea I stuck out one hand. As the hot liquid seeped down my throat, I began to warm up. "No time to lie in, you've got lots to do before Dad takes you to the train station," said Mom.

I only had one school uniform. I didn't wash it every night but sometimes it was so filthy I just had to. We played hopscotch and dodge ball, climbed trees and ran around the sports field in P.E. so I got very dirty. After washing my uniform I hung it on the piece of rope strung across the kitchen near the stove and hoped it would dry by morning. When it was really cold we went to bed early with a hot-water bottle to warm our feet.

Sometimes the stove would die down sooner than usual and my uniform would not be dry.

Six old flat irons always sat on top of the stove. With the morning fire raging, they heated easily. "Miriam," I would shout from my bed, "please iron my uniform for me and make it nice and hot so I can put it on while it's still warm." I could hear her grabbing the iron with its clip-on wooden handle and banging it on the blanket covered enamel table, which stood in the middle of the kitchen. "Don't burn it Miriam." The hot stove-heated irons had already made a pointed brown burn mark on the hem at the back the last time she ironed it.

Aunt Vida always knit white socks for each of us. They stretched during the day and slid down inside our shoes by afternoon. I couldn't stand to start the day with dirty slippery socks so I had to at least wash them every night. I stretched them out long and narrow and pegged them on the piece of rope above the stove.

In the afternoon when we arrived home, Miriam usually made another pot of tea. During the winter we sat around the table in the kitchen, but in summer we'd sit out on the front verandah. When Miriam cooked the dinner the kitchen was like an oven. All sorts of pipes traveled from the stove up into the ceiling. We didn't dare touch them, they were boiling hot. "*Mnige Sheesa!*" Miriam warned us, tapping the pipe with a spoon.

Some pipes went to the kitchen sink. One went outside to an old bathtub where the natives did all the washing. Others crawled into the roof and over to the bathroom so we could have a nice hot bath. The water bubbled and gurgled out of the hot tap when we turned it on. We had to make sure to run the cold water from the other tap at the same time as the water was so darn hot.

Over time, Mom figured out the oven so she could bake a cake. She had to wait until the middle of the day when the fire died down and turned to red hot ashes. We knew if she had it right by the size of the cake. Just right meant it was high and puffy. Flat and level meant the oven wasn't quite hot enough. Sunk in the middle meant it flopped. We didn't mind the flops. Mom filled the sunken part with icing to level it off and we lapped it up, licking our fingers, savoring the sickly sweet icing.

The kitchen was the gathering place for the whole family, the natives and ours. One of those mornings when we were sitting around the kitchen table having tea, Bigiswe came in for his. Four-year-old Trish trotted over and lifted up his *beshu*. Startled, Bigiswe crossed his legs clutching his *beshu* into his crotch.

"*How! How!*" he exclaimed as he rushed outside.

"I just wanted to see what was underneath," she said. The native girls screamed with laughter.

"You mustn't do that. It's very rude!" Mom groused at Trish. Sheila and I both wished we'd seen what was underneath. We didn't know much about men and our family didn't talk about it with us.

◈

Dad worked all day on the farm so I asked Mom where we got money now. He didn't have a real job. She explained how everyone had to work hard to sell things. When we got paid that gave us money to buy the seeds, food and other things we needed for farm life. Each week the native families would get flour, corn meal, sugar and rice to take home to their *kraal*.

We soon learned to work hard so there was some money every now and then. We had enough to eat. The vegetable garden was productive and supplied all of us. The Africans loved pumpkins and they grew profusely. I liked cabbage and green beans. We grew lettuce, big juicy tomatoes and an abundance of potatoes. I had never seen potatoes growing before. When you plant one potato, a leafy bush grows above the ground. A few months later when you dig it up the roots have produced ten to twenty fresh new potatoes.

Although there were many places to play and explore on the farm, we began to understand how important it was that everyone needed to help with daily chores. There were jobs for all of us. "If we are going to survive we all have to pull our weight kids. No complaining," Dad said. Whenever we had spare time we jumped in the prickly haystacks and rode our bikes for miles on the dirt roads, splashing through puddles and making dams in the stream. We even played dolls with Jabulile's baby Sibongile. We were never at a loss for things to do.

At last when the mealies were ready to be harvested Bigiswe and Mkovo did most of the work. They chopped the stalks off low down and stacked them together in standing bundles to keep the rats away. Jock and Trixie had a field day chasing the rats as the bundles dried out over the next week or so. Once they dried, Dad drove out with the harvester. Bigiswe, Mkovo, the two *umfaans* and sometimes Sipufwe if he was able, tossed the stalks into the trough of the harvester. It chewed everything up separating the full, rich, yellow mealies from the dried up stalks and spewed the chopped stalks back onto the field. Later the mealies were tossed into a grinder, ground and bagged for sale as cattle feed during the winter. This annual yield was the main source of income for our farm. It took Dad several trips with the truck loaded to the gills to get it all to market.

When the check for the mealies Dad sold from our first crop arrived in the mail, it was not nearly enough to cover the expenses for the following year. "How can we manage any longer Dave?" Mom turned to her books and the list of bills trying to figure out how they could pay their suppliers and still have money left over to buy seed for the next year. She sniffed and wiped her nose as she fiddled through the stack of bills.

"God Con, we'll have to find a way. I'll talk to the Klingenbergs tomorrow and see if they can offer us some advice." Mr. Klingenberg suggested Mom and Dad buy crop insurance to protect them from future disasters. They even offered to lend them the money to pay for it. Dad wanted to accept their help, but in the end decided they wouldn't.

"Next year we'll know what we have to do and we'll plant early and make a go of it on our own."

"There just isn't enough money left to buy crop insurance," Mom said after adding up the bills. So they decided to borrow from the bank to buy enough seed to plant a full crop the next year. When I saw them kissing I didn't worry any more that day.

A few days later, Mom was wheezing and puffing on her inhaler when I got home. They had been talking about money again, going through the bills trying to make a plan on how to manage. "I have to go and lie down," Mom said. She got up and walked slowly to the bedroom. I peeked into her room and saw her ease her way onto the bed struggling for every breath. I tried to help and covered her with a blanket. "Don't put that army blanket on me," she snapped, "I can't stand the weight." I looked around and found a light crocheted shawl and dropped it over her.

When she first developed asthma, the attacks occurred early in the morning. I'd wake and hear her wheezing, gasping for every breath. Dad would bring her a hot cup of tea hoping it would help. We stood by her bed anxiously watching, as she lay propped up on pillows looking so strained. In one hand she clutched her handkerchief, and in the other the inhaler she puffed into her mouth every now and then. It sounded like she'd never manage another breath. "Is she going to die?" I asked Dad some mornings as she struggled to breathe. I was so scared as I imagined our house without Mom. She did everything for us. How could we ever manage without her?

She went away once to hospital to get fixed. I was terrified she would never come back. Our Aunt Dolly came to stay. "No one dies of asthma," she assured us, but I didn't believe her. She hadn't seen Mom gasping for air, her chest heaving and rattling as she fought to breathe. She hadn't seen her eyes bulging as she tried to get out the words to tell us she'd be ok. Two weeks later Mom finally came home from the hospital, thin but smiling. She showed us her new inhaler with the latest medicine. "I think I will be a lot better now," she said. But she wasn't.

❖ 8 ❖

The Big Hailstorm 1950

Dad plowing
Bigeswe, Tegwaan, Trixie and Jock

About six weeks after Dad planted the mealie crop I rode the train home as usual. I looked out the window across our fields, which we passed just before arriving at Umvozana station. I could see Mkovo on the tractor in the distance, dusty clouds filling the air as he harrowed the weeds between the lush green mealie stalks growing in the warm summer sun. I had become fond of the Zulus who worked so hard beside my Dad every day. I contemplated the things that brought happiness to us now. The vegetable garden, the pigs, cows, ducks and chickens, all the parts that made our farm life experience so rich. The train slowed and pulled into the station.

I jumped off and headed over to the pile of mailbags. I was alone because Sheila had stayed home from school that day. I kicked the mailbags about until I spotted ours and slung it over my shoulder. As I wandered down the road towards the house I noticed unusually dark clouds behind the hills on our farm. Many afternoons the clouds built up and a quick summer shower or brief hailstorm would settle the dusty fields and water our needy crops. Usually the clouds passed quickly once the rain stopped. But the clouds looked ominous, darker and more intense than usual. I picked up my pace and hurried along the road to beat the coming rain. As I scurried around the corner, our comfortable old farmhouse came into view. I saw Mom still sitting on the verandah gazing towards the clouds. "The tea's nice and hot. I made a cake today so drop your bags and drink up. I plopped down in a chair and put two sugar lumps into my tea and sipped contentedly. Just then Dad walked on to the verandah, a worried look on his face.

"Bigiswe tells me there is a really big storm coming and we'd better get ready for it. I don't know how these Zulus know it, but when they say it's going to be bad, I know we'd better listen to them." He swigged his tea hastily, giving us a sense of urgency.

"Hurry Con. Doff you go and help Sipufwe shut the chickens and ducks into their pens. I am going to see the cows and pigs safely in the *kraal*." I looked up at the sky again. The dark, yellow and black clouds were coming much closer and I heard a loud clap of thunder followed by a scary flash of lightning.

"I hope it doesn't rain too hard Dad. I saw Mkovo harrowing the fields this afternoon."

"Get on with your jobs now you lot, we haven't got time to waste." We picked up the tea things hastily and carried them into the kitchen. Dad went off to the cowshed and I ran to the back of the house to help Sipufwe get the chickens shut in. The sun disappeared as the clouds moved rapidly nearer and although it was only about half past four in the afternoon it seemed like night. At first the air was very still, then another clap of thunder followed by a close bolt of lightning broke the silence and a strong wind blew the smell of hot earth, cow dung and eucalyptus into my nostrils. I could sense the tension amongst the Zulus gathered in the kitchen. Bigiswe had brought his family and Minnie down from the hill. He must have known what was going to happen. He left their chickens behind at their *kraal*. "They will hide in the trees," he told us. Another crack of thunder, followed by bolts of lightning lit up the sky and scared us all. The Zulus huddled together and chattered nervously at the crack of every thunderbolt.

Dad came in looking worried and plopped down in his usual old chair. Mom sat close at his side resting on the arm. We four girls huddled around his feet while Jock and Trixie scrambled and cowered as close as they could get to us. The thunderbolts rumbled and cracked, the windows rattled and the lightning bolts flashed. Moments later the rain began to fall on the corrugated iron roof. The wind blew and howled through the plantation. The continuous dull roar of pounding rain suddenly changed. It sounded like rocks falling. "Oh my God!" Dad jumped up, "I think it's hailing." We followed him to the window and I pressed my nose against the glass to see. The lightning flashed again and lit up the whole garden. The lawn was pure white, covered in hailstones. Just then the dining room window smashed, glass flew everywhere and rain and hail poured in. The curtains flapped and blew up towards the ceiling as hail stones bounced onto the dining room floor. "Get away from the windows!" Mom screamed. The hailstones were as big as golf balls. The pounding on the roof was so loud it sounded like a herd of cattle running across the rooftop and we couldn't hear ourselves speak. The lamp blew out and we huddled together in the dark. Trish and Ebe started bawling. The flashes of lightning gave us our only glimpse of the destruction as we sat frozen with fear. At last the hail stopped and an eerie silence crept over the house as the storm clouds passed. The sun peeked out and we could see again.

Slowly Dad opened the front door, Mom at his side, the silence broken by the rain dripping off the roof. The front lawn looked like a winter wonderland, completely white, covered with hail. We girls rushed outside throwing the hailstones about and popping them in our mouths, yelling to each other as if we were at a picnic unaware of the devastation around us. Then I heard Mom.

"Oh no Dave! Just look at my fruit trees, not a leaf on them." I stopped. The tree branches were bare. Most of the tiny apples were knocked to the ground and the vegetable garden lay in tatters. Dad rushed out the back door to the fields nearest the house where cousin Dave had ploughed the year before. "Oh my God, the mealies! They're ruined." We ran up behind Mom and Dad to look at our once thriving crop. All we could see was row upon row of torn shredded stalks. Mom buried her face in her hands as Dad put his arms around her shoulders. He stared in stunned silence at the ruination around him. Shocked at the sight, Bigiswe and Mkovo rushed to Dad's side, their mouths agape.

"*How! How! Bass.*"

"Will it grow back Dad?" I asked, wanting to cry too.

"Not like they were. Right now they looked ruined to me. I don't know if they will recover or what we'll do."

"We should have bought crop insurance like our neighbors told us." Mom turned away and walked back towards the house.

Tree branches were broken down and stripped of foliage. The beehives had blown over and honey dripped slowly out of the honeycombs as the bees buzzed about circling their nests. The once white washed walls of the house looked dirty brown. They had been pounded so hard the mud from the wattle and daub structure showed through. As we walked around Dad counted the broken windows, at least half of them smashed.

"How are we going to manage?" I asked Dad.

"I don't know kids, we'll just have to wait and see what tomorrow brings. Let's go inside and make a sandwich." Mommy began wheezing. I was afraid she might die.

Dad said there was no use in staying up worrying. We would be able to see a lot more in the morning, but we could hardly sleep that night. Outside my window I could hear the constant dripping of rain from the trees even though the storm had passed. Eventually I fell asleep.

In the morning, rays of sunlight poured through my bedroom window. I heard Sipufwe come into the kitchen for his morning tea. The natives were talking all at once about the storm. I jumped out of bed expecting to see the lawn covered in hail, still white, but it had melted away. Only the leaves strewn everywhere and the naked trees told the story of what happened the night before.

Dad took Mom a cup of tea in the bedroom. She was sitting up in bed leaning against her pillows wheezing and coughing. She took the hot tea gratefully. I stood in the doorway staring at her. I hated that wheezing sound. It was so frightening but it seemed to be a part of our lives now. She would slowly improve after her tea and a few puffs on her inhaler.

Dad picked his shorts up off the floor from the night before and put them on. Slowly he pulled on his dirty socks and boots and stood up.

"Well I suppose I had better go outside and see how bad things really are." I rushed to my bedroom to find something to wear and followed him outside.

"Aren't we going to school today?"

"No, the roads will be so muddy we'll only get stuck in the mud and there is so much to worry about here. You're lucky. You get the day off."

I didn't feel a bit lucky that day, everything looked so broken. The sun streamed through the plantation with more light than I had ever seen. Several enormous eucalyptus trees stripped of bark and leaves had blown down and lay across the path we played on when tricking Mom. Dad trekked back up to the fields to check on the mealies. He stood there silent, looking at the sun glinting on the stalks, transparent green sticks, just row after row bare of leaves. He turned around and walked back to the house. "We'll need a miracle from God to survive this mess."

Mkovo came into the kitchen to report all the animals had survived. I ran around the house counting how many windows were broken. The most damage appeared to be on the one side where the house had been hit the hardest by the hail. Dad made a list of things we needed, white wash, glass, rakes, a big saw. It would take weeks to bring our beautiful farm back to normal.

Gradually things were mended, painted or fixed. We planted two fields of potatoes instead of one and Mom and Sipufwe worked hard to get the vegetable garden growing once again. The roses were so badly damaged it would take six weeks before we could pick and sell another dozen flowers.

Dad said we had to think of ways to make extra money while we waited to see if the mealies recovered. Mkovo and Sipufwe planted a new field of gladioli bulbs. The florist said they would take all we could grow. Mom and Dad didn't know the pitfalls of growing gladioli. A nasty black and yellow beetle soon found the growing plants and they were crawling all over chewing holes in the leaves. Dad offered us a farthing for every beetle we picked off. Daily, for a week, we each took an old jam tin filled with an inch of motor oil and picked beetles until it was too dark to see them. We conquered the pest and Dad promised to pay us when the checks came in.

A few months after the storm, Bigiswe came to Dad and told him he had heard about working in the gold mines in Johannesburg where he could make a lot of money. Many other natives in the area had been going to the mines for money and word spread fast. He made up his mind to go and work for six months of the year. He'd go in the winter after the mealies were harvested when Dad wouldn't miss him so much.

Mom and Dad tried to warn him of the dangers of crime and loneliness in Johannesburg. He was a good man and they worried he would never come back. But he had made up his mind and promised he would never desert his family. When the time came Dad gave him a pair of shorts and a shirt. He looked like a different person without his *beshu*, wearing clothes. Finally one day he was ready to go. Jabulile packed a meal of Putu balls and a couple of apples wrapped in an old doek. Dad said he'd drive him up to the station. He had a long way to go, catching a train to Greytown, then Durban and finally to Johannesburg. When he hopped into the back of the truck he waved as they drove off. No hugs or goodbyes, no kisses or promises, just Jabulile staring at the vanishing truck, tears trickling down her cheeks. The *umfaans* waved and took Bongi from Jabulile when she walked back into the kitchen to do her work.

The months flew by and one day Bigiswe came walking down the drive, *knobkerrie* in his hand, dressed in long trousers and wearing a hat. Everyone ran around him jumping with excitement, talking in Zulu so fast I didn't know what they were saying. Bigiswe settled back into the farm working as hard as ever. I never knew what happened in Johannesburg, but he didn't go again the next year.

❖

In the summer on hot rainy nights the frogs came out by the million. We could hear them popping under the car wheels when we drove home in the dark. Pop! Pop! Pop! We could see them all over the road in front of the car lights as Dad flew down the driveway. Impossible to avoid them, we shrieked in delight. "See how many you can squash!" Then we'd amble back up the driveway to look how many he'd got. They were big fat bullfrogs with bulging eyes and brownish lumpy skin. As we wandered amongst the destruction, nervous frogs hopped away into the grass on the side of the road, seemingly unaware of the fate of their brothers and sisters. "Ag shame, poor things!" we'd say as we examined the details. Some squashed totally flat, some just flat on one side, one half still round and bulging like a balloon. We could see their innards squeezed out where their belly had popped open and their little legs splayed out from their last leap for life.

It wasn't easy to catch a frog and hold onto it. I hated the slimy feeling of their underbelly in my hand. I really didn't want to hold one at all but Sheila loved them. Cupped in her closed fingers, she held on tight while she stroked and patted one, the poor frog blinking and wiggling with panic until she let it go.

Sheila had warts, lots of them, on her hands and fingers and all over her knees. Mom said she got them from touching the frogs. "If I got them from touching frogs why doesn't anyone else have warts?" she'd argue. Mom didn't have an answer but she had lots of wart medicine. Some of Sheila's warts were big and scaly, some small and round covered in reddish flakes of skin. You couldn't pick them and if you did they bled all over the place. For a while Mom dabbed every wart with a sickly smelling liquid the doctor gave her in a bottle with a small black brush attached to the lid. After weeks of dabbing the warts were still there and a couple more appeared. We were sitting outside on the back verandah examining the warts and counting them, five on her pointy finger and four on her ring finger. There were twelve warts on her one knee and two on the other. "I think they are spreading, soon I'll be one big wart," Sheila complained. I looked at a big round black wart peeling and nubby and pictured her whole body looking that way. It sent a shiver down my spine. At that moment Jabulile walked out onto the verandah with a mug of tea in her hand, "What you doing *nkosazanas*?" she asked, seeing our heads bent close over her knees. Sheila showed her the warts. "*How, mnigi!*" she backed away as if Sheila had leprosy. She looked into her tea mug quietly for a few minutes and then told us she knew how to get rid of them. She knew the perfect cure. All we needed was a rooster's head. "This mooty, it's fixing lots of warts, many long times."

So next Friday when Dad killed the chickens for Saturday delivery to Aunt Dolly, he killed off one of the young roosters. He wiped the blood off and handed the head to Sheila. It was still warm, it's eyes open unblinking. "Don't look at me like that!" she said. She held up the rooster's head topped off with a nice red comb and looked into its eyes. "You may be dead but you are going to do me some good." Jabulile told us to rub the cock's comb on each and every wart, then bury the head in the ground and wait for it to rot. When it's all gone the warts will fall off," she explained. I ran out to the farm shed and found Mom's garden spade. Sheila carefully rubbed each wart. The comb bobbed about as she swished it back and forth, the rooster's lifeless eyes glazed over, bulging in and out as she gripped the slippery head. The job completed, we looked around and pondered where we should bury this precious mooty. "It'll have to be somewhere the dogs can't find it and dig it up before the cure has time to work." We decided the eucalyptus plantation was the best place. The dogs hardly ever went there and they would never smell it. I dug a nice deep hole, about six or seven inches across and Sheila dropped it in.

We took one last look at the rooster's head, shoveled the dirt over the top, covered the newly dug earth with leaves and placed a small rock on the top so we wouldn't forget where we had buried it. A few weeks later we went out and dug it up. The rooster's head was covered in maggots, crawling around his beak and eyes. His last few feathers were wet and stringy, caked in dirt.

"Jabulile," I shouted from the edge of the plantation. "Come and see the chicken's head! Please, please." She was busy ironing and did not want to be bothered with us but she finally came.

"*How, how!*" she exclaimed. Put it back. Put it back quick. He's not ready." Sheila looked at her warts, still all there. We covered the old rotting rooster head back over. The next time we looked at the head it was mostly bones, but the cock's comb had not rotted away completely. Sheila still had the warts but we wanted to believe they were smaller. Six months later we foraged around in the ground and could only find the neck bones and a very rotten beak. Most of the warts on her knees seemed to have faded away. By the time the rooster's head turned to dust she hoped they would all be gone.

I'd been playing tennis on a hot day when I noticed it was almost three o'clock. I grabbed my satchel and ran down the hill to catch the train. Fortunately it was still there, the engine warming up. The Newmarch boys sat in the *Whites Only* coach. "We've got the windows," they shouted as I jumped onto the steps of the compartment, climbed inside and slammed the wooden door. Puffing heavily from running so fast, I pulled down the sliding window on the door and stuck my head out as the train slowly inched its way out of the station. With my elbow resting on the sill, I leaned out as far as I could to catch the breeze. It felt good blowing on my sweaty hair. The train picked up speed and wound its way around the corner, across the river and out of town towards the hills and farms. Acres of young wattle trees grew in long straight rows alongside the track most of the way, blocking the view on either side. The wheels squeaked along the track as it sped in and out of the plantations. Smoke and soot belched from the funnel and I relaxed to the same repetitive sound I loved. Gradually my panting eased.

Googly, our Afrikaans train conductor strolled through the compartment checking passenger's tickets. We had season passes. He snipped a hole in them every now and then but I couldn't find mine. "You just better have your ticket tomorrow or I will tell your Dad," he threatened. I didn't care, he never told on us anyway so we just laughed and promised to find it the next day.

I hung my head out of the widow and I could see the *Blacks Only* compartment. It was always full of natives going to Kranskop where many Zulus had their home *kraals*. Every window had three or four heads jammed together leaning out, pushing and shoving for some cooler air. They waved and shouted to their friends walking home along the side of the tracks.

Our compartment wasn't very full, mostly kids going home from school. We settled into our seats and everyone calmed down. I flopped into my seat when all of a sudden an enormous jolt threw everyone flying. The wheels screeched and screamed to a halt.

"What's happening?" I shouted. The Newmarch boys were at the windows on the curved side so they could see up ahead.

"I dunno, can't see much!" I rushed across to the other side of the car. A native came running alongside the train yelling in Zulu, waving his whip and his *knobkerrie*. He appeared to be a cattle herder. Googly jumped off the train and ran towards the engine, shouting at the natives in Zulu. They were running everywhere and we saw a couple of cows standing near the train. "I bet we hit a cow," John Newmarch guessed, "let's go look." Googly ordered everyone to stay on board but the natives poured out the back like syrup. Running to see what had happened, they weren't waiting for Googly to tell them what to do. They didn't trust trains most of the time anyway.

We couldn't resist. Nobody was paying attention anymore so we jumped off and ran to the front of the train. When I got there, crowds of natives were gathering and shouting in Zulu. I pushed my way through to see a terrible bloody sight. The train had hit a cow crossing the track. She must have been smack in the middle as the engine rounded a corner between the trees, too late for the driver to stop. He was standing there looking with dismay at his train, then at the mess that had been a cow. The cattle boy, a young *umfaan* sat on the bank crying. He didn't look old enough to tend the few cows standing there chewing the cud. I edged my way in closer to get a good look.

"Get back you kids!" Googly shouted to us.

"Ah man, we want to see," we begged.

You could hardly recognize the cow. Blood, legs, insides and black and white hide were stuck all over the front of the train. The head hung to the side and the horns stuck up in the air crooked. Blood had spattered everywhere and skin hung on big lumps of red bloody meat. "Look at that hoof lying on the ground, it's chopped right off." One of the Newmarch boys pointed down by the engine, "Gee man that cow made a hell of a mess."

The crowds grew. Some came off the train and others had been walking through the rows of wattle trees taking a short cut home. As if by magic they gathered around exclaiming back and forth in Zulu. We were the only English speaking kids there. Chunks of cow were spread for several feet along the track. Natives began dragging bits out and stuffing them in their bags creating an even bigger commotion. The *umfaan* who had been tending the cows was still crying. It was his cow but no one paid any attention to him. He would be in big trouble with his father. Before we knew it most of the pieces of meat had been picked up and the tracks were cleared, so the train could get on its way again.

Surprised that Googly spoke Zulu so well, he ordered everyone back onboard as he ran up and down. Gradually everyone climbed back into their seats and we moved off. The wheels squeaked and hissed through all the blood towards our station not far down the track. We left the chaos and the crowd behind.

When we reached our siding Googly threw out the mailbags, stirring up the dust on the platform. We jumped off the train, grabbed our mailbag and took one last look at the gory mess on the front of the engine. We walked to the end of the station and crossed the road towards our long, berry bush lined driveway. We could hardly wait to tell Mom why we were so late.

"Where the heck have you kids been?" Mom jumped up from her chair as she spotted us running down the driveway. "I was worrying that the train had broken down somewhere."

"The train hit a cow, you should have seen the mess!" I told her breathlessly.

As we described all the gore and guts Mom sat down calmly and poured the afternoon tea as if nothing had even happened. The next morning when the train stopped at the station to pick us up for school, there was no sign of the excitement from the day before, the engine washed clean.

❖

Dad read in the Sunday paper about the police department hiring men to return to the police force. With the loss of the mealie crop and the devastation on the farm, Dad realized he had to find another way to make some money so we could survive. He had left the police force when he went off to war so decided to apply to re-enter and became a mounted policeman. He rode around the countryside from farm to farm checking on various crimes such as thefts, fights and stabbings amongst the natives. He often stopped and had tea with Mom or some of the neighbors if he was close by.

The horses were kept in an old fort in Greytown. On workdays Dad drove into town, saddled up and went out on his rounds. That meant I could stay after school to play tennis and get a ride home with him later, if he left his horse at the fort. Sheila hated the idea. She wanted me on the train with her, but I was growing up and I didn't really want to be with my nine-year-old younger sister all the time.

So Sheila rode on the train without me. One day she found herself alone in the compartment except for an older man. Right after the train left the station, Googly collected the tickets and headed towards the back of the carriage. The old man sidled up to Sheila and told her how pretty she was. He began touching her legs and fondling her. She cried and begged him to stop. "Please, please leave me alone," she whimpered. He took no notice. He pulled her legs apart and licked her legs. Then he pulled her pants down and tried to lick her genital area. "You like that, don't you?" He smiled and looked up from what he was doing, his pock marked leathery face with his red, lumpy tongue wobbling in his mouth. She froze in terror.

Googly came back through the train talking loudly to another passenger, so the disgusting old man moved hastily to the other side of the compartment and pretended to look out the window. Googly could see Sheila looked very upset. "Are you all right?" Too terrified to speak, she just nodded as she held her legs closed tight with her pants halfway down under her dress. As soon as Googly left, the man smiled across the aisle at her. "I'll be seeing you again sometime. You are such a nice little girl." She jumped up and ran into the next compartment. Fortunately the train pulled into our station, so she leapt off and ran all the way home terrified he was following her. She told Trisha, the first person she saw, what had happened. Trish was too young to understand. Sheila never told me or Mom and Dad about it for many years. We continued to take the train every day. My twelfth birthday came and went. "Please don't stay after school anymore," Sheila begged continuously.

One morning an older student handed me a note from a teacher I didn't know. A Mr. Cannon wanted to see me. With fear and trepidation I knocked on his door. He sat behind his desk and greeted me with a smile.

"I saw you running the other day, you looked like a gazelle," he said. "I want you to come and try out for the running team after school." Stunned, I didn't even know I could run fast, let alone like a gazelle.

"I only have one problem," I told him. "Most days I have to take the 3.25 train home because my younger sister is afraid to be on the train alone. I'll ask my Dad if he can work something out."

"Don't you worry there has to be some way to handle this," Dad said, excited when I told him the news. Mom and Dad found out that Sheila and I could stay during the week at the local convent in town where lots of other farm kids boarded. "It's not very expensive," he said. "Those nuns will keep an eye on you and you'll be able to run every day."

Mom called Granny to tell her. "Your Granny is going to help out with the cost. She's almost as thrilled as us about you running." I could hardly wait to go to the convent. I packed my school uniforms, my shirts and bloomers, my new running shorts, some socks, my hairbrush, toothbrush and a new tube of Ipana toothpaste into a cardboard box. I had never been away from home and was much too excited to worry about missing my family. It would only be from Monday to Friday.

On Sunday we drove to the convent, a stark brick building with symmetrical windows evenly spaced. A stern looking nun greeted us at the door wearing horn-rimmed glasses. A starched white band framed her pale pasty face, attached to a triangular veil that covered her hair and hung down her back. She fidgeted with beads dangling from a rope belt. Sister Bernadette introduced herself and led all of us up the stairs to show Mom and Dad the girl's dormitory where the borders slept.

We walked into a large room with several rows of iron beds on creaky wooden floors. Sister Bernadette pointed to a corner cubicle where she slept. Just outside the dorm, another room housed a large padlocked cupboard and four washbasins. "For evening and morning ablutions," Sister said, pointing around the rooms. The two showers and the toilets were down the hall. She unlocked the padlock on the cupboard and allocated one shelf to me. Mom unpacked my stuff neatly and Sister closed the cupboard, clicking the padlock shut. "The cupboard is unlocked from 2 to 4 p.m. daily," she informed my parents. I was much too scared to ask how I would get clean clothes. I would have to worry about that later. She showed Mom and Dad the dining room and music room. They hugged us goodbye and left.

Sheila began crying but I didn't. I was going to be a fast runner and I couldn't wait to get to my first practice. "Now stop that silly nonsense," Sister Bernadette scowled at her, "no use crying like a baby. Follow me, it is almost time for supper." We walked down the stairs behind Sister. Sheila wiped her tears away as she followed along behind me to a large room. The borders, both girls and boys, knelt on the floor in rows, swaying as the nun reciting prayers went on and on. We knelt down and joined them.

After what seemed like forever, they all shouted "Amen" in unison, jumped up and dashed into the dining room. I was starving. Sister Bernadette stood behind a long table ready to serve the food. The kids were all pushing and shoving to get in line in order of height. Sheila clung to me. Sister waved her spoon like a conductor shouting for Sheila to get into her right place in the line.

"It's by height, stop hanging onto your big sister now."

"Please Sister, she's scared. Can't she stand by me her first night?" Sister nodded reluctantly.

We held out our plates while she slapped down a hunk of brown bread and a dollop of pink blancmange, all wobbly and disgusting with a tablespoon of marmalade. The blancmange was unsweetened so we spread our marmalade over the top and ate it with the bread.

The first night in the dormitory we noticed only some girls showered but everyone went to the toilet. At eight o'clock Sister Bernadette rang a bell and called to everyone to clean their teeth and get ready for bed. She locked the door of the dorm and retreated into her cubicle.

"Are we locked in?" I whispered to a girl I knew from school, my hand cupped over my mouth.

"Yes, and she only unlocks the door when she goes to mass at half past five in the morning."

"Where do we go in the night if we have to?"

"We go in that bucket." She pointed to a large white enamel bucket with a lid. I made up my mind I would not go in that bucket even though I'd just guzzled down a lot of water with the horrible blancmange and bread.

My full bladder woke me early. I was dying to go but lay fidgeting in bed trying to pluck up the courage. Eventually I tiptoed over to the bucket and lifted the lid. In the dim light I could see it was half full of stinky yellow pee from all the others. I thought I just couldn't do it, but my full bladder was stronger than my brain. I squatted, wobbling over the bucket, trying to pee down the side so the whole dorm wouldn't hear me going. It made a loud splashing noise that echoed through the silence. Surely Sister Bernadette and everyone else heard me. I tiptoed back to my bed, the moon casting my shadow across the wall so everyone knew who it was.

At six o'clock Sister rang a loud bell. Everyone clamored out and hastily made their bed. I went over to help Sheila who started crying. Too afraid of the bucket, she had wet the bed. I grabbed the sheets off the bed, pulled up the bedspread and smoothed it over. I rolled the sheets up into a ball and chucked them out window into the garden below. There was no way Sister Bernadette would know. I went to the telephone box near the school and rang Mommy, telling her the whole story. When I walked home past the dorm after running, I noticed the sheets were gone from the garden.

At a quarter past six we knelt down for morning prayers. At half past six we dashed to the dining room for breakfast. Sister stood behind a huge saucepan of porridge balanced on a hot plate. She dished out a big helping, dumped a tablespoon of brown sugar in the middle and poured boiled milk over it to finish things off. The milk had a thick, yellow congealed skin floating on top, with little bubbles around the edges.

"Please don't give me any of that skin Sister," I begged.

"Why not?" she said. "It's good for you." She spooned the lumpy yellow blob into the middle of my porridge. The only thing that got me through breakfast was the thought of how much fun I was going to have running in the afternoon. I could hardly wait.

At lunchtime, I felt really hungry so I trudged up the hill from school to the convent. I was relieved that prayers were cut to ten minutes. I didn't want my knees sore for running. They served a big plate of beef stew, more vegetables that beef, but it smelled great and filled me up. I sopped up the gravy with my bread. Sister Bernadette reminded everyone the cupboard was open from two until four. Too excited about the running, I didn't worry about not being there on time.

I trotted out to the running field in my old school shirt and new shorts, barefoot. I looked anxiously around. Most runners wore spikes and were bobbing up and down jiggling their arms and loosening up. "Greenland," shouted the coach, "come over here and meet the team." I cringed. I hated hearing my last name out loud but no one seemed to care. We took off jogging around the field to get in shape.

I arrived back at the convent tired, sweaty and happy, long after four o'clock. I marched up to Sister Bernadette nonchalantly and asked if she would open up the cupboard so I could get some clean clothes from my shelf.

"No, you'll have to wait until tomorrow."

"But Sister, I'm all hot and sticky and dusty. I was at running practice and can never be back before four."

"That's too bad, you know the rules." She turned and marched away.

I showered and put on my dirty clothes and had to wear them to school the next day. Fortunately Mom came up with a solution. The plan was to leave the dirty clothes in a pillowcase hidden in the garden. Dad would pick them up and bring them back washed and ironed in a couple of days. Sometimes I would look out the window early and see Dad riding up the road through the morning mist with the bag of washing slung over his horse. I waved as he tucked the bundle under a bush. Sister Bernadette would never know. Our little secret worked for a long time and I ran every day.

After a few weeks the coach decided to clock our times. We would all run the 100-yard dash five at a time. I lined up and took my position. "On your marks, get set, go," he shouted. I ran like a gazelle. To my surprise I could run faster than the other girls in my group. One of the girls, who was used to winning all the time, burst into tears and fell to the ground, clutching her ankle and whining about the pain. She was just a bad sport. I had never been the winner of anything before and I loved the attention. I discovered I liked it, so I kept running as fast as I could in my bare feet. Coach asked me if I wanted spikes, but I was more comfortable barefoot. I never wore shoes at home and my feet were tough as leather. Besides, I knew we couldn't afford them but I wasn't about to tell him that. Every time coach used the stopwatch, the girl with the spikes would get a pain in her side or a headache. Sometimes I would only beat her by seconds but she cried and complained. It was the first time I experienced bad sportsmanship.

While boarding at the convent Sheila suddenly developed a tick in her face that she couldn't stop. No one knew what caused it and Mom took her to several doctors. One prescribed giving her a sip of Port every morning and evening. We were instructed not to draw attention to it as she was very self-conscious. Mom asked Sister Bernadette to administer the Port and not mention the facial tick. At breakfast she would give Sheila a teaspoon of the alcohol and tell her to stop fidgeting. "You're just putting it on," she said. "You'll grow out of it."

I thought maybe she hated the wee bucket like I did. "Don't be scared of that old bucket. I hate to use it too but it's better than wetting the bed." Nothing I said seemed to help. She would wake up wet and sweating, creep over to my bed and tap me gently on the shoulder, "Da," I'd hear her soft breathing right in my ear. "I had a bad dream," she'd whisper. I'd tuck her back in bed under the blanket and the bedspread and hope Sister Bernadette wouldn't discover she had no sheets. We could see Sister's shadow on the ceiling from her cubicle as she got ready for bed and when she began shuffling about getting dressed for early morning mass. She had good ears. "Be quiet or you will be punished," she'd yell out from the cubicle if she heard us whispering. Punishment usually meant bending over the bed to be smacked with the back of the hairbrush and then writing one hundred times, "I will not talk after lights out."

I hated the convent and how Sister Bernadette treated my sister, but my running life meant everything to me. When I told

Mommy about the Port, she decided Sheila should live on the farm once again. Sheila told Mommy she would not catch the train alone but never said why. They agreed she could walk down to the Fort after school and wait for Dad to take her home.

I stayed on at the convent so I could keep running. Sister Bernadette hindered me in every way she could. She forbid me to share a book to study with a friend. She hit me with the hairbrush bristles if I was one minute late for the endless prayers and she locked me in a bathroom if I protested. I ate the disgusting blancmange with marmalade. She could splash all the boiled milk she liked on the porridge, but she couldn't stop me. The coach chose me for interscholastic competition and I found myself running against the best of other schools. I didn't win all the time but I won a lot. I grew taller, my legs were longer and they just flew.

Sheila seemed happier living back at home but the tick didn't ease up. I didn't know she was living in fear every day, afraid that horrible man might be lurking around a corner waiting for her.

I loved being able to run every day after school. I adjusted to living at the convent and made new friends. I had never been able to hang around after school with other girls before and I enjoyed, socializing, laughing about silly things and not having to rush home and work out in the rose fields picking flowers.

I began to feel more grown up. I was growing "bosoms". Mommy told me I would begin seeing changes in my body but she never really told me what would grow. I felt uncomfortable with the tiny bumps on my chest and thought everybody noticed. When I wet them and blew on them in the ladies room just before I went out, they shrunk and I looked my usual flat self. That seemed to work for a while. Eventually they simply would not shrink or melt away. They were growing quite permanent but fortunately my running shirt was baggy so the bumps didn't show too much.

One day I walked back to the convent from school with my friends. Some boys dressed in the school uniform were wandering up the road ahead of us. They slowed down and one of them made a joke to me. "Shut up you silly buggers!" I said, embarrassed and coy. I don't know what made me say such a stupid thing and immediately I wished I hadn't. Boys had always seemed like pests. I had no clue how to speak to them but I liked the flirtation and the unexplained flutter of excitement. I looked down at my feet and carried on walking up the road ignoring their giggling. They snickered and called us names. This was my first brush with the opposite sex.

❖ 9 ❖

Selling the Farm
1952

The family just before we sold the farm

When Dad picked me up at the convent at five o'clock one Friday afternoon, I flung my bag into the back of the truck excited to be going home for a couple of days. I hopped in, hot and tired from the afternoon's running. Anticipating his usual silly joking I expected to see a big smile on his face. Instead he looked tired and strained.

"What's up Dad? You're looking a bit grim this afternoon."

"Well I really hate to have to tell you this," he heaved a long sigh. His Adam's apple wobbled up and down as he swallowed hard. "We've sold the farm." I gulped and felt a huge lump stick in my throat. I tried not to cry. Dad clenched his jaw and the little veins in his cheek wiggled. I knew he hated to tell me so I scrunched my eyes shut trying to be grown up. "Are they nice people? Do you think they will they look after all our animals?" I said, attempting a show of bravery. Without a word, Dad roared along the familiar dusty road towards the farm and I reflected on the recent events in our lives.

We understood Mom and Dad had almost no money left after the hailstorm had damaged our crops so badly and the harvesting was over. Sheila complained one day her feet hurt because her shoes were so tight. "Well, you'll just have to find a pair from this box to wear," Mom said. She fished a box out from under the wardrobe with all my old shoes packed neatly in it. Sheila looked in it to see the shoes grey with mold, growing like a tiny white field of grass.

"Why do I always have to wear Doff's old shoes? She always gets the new pair."

"Doff's the oldest, we can't afford to buy anything right now so you will just have to make do. Dad will shine them up — nothing a bit of spit and polish can't fix." Secretly glad I didn't ever have to choose from those moldy old shoes, I hoped my feet wouldn't grow too fast. I would probably have to wear my shoes until my feet grew right through the front of them.

To make matters worse, when Bigiswe went away to the mines Mom thought she could cope with running the farm while Dad worked. His job didn't seem very difficult. He rode a shiny black horse from farm to farm, often being invited in for a cup of tea by some of our neighbors. Once in a while he'd come home with a story of a stabbing, or a fight, or a native beating up his wife, but most of the time things were pretty tranquil in the farmer's world. When close to home he'd stop in, have lunch with Mom, and check on Mkovo and old Sipufwe. "I suspect those bloody natives are taking advantage of your mother," he told me.

Mom didn't speak much Zulu and found it difficult to manage everything. The corn was growing tall and so were the weeds. The hay fields needed cutting, there were pigs to feed, cows to milk and chickens to kill every Friday. Her asthma got worse as she got more impatient with us and yelled orders to everyone. Old Sipufwe hid in his hut pretending to be busy in case Mom wanted to boss him around a bit more.

As we drove along the driveway towards the house I finally realized the worst thing of all, we'd have to move. I began crying, I couldn't hold it back. When we walked into the house Mom could tell by the look on my face that Dad had told me. I ran into her arms. "I don't want to leave here," I cried. "I love this place so much. I've been so happy here, I'll never be happy again." As we sat picking at our food that night Dad tried to reassure us how much better things would be. "It's all for the best kids. We can take Jock, Trixie and Patches and the new people will take over the animals. Your mother won't have to work so hard trying to keep this farm going. Her asthma might even get a bit better." Dad picked up his lamb chop and chewed the meat off the bone.

"We'll move into town and you won't even have to change schools right away. It'll give you time to adjust while we wait for a transfer to a bigger city."

"What are the new people like Dad?" I changed the subject, not ready to talk about the future.

"Well they came from Britain to South Africa after the war and now they want to farm again. The man is a typical pommy, long socks, army shorts, lily-white legs and arms and ruddy pink cheeks. He looks bloody ridiculous with his cravat tied around his neck, but I suppose it doesn't mean he isn't a farmer." Dad could still make us laugh imitating the pompous English accent as he told us about the new owners, the McCauleys. The next morning the warm sun woke me early, as long shadows from the eucalyptus trees flickered across my bed and reflected on the wardrobe door. I lay quietly in my cozy little bedroom with my cat Patches cuddled up, purring loudly. I could hear cups clinking in the kitchen. Mom usually brought me tea in bed when I was home for the weekend, a special tradition I loved.

Staring at the wardrobe, I thought about the time I had tried to reach on top for a hat. I climbed onto the shelves with the door open when suddenly the whole thing came crashing down on top of me. I screamed like a banshee and Dad came flying to the rescue, heaving the wardrobe off me, lucky to be alive. "You bloody idiot, you could have been killed. Don't you ever think about what you're doing?" He hugged me with his brown hairy arms, smelling of hay and eucalyptus. Remembering that moment made me think of all the things I loved about the farm, especially the smells. A sweet grassy, fresh warm dirt smell after a summer rain, the aroma of green mealie leaves wafting through the air as I kicked the mailbag home. Mom's roses in the field, grown and sold for their strong scent, even the smell of cows, pigs and the other animals made me happy.

As I lay watching the eucalyptus branches make shadows on the wall, I thought of all the times we had played in the plantation. We dug holes and covered them with branches and begged Mom to come and see the house we had made. Giggling naughtily, we waited for Mom to trip in the little holes we'd camouflaged, so disappointed when she stepped right over them. Many times we had played cruise ships on a huge pile of eucalyptus logs, balancing carefully as we skipped from log to log, "The Deck" as we called it. I was "Daphne" and Sheila was "May". "Let's play May and Daph," Sheila would say to me. We spent so many hours in that imaginary world.

I heard the cows mooing outside my bedroom window as Tegwaan herded them off to the fields to graze for the day. Molly and Daisy and all the rest of them we knew like friends and called by name. Tegwaan had taught us how to crack a whip at their feet to keep them in check. I loved to do that.

Later I overheard Dad talking to Mom. "They're stealing this bloody farm, but we haven't had any takers so we'd better be thankful."

"I just hope we get enough to pay all the bills. I'm so tired of eking out the money." Poor Mom, she never bought any new clothes for herself, she always put our needs first. She had big holes in her undervests so she'd wear two, one to cover the various holes in the other one. "Layering them keeps me warm on a frosty night," she'd say, "even if they are a bit tatty." Maybe Mom would be able to buy some new vests.

We'd never be able to go hunting doves again like all those wonderful summer evenings Pete and I crept along the river bank sneaking up on unsuspecting birds and shooting them with our Beebe guns. I turned my eyes towards the legevan skin tacked to the wall. Pete and I had spotted that big spiny lizard sitting on a rock and we both shot him at the same time. He was at least eighteen inches long. We dragged him home so proudly showing off to the family and the Africans. They were always enthusiastic about our hunts.

I worried about leaving Begiswe and Mkovo, Minnie and Miriam, all the *umfaans* and our own little brown baby girl Sibongile, now running about the farm following her mother. "They're all staying here," Dad explained. They could not go with us, they couldn't read or write and only knew this place, this way of life. This was their home.

Poor old Sipufwe, we'd miss him, we'd grown to love him. He was always around making *Putu* and offering us Zulu food, which I had never got used to. They covered everything with *maas* or sour milk. It was greenish, separated into a watery liquid and a cheesy, white shiny lump. I almost vomited every time they persuaded me to try it.

I looked at my yellow shorts and running shirt hanging on the wardrobe door, washed and ready for another race. On Monday morning I would be back at the convent with mean old Sister Bernadette. I had grown used to her and found some allies amongst the other nuns so that her cruelty didn't upset me so much anymore. My running successes made me so happy I could tolerate anything. At least I could still run when we moved into town.

I rolled out of bed and ambled into the warm kitchen, the smell of mealie meal porridge cooking on the wood-burning stove. Our native women bantered and laughed as they went about their work. It was only eight o'clock and I had the whole day ahead of me to enjoy our farm.

The next time I came home for the weekend Mom and Dad were packing things up. Big boxes sat in the middle of the lounge. My farm life was coming to an end. Granny's china flowers were wrapped in newspaper and carefully packed. The dining room walls were bare. All Dad's rugby pictures had been taken down leaving only pale dusty squares to remind me of Dad's pride in his team photos. The kitchen cupboards were empty and there was no clinking of hot irons on the fiery old stove. I missed the sound of them banging down on the ironing board, now leaning against the wall, a forlorn old thing with iron shaped burn marks all over the cover.

The party line phone rang, two longs and a short – our ring. Mom picked up the receiver and held it to her ear.

"Hello," she listened to the voice on the line.

"We hate to go, we're almost packed. It's been a long couple of days," she said. "No the kids aren't doing too bad." What did she know? I ached inside and could hardly look at Jabulile or Miriam without crying. Little Bongi hung sleepily from the blanket tied to Jabulile's back, drool leaving a wet patch on her pink uniform. How we would miss her happy giggle and Zulu chatter as she toddled around the garden with us.

Jock lay on the kitchen floor scratching and shooing off the flies. Thank goodness he was going with us. Dad had managed to give away all Trixie's ten pups so she could come too, but all the other animals would be staying.

I wandered out onto the back verandah and clung to the wattle tree pole that supported the roof overhang, running my fingers over its smooth knotted surface. Jabulile was bending over the old peeling enamel bathtub scrubbing the last of our washing. She rinsed ir, twisting the water out of each garment. I stood and watched her peg the washing on the line just as she had done for years. When it dried in the breeze, she'd iron it for us for the last time before we packed our final things.

"Will you miss us when we go?" I asked her.

"*How*, Ma'am! It makes me cry. I velly sad." Her eyes filled with tears. "I am hurting in here." She pointed with a sweeping gesture at her chest.

I wandered down to the old cowshed. Mkovo was raking out wet stinky hay and getting ready for milking time.

"I am so sorry we are going away. I don't want to leave but we have to. I hope you can be happy with the new owners."

"Ma'am I am worry a lot, I will miss the *Baas* and the Madam so much."

"What will you do?"

"I have nowhere to go Ma'am. This is my home. I must stay for Miriam and Granny. She is getting very old now."

I turned away and walked slowly back to the house, looking at the green roof and the pretty garden before I went inside. Miriam was making tea. All the china had been packed so she set out some old mugs on the tray. As usual she'd made a big pot because Bigiswe and Sipufwe would be coming to the back door for their afternoon tea too.

"My life will never be the same again," I moaned at Mom.

"I know that Doff, it will be different but you will survive. We're going to miss this farm we've grown to love so much, but we can't make it here. We have a chance to sell and make a better life. We're doing it for you kids." She held me tight and I cried hard feeling better letting it go. I'd been pretty brave until it came down to actually going.

"Come let's sit outside with our tea," she wiped my eyes and tried to smile.

"Let's not spoil our last days here crying."

Miriam loaded the tray with the teapot, mugs, sugar and milk and carried it out onto the front verandah. Jock followed us and flopped down beside Mom. Bigeswe and Sipufwe made a hasty stop to fill their big enamel mugs before going back into the fields.

"I'm going to miss them all so much Mom."

"I know that, I feel just the same as you do. They've taught us such a lot about the Zulu way of life, and they learned a lot more English than we did Zulu, I hate to admit." Mom sipped her tea in silence. I sipped mine and made a loud gulp as I swallowed hard, trying not to cry again.

❖ IO ❖

Greytown
1952

In our holiday dresses

Mom and Dad rented a place in Greytown surrounded with a big overgrown garden covered with fruit trees. The old square house had highly polished verandahs on all sides and a black corrugated iron roof. We thought that Jock and Trixie would be happy.

When moving day finally arrived, an old Indian drove up in a big lorry with *Naidoo's Moving Service* painted on the sides. "Hello Madam, I am coming to take you to your new house." Everyone helped carry things outside onto the front lawn and slowly filled up the truck.

Our old farmhouse echoed with a hollow emptiness. We girls ran through the house for the last time shouting to each other. The floors creaked and the noise bounced off the bare walls. I looked into Mommy's bedroom. It seemed so bare without their furniture and I thought of the many times I had crept into that room for comfort when I heard a strange noise in the night or saw a suspicious shadow on the wall. I pictured Mommy gasping for breath during one of her asthma attacks.

As the time came for the last goodbyes the natives stood in a row, with the *umfaans* and babies looking forlorn and sad. We shook their two hands in ours, up and down, up and down, not wanting to let go. Tears streamed down their dark cheeks, all of us blowing our noses and sobbing as we said our goodbyes. We didn't promise to visit or come and see them, we just said "*dankie dankie, hamba gashli,*" over and over. It felt like dying. I didn't know what lay ahead but I knew I was leaving something I had grown to love very much. Naidoo's lorry pulled out of the driveway up the road, leaving a huge cloud of dust. "Load up the dogs and cats, kids," Dad shouted. "Hop in the back, it's time we were off." We waved furiously to Bigiswe, Mkovo,

Sipufwe and their families. The *umfaans* ran up the road behind the truck until we couldn't see them any more for the dust.

❖

We moved into the rented house in the afternoon. I helped Mom unpack most of the kitchen things until late that night. It was much easier with the flick of an electric switch. We worked under the light of one bare fly-speckled light bulb, dangling in the middle of the room. Having electricity was about the only thing I liked about the house.

Spiders had been busy weaving webs in the corners. Creepers crawled over most of the verandah walls, tangled dark tendrils dangling everywhere. Dad said he'd have to chop them all back in the morning. Mom handed me a long pole with black ostrich feathers attached with electric tape on the end. I swung it wildly, swooping at the spiders, destroying their webs and knocking down the dried out carcasses of various insects they had ensnared. As I swished about, geckos ran across the ceiling, ducking behind the light fixtures. A green praying mantis clinging with its spikey legs right above my head surveyed me with big round eyes. I didn't dare touch it, it might land right on top of me.

Mom shut Patches in our bedroom and we smothered his paws with butter so he wouldn't be able to smell his old life once he'd licked his feet. He was to stay in the bedroom for a week so he'd forget, but he was so quick he escaped the second day. We couldn't find him anywhere. We called and called. He never came. I put food on the verandah hoping he'd get hungry when it got dark. I lay in bed wondering what would happen to him, imagining the worst things, never dreaming he was on his way back to the farm.

Three days later the new owners of the farm telephoned to say Patches had meowed loudly at the kitchen door. He was very dirty and hungry so they fed him and he'd curled up by the old kitchen stove falling asleep quickly. Dad drove me out to the farm the next day to pick him up. He purred happily when we arrived. We cuddled and stroked him, took him home and shut him in the bedroom with us.

After a week and no escapes, Mom decided he would settle down so we let him walk around the house sniffing the furniture. He sniffed and sniffed, poking into every corner, then suddenly out the window he went. We chased after him but he disappeared, nowhere to be found. I couldn't imagine him padding along the six miles to the farm over hills and valleys, crossing roads and train tracks.

This time when the farm people called we knew Patches had shown up again. When we picked him up he seemed much more anxious, the ordeal had clearly worn him out. I hugged him and stroked his back, smothered his feet in butter, fed him and gave him a large saucer of milk. Surely he would stay this time. I pulled him down under the covers and cuddled him as much as he'd allow that night, but he was restless and did not want to lay next to me.

Two days later he escaped again and went straight back to the farm. This time the new owners suggested to Dad that we let them keep him if we thought it best. Mom and Dad urged me to let him go. I lay awake all night worrying about the cat I loved. It was very hard for me to imagine he could be happy without me. I certainly wasn't happy without him. I cried when I thought about him all alone out there, but I had loved the farm so much too, why shouldn't he. By morning I made up my mind to let him stay. Dad phoned the McCauleys to say we'd leave him with them.

We drove out to see him one more time. He was lying outside in the dirt as we drove up. He rolled over and purred when I stroked him, content and happy. I picked him up, hugging him to my chest but he wriggled away and lay down under a tree in the shade and licked his paws. I never saw him again.

❖

We settled into the ugly old house on the hill outside Greytown quite easily. It was not nearly as difficult as I expected. Dad worked from the police headquarters, an old fort that consisted of a square building surrounding a large grassy courtyard. He wore jodhpurs, riding boots and a smart tunic to work everyday. He kept his horse at the old fort located at the bottom end of town right near the river. It was built in the early 1800s for the easy access to water and housed the British Army in those days.

The heavy old wooden doors were open all the time. One door featured an enormous rusty keyhole about two inches across. No one knew who had a key. The hinges creaked and groaned when they tried to close the doors so they simply did not bother.

Dad's native assistant Mbongi waited for us every morning. He took great pride in keeping Dad's black horse shiny and well fed. He even polished his hooves with black shoe polish. As we drove into the fort he'd wave to us enthusiastically, greeting us in Zulu. Mbongi's hair was specked with grey. His big brown eyes sunk deep in his wrinkled face were shaded with bushy eyebrows. The minute he spotted Dad his thick lips broke into a smile. "You know that Mbongi gets up at four o'clock every morning to walk from his *kraal* to the police station so that he can be here before me. His feet must be like bloody leather."

"The horse is ready for you *Baas*. He is looking for a good ride," Mbongi said. "And the *nkosazanas*, they go to school today?" Even though we did the same thing every day, he always asked if we were going to school. He wore brown pants bound tight from the calf all the way down to the bottom with frayed khaki colored wraps from World War II, which looked a bit like bandages. Even in the coldest winter, his feet were bare.

In the afternoons, I was free to run. I could train and did not have to worry about the convent and Sister Bernadette any more. In the heat of summer we went to the public swimming baths after school to strengthen our legs and cool off in the brackish green water. I found I was getting stronger and stronger swimming back and forth, instead of running around the field.

The first half of the year my days were filled with school, tennis and running. I had little time for anything else by the time I had done my homework. During the school holidays we played hopscotch in the garden under an old pergola covered in granadilla vines. We'd suck the juicy pips from the granadillas until our mouths were sore. We each had our own special hopscotch stone. You threw it into the square and if it touched the line you lost your turn. If you stood on a line hopping from square to square you were out. We'd scrap and fight over the game until Mom threatened to shut us all in separate rooms for the rest of the day. "Fight quietly," I would whisper to my sisters, as we pushed and shoved, argued and accused each other of cheating, "We don't want Mommy to hear us."

One sunny afternoon about six months later, Mom and I were sitting on the verandah. I was doing my homework and Mom sat sipping her second cup of tea when Jock jumped up at the sound of the truck tires crunching on the gravel driveway.

"I've got some good news." Dad waved some papers excitedly as he climbed out of the truck.

"I'm being transferred to Pietermaritzburg and we'll be moving in a month."

"So soon," I whined, "we don't want to move again."

"We'll have more money, I'll have a better job and you will be able to go to a better school."

Dad didn't seem a bit bothered but I was stunned. I liked my school and I didn't need a better one. "We'll pack up and move during the July holidays," he said. "Meanwhile we have to buy a house so we'll all go to Maritzburg this weekend."

It poured with rain all the way. All four of us were jammed into the back of the truck. The canvas cover Dad had made for the truck years before leaked all over the place so we were drenched by the time we arrived in town. The plan was to stay with our Aunty Dolly who used to send us the dressed chicken orders every week when we lived on the farm.

Tall, with a long thin face and greying hair tied back and twisted into a bun, Aunt Dolly was warm and friendly. I didn't think she wore a bra. I could feel her floppy old bosoms against my body when she hugged me. She wore a green overall tied around the waist that covered her dress. She'd spread her arms out wide to hug us as she marched down the steps bellowing loud greetings.

Our cousins Pete, Dave and Mike slept on bunk beds on the verandah. When we stayed there we had to share the beds with them. Dave made jokes and Pete teased us as we lay on our backs crowded on the two beds watching the rain drip off the verandah roof. We giggled and talked until Aunty Dolly was tired of the noise. "Shut up you kids," she'd shout, "go to sleep!"

I loved to visit Aunty Dolly. She would tell stories about the church and Child Welfare. She helped at Child Welfare every week. They supervised clinics for babies and helped the native women learn how to care for them along with their many other health problems. Aunt Dolly also told us stories about black families, deserted wives who walked miles into town often leaving two or three children with the granny, so they could look for their husband. She told Mom about bad husbands who found new girl friends and sometimes stabbed their wives and were dragged off to jail. All natives had to carry a pass and obey a 10 p.m. curfew. Mom and Dad didn't think that was very fair and it caused many problems with arrests for simply being out late. Even if they missed the bus it was not considered a good excuse.

Mom and Dad soon found a house to buy. "Perfect for us, with a big garden for Jock and Trixie to romp in," Mom told us happily. "We'll go to church with Doll tomorrow and see how we like it." We got up early as Dad insisted we braid our hair. Aunty Dolly loved St. Peters. "It's the oldest church in Maritzburg." She sang in the choir every Sunday so we had to sit by ourselves. The priest followed the choir procession into the church singing a hymn. We could hear Aunt Dolly bellowing louder than anyone else. "Listen to Aunt Dolly," I whispered to Sheila and we giggled. Mom gave us a filthy look.

The priest wore white garb and heavy embroidered vestments draped over his shoulders. His back bent forward as he walked and his beak nose poked back and forth with his steps. He sang almost as loud as Aunt Dolly. Throughout the service he droned on and on. I stole a few sideways glances to see if there were any young people in the church. A boy across the aisle stuck his tongue out at me when he saw me staring at him, then his Mom poked him on the shoulder and he looked back down at his prayer book. Maybe things would not be too bad in this town they called Sleepy Hollow.

After fidgeting around kicking stones in the pathway while our parents shook hands with the vicar and said hello to Aunty Dolly's friends, we hopped into the back of the truck ready to drive out to see the house they were buying. We found it on a narrow street amongst lots of similar small houses. They all seemed to have large front gardens bordered by low brick walls. Dad pulled up on a grassy patch alongside a brown brick wall and waved his hands. "There it is, what ya think kids?" he said, hoping we would be wildly enthusiastic. "Doesn't look too bad does it?" It had finally stopped raining so Dad rolled up the sides of the canvas and we stuck our heads out to take a good look.

We stared at a plain, brown brick house with a green front door and an enclosed verandah across the front. Disappointed, it didn't look very exciting at all. "Wait 'til you see the back yard, you'll love it," Dad enthused. Everyone trooped out of the truck. Dad opened the big wooden gate and we followed him up the driveway to the empty house. We peeked into some of the windows on the low side. "I bags that room at the back," I shouted. I could tell it would be in the corner so my sisters would not bother me all the time. The back verandah was similarly enclosed. It didn't look inviting at all. I followed the family around drearily, not feeling very excited about any house in town and particularly not this one.

As we drove away Dad suddenly announced that he had a surprise for me. "We're going to drive past the school where you'll be going. Mom made inquiries and saved the news for now." At the top of a long tree lined road I spotted an enormous brick building with lots of square windows evenly spaced across the front. "There you go Doff, your new school." I read the sign painted in dark green ink, *Pietermaritzburg Girls' High School*. I could hardly believe it. I could go to Girls' High! Lots of my Greytown friends were borders there. The move didn't seem so bad after all.

We drove back to Greytown that night in silence. It wasn't very cold and the stars twinkled in the sky. I followed the milky way all the way back as I lay on my side next to my sleeping sisters wondering what our new life in town would bring.

A month later we packed up and loaded into the same Indian lorry, which had moved us from the farm. I was filled with excitement at the thought of being a student at Girls' High, a posh school with tennis courts, hockey fields and a huge crystal clear swimming bath. You could actually see the racing lines on the tile at the bottom. Dad loaded the dogs and our only cat into the back of the truck with us and we set off down the dusty road for the last time.

Maritzburg lies in a valley with the Umgeni River running right through the town. As we drove down the hill on the tarred road the heat and humidity hit us.

"It'll be a hell of a lot hotter here." Dad warned.

"We'll miss the cool morning mist that kept Greytown more pleasant, but I suppose we'll get used to it." Mom rolled down the window in the front of the truck trying to cool off, a slight breath of air blew into the back where we sweltered. Dad had the canvas canopy closed all around us to keep the dogs and the cat safe.

We drove straight down the main road through the middle of town. The sun sank behind the hills and the five-o-clock bustle was a new experience for us. We lifted the canvas corners so we could see into the street with most of the native shops situated at the lower part of town. You could tell because there were piles of fifty pound bags of mealie meal and potatoes, lots of fat green cabbages stacked on tables, and plucked chickens hanging by their feet across the front of the stores. One shop sold brightly colored dresses, hung out in front flapping in the breeze to attract attention. Shoes tied together with string dangled from a verandah ceiling. Natives milled about everywhere, some waiting for the bus to the Edendale Township. Women sat on crates or boxes feeding their babies, chattering and shouting to their friends in Zulu. The smell of curry and odd spices floated into the hot truck as we passed them by. An old man sat at a treadle sewing machine on the porch of one of the dress shops mending clothes. Women lined up with their torn garments waiting their turn. Native men gathered at the corners smoking, talking and shouting to their friends in crowded trucks as they inched by in the heavy traffic.

As we approached the center of town an old three-story Victorian brick building towered above us with ornate architecture, gargoyles and ledges protruding everywhere.

"That's the Town Hall built long ago when Maritzburg was first established," Mom yelled to us through the back window. There was a large statue of Queen Victoria in the grounds across the street. Past the Town Hall the shops changed and we could see posh dresses in the windows, school uniforms, hats and high heel shoes. Only white people came out of the shops and walked on the pavement. The sidewalks were swept and uncluttered. We passed the Cathedral on our left and Grey's Hospital on our right. "Not long before we get to the new house," Dad said. We have to cross the river, pass the Bowling Green and turn left at the first road." He crept along with all the other traffic.

Jock didn't like it one bit. He barked and pulled at his leash tied to a cleat in the back with us, scaring the cat tied in an old mealie sack. Trixie lay placidly at my side. She never got excited over anything.

We drove into Riverton Road away from the hustle and bustle down a quiet street, past a mixture of brick houses, some with big trees in the front garden and beautiful lawns, others very ordinary. "Open the gate Doff," Dad shouted as he pulled in the driveway. Glad to get out of the heat in the truck, I hopped out eagerly. He drove in and jerked to a halt. Everyone bundled out after the long day, anxious to explore the inside of our new house. "Shut the gate quick Doff, we can't let old Jock loose yet." I ran back to the gate, Jock barking constantly. "It'll be fine here Jock, just wait and see," I patted and hugged him, trying to calm his anxiety. Trixie sniffed about, peed thankfully on the lawn after such a long hot drive and plopped down in the shade.

Mom took the sack with the cat into the house and shut him in the bathroom. We hadn't buttered his paws and he was very unhappy. The house was empty and hot. We ran around bagging rooms and I had to settle for the smallest bedroom again because my sisters had to share the big corner room.

Since our furniture had not arrived, we all went back to Aunt Dolly's for sausages and mash and spent the night. Jock and Trixie slept on the bed next to me. They didn't go far from us as they could tell something was changing. Mom left the cat at the house. Tired and excited we fell asleep ready to begin our new life in town

❖ II ❖

Pietermaritzburg Girls' High
1952–1954

Pietermaritzburg Girls' High

After we unpacked Mom drove us to our new schools to sign in. She bought us each one uniform, "to get us started." Sheila looked quite nice in her yellow check dress, with a belt and puffed short sleeves, but I thought mine was much smarter. A short sleeved, white cotton shirt with a square neck and a

189

green sleeveless tunic to wear over the top. We each got a white panama hat with our school colors on the headband and a new pair of black lace-up shoes.

Dad had a new uniform too, a tunic and long pants with a shirt and tie. No more jodhpurs. He was going to be a regular policeman. The next day we started in our new schools and for the first time I felt very excited.

Girls' High sounded so posh. I never thought I'd be going there. I could hardly believe it was happening but I was thirteen and a half and grown up. Mom took me into the Principal's office, which was right near the front entrance and after a few words with Miss Grundy, she left.

Miss Grundy sat behind a long, shiny, neat desk. There were no papers on it just a gold pen set on a wood stand. The office was lined with books, mostly history books. She must have been a history teacher once, I thought. "Well," she said, looking at the paperwork Mom had filled out, "let me see where you fit in. I think we'll put you with Miss Banks. She'll be your classroom teacher so let's go up to her room right now and you can meet her." A loud bell rang and hundreds of girls dressed in green uniforms rushed up and down the stairs and the hallways. I followed her along the hall. "Good morning Miss Grundy," the girls greeted her with deference.

When we arrived at Miss Bank's room on the second floor at the end of the long verandah, Miss Grundy led me into the room. I stood scared stiff as a sea of faces looked up from their books and stared at me. "Good morning girls. This is your new classmate, Dorothy Greenland." I cringed at the sound of my surname spoken out loud, half expecting everyone to laugh. I wondered what they must think.

Miss Grundy left and I stood there, tall, skinny and quite self-conscious. I gaped at the class wishing I could fade into the background. Miss Banks pointed to an empty seat in the front row. "Why don't you take your place in that seat next to Joan." I sat down beside her and pushed my new satchel under the seat. The desk was very old with lots of names carved into the lid, some filled with ink. It smelled of pencil shavings and books. I glanced at Joan. "Hello," she muttered, seeming as awkward and shy as me. Miss Banks was in the middle of handing out past test papers. As she handed them to the person whose name she called she would make a comment.

"Nice work Ruth. Not much effort put in here, Diana. Well, well Joan," she peered over her glasses, "one out of a possible ten for you. I wonder how much time you put into it?" She glared at Joan with raised eyebrows. Joan sunk lower in her seat as Miss Banks plopped the paper down in front of her. "I don't know," Joan answered so softly that I doubt Miss Banks heard her. She snorted and moved on to the next pupil's paper.

I sat watching the process. Miss Banks seemed like a real sergeant major. I liked the way Joan appeared unperturbed by her. When the bell rang for lunch, Joan offered to help me through the day and the beginning of a very special and lasting friendship began.

Miss Grundy came back later to tell me of my choices for classes. "Biology or Physical Science? Geography or French?" Biology sounded easy and I already loved Geography so it wasn't difficult to choose. Later that day we went to the P.E. class and I met the pretty young gym teacher, Miss Basson. She checked everyone in with her clipboard and when she came to me I told her I was a runner. "Well, we don't do running here at GHS," she said. "Young ladies have been known to faint so the running program was cancelled many years ago." Stunned, all the excitement of the new school evaporated in a flash. I wouldn't be running. What could I do? That was my life. Miss Basson, not knowing my reaction to her statement about running, smiled. I stood and stared at her blankly. "Field hockey or net ball?" I had never played either, how could I decide? Joan leaned forward and tapped me on the shoulder. "Choose hockey, only drips play net ball." At the end of the day I learned my subjects would be English, English Literature, Algebra, Biology, Geography, History and playing hockey after school during the winter months, swimming and tennis during the summer. I decided I would survive GHS after all.

A few days later, Joan spotted me sitting on a bench by myself at lunch break and wandered over. "A bunch of us sit together," she told me as I grabbed my lunch box happily, so thankful not to be sitting alone again. Joan introduced them one by one as I munched my jam sandwich and they smiled pleasantly. Millie, a round-shouldered, skinny, flat chested girl with a few pimples on her face and forehead laughed merrily.

"We're an easy bunch to get along with." Joan said she always had the best lunch. Next Sheilagh, a big girl, taller than me with curly hair and a crooked smile, greeted me warmly as she spooned fruit out of a washed baby jar.

"Where did you go to school before? Climb up here and have a seat." She patted the big wooden storage box she was sitting on.

"Thanks, I've just moved here from Greytown." I hopped up onto the box. "It's so nice of you to let me sit with you."

"I'm Norma," said the tall, blonde skinny girl with a narrow face and big eyes. "Sheilagh comes from Richmond,

Lunchtime at Girls' High, Norma, Eugene, Sheilagh and I with Millie
Winter Uniforms

that's not too far from Greytown." I knew where Richmond was. We'd been there once to look at a beautiful farm with a lovely house which Mom and Dad couldn't afford. It stuck in my memory I wanted it so badly. An old gum tree sheltered us from the hot sun as we ate our lunch. "They keep all the net balls in this box for the drippy netball players." I looked about this group thinking they looked a bit drippy too. I said nothing and peeled my orange.

Millie fished a big slice of cake covered with thick icing out of a neat little tin and bit into it. "I hate sports, I only play because I have to." She turned out to hate gym classes, tennis classes and swimming. She always played back on the hockey field because that way half the time she wouldn't have to do anything. Usually when the ball came her way she was daydreaming and missed the tackle anyway. A quiet student in the classroom, Millie didn't say much and never put her hand up if she knew the answer, but when we wrote a test or an exam she'd get top marks in the class. Sometimes Joan and I spent days swatting hard for a History or Geography test, asking each other questions, going over and over the facts only to get a C.

Millie, Joan and I became close friends and rode our bikes back and forth to school every day. The roads we took were lined with pretty houses and tall jacaranda trees. We loved to hear the popping sound of the blossoms as we sped along the road in the springtime. During summer, I rode up the hill and across the main road to Joan's house, early enough before it got too hot. The main road ran right through Maritzburg from one end to the other. You just waited on the side until you could leap on your bike, peddling like mad and make a wild dash between speeding cars. When I pulled up at Joan's house perspiring and breathless, I'd ring the bell on my bike. On cold mornings my nose would run and I'd give it a loud honking blow while I waited. The day Joan got married, her Dad toasted her bridesmaid, me. Mortified, he said he always knew when I arrived because he heard me blowing my nose.

Maritzburg lay in a deep, hot valley surrounded by hills. The muddy brown water of the Umzinduzi River flowed slowly through the middle of town dividing the neighborhoods. We lived on the north side where the houses were bigger and the gardens large and well kept. On the other side, the houses were much closer together and older.

Joan was always late, so we'd have to peddle furiously down the street to Millie's house, ringing our bike bells so she'd come rushing out. From her house we rode down to the bottom of a long hill, only to have to push our bikes up the other side, then fly along Alexander Road at full speed. When we were out in public in uniform we were taught to behave with lady-like decorum. We often had to abandon our genteel behavior in favor of peddling as fast as we could — three wild windblown students racing to beat the bell. We'd fling our bikes into the rack, never locking it, and run like mad to our classroom just as the bell for assembly rang. In the afternoons when we rode home, Millie's mother would see us coming and would send their *umfaan* down to the bottom of the steep hill so he could push Millie's bike up the hill. When it was very hot, Joan and I would beg Millie to let her *umfaan* push one of our bikes. "No, he's our *umfaan* and he's to push my bike." We did not think about the difference between black and white children. It did not even enter our heads that a young black kid was sent to push the white girl's bike up the hill. Many years later Millie told me that she was embarrassed when her Mom sent the *umfaan* down to meet us, but she never said anything. Sometimes we stopped in at Millie's house on our way home because her Mom often baked delicious cakes and we would eat a lovely big slice, moist and tasty, smothered in thick buttery icing. The *umfaan* took Millie's bike, wiped it down and put it away in the garage.

I soon found out what Joan meant about Millie having the best lunches. In addition to a different sandwich every day, she always had cake or biscuits, fruit cocktail in a jar, a drink or some other delicious item. Lucky thing, I used to think. Whatever it was we were all envious, and we'd try to swap.

"Aw come on Mill, I'll give you my jam and cheese sandwich for a ham and tomato?"

"No, I don't want any of your boring old sandwiches."

"How about a bite of that cake for a biscuit?"

"No, I think I'll stick to my own lunch. I don't want your germs."

Most of us had pimples. I hated them. Every couple of weeks I'd get two or three new ones, first a sore red spot, then a big yellow head. I'd squeeze it out and feel better.

"Stop picking at your face," Dad said. But as they collected I prolonged them by picking the scab off every time it felt nice and hard. I was always buzzing my fingers over my face like a Geiger counter feeling for something to pick. No amount of nagging from Dad helped. We didn't have a lot of mirrors in our house, only one in the bathroom and one at Mommy's dressing table so I didn't pay much attention to how I looked. I was much more interested in sports. One day Sheila and I were having one of our usual fights. "Shut up pimple kite," she shouted. Hurt, it stopped me in my tracks. I hadn't thought of it that way.

"Mom," I yelled. "Sheila called me pimple kite!"

"Well Doff, you ought to take a look in the mirror once in a while, maybe you'll stop picking at your face." She gave Sheila a talking to that day. "Doff's at that sensitive age now, so be kind." I glared into Mommy's dressing table mirror and saw that pimply face staring at me. Spots on my cheeks and forehead, small ones, big red ones, freshly picked ones and a couple of juicy new ones. I looked a real mess. I realized then how much I was always feeling around for a scab and I had to try hard to stop. That day I resolved to resist but it proved very difficult.

I also became a regular nail biter. Dad bit his nails so I didn't think much about it. I just seemed to have hang nails that needed trimming or I broke the nail and would trim it with my teeth. Dad and I sometimes talked about the comfort of trimming our nails that way. "I just can't help it, there is always some reason why I have to bite them." I just couldn't resist. Ever practical, Mom said our nails were ugly and we were ruining our teeth. So one day we both agreed to try and stop. Dad showed me his growing nails every day or so. "I'm trying to stop but I just had to bite this little bit off." I made excuses every day. I managed to grow my thumbnails for about a month and they looked quite nice, but Dad won the contest because he never bit his again once he stopped. After a few months Dad declared himself the winner. I just carried on the same old way.

At Girls' High they gave out posture buttons, a large round button, half green and half white, which you could pin to your uniform like a badge. Millie had scoliosis so she would never get one. She had to go to remedial exercises every morning and swing from the bars by her arms to straighten her back. Joan received a posture button. Her back was straight as could be. Envious of Joan's button, I believed if I tried harder to stand up straight I might be awarded one too. Every time I happened to think of it, I would straighten up, pull my shoulders back and march along stiffly, until I forgot or something else more interesting distracted me.

"You'll never get one," Dad said. "You have been slouching too long."

"Shame Dave, you should encourage the kid." Mom always stuck up for me.

For my entire time at Girls' High I remained in a constant state of shoulders back or slouching happily. I never did get a posture button. My only consolation was that Millie didn't get one either.

When a new term began Joan and I giggled and fooled around as usual. We entered the classroom and rushed straight to the desk in the back corner and unloaded our books. The desks were wooden two seaters with sloping lids covered with the names of the many girls who had preceded us carved into the surface.

Miss Alstrup, our new classroom teacher introduced herself. Her specialty was Mathematics and she would be drumming Algebra into us for the next six months. After that we would move on to Geometry and Trigonometry. Straight out of university, Joan and I looked her over. She wore an old fashioned frock with a flared skirt, frumpy shoes and hardly any makeup. She wasn't too thin but she wasn't fat either. Her hair waved naturally, scraped back with a headband revealing a high smooth forehead. Her eyebrows were thick and bushy, she had a nice shaped nose and a pretty mouth. We sensed she was trying to make us like her, but she was afraid to give too much leeway so she treated us strictly. Miss Alstrup began the Algebra of the day.

"Please open your books on page forty-two, class."

"Do you have your Algebra book?" Joan whispered. I scratched around in my desk, holding the lid open with my head so I could use both hands to push the books around, when the lid slipped of my head and shut with a loud bang. Miss Alstrup jumped, the entire class looked our way, Joan smiled sheepishly and I peered up to see all eyes in our direction.

"Sorry," I croaked.

"What do you think you are doing Dorothy?"

"Well, I was searching for my Algebra book, I didn't mean to let it bang shut."

"Don't let it happen again please. You should have had your book ready at the beginning of class."

"I've found my book," Joan whispered, "let's share." We huddled close together with the book open in front of us and tried to pay attention.

"I don't understand a word she is saying," Joan giggled.

"Neither do I. I hate Algebra."

"I think I hate it more than you."

"I'm not sure she knows how to teach, she's just rattling on and on."

"What are you two girls talking about?" I looked up at Miss Alstrup standing in the aisle right next to us. "I can see you're not paying attention sitting here at the back of the room. Pack up your books and move up to the front right now."

"Aw Miss Alstrup we weren't doing anything."

"I know that, that's why you are moving up to the front." Her hair swung around her ears as she pointed towards the desk. In the middle of class, with everyone staring at us she made us move right near her table. I slunk forward loaded down with all my books, keeping my eyes pinned to the floor. The room remained silent except for the creaking floorboards.

It wasn't really hard to sit in the front row and we learned a lot more. But every new term Joan and I headed for a back desk and within weeks we would find ourselves relegated to a front seat. The inclination to talk to each other was so irresistible we could never keep our hold on the outer limits of the room.

We moved from classroom to classroom when the bell rang. My favorite subjects were Biology and Arithmetic. Once a week we went to an Art class that I looked forward to as the teacher gave me my first lessons in painting. I discovered I could actually paint quite well and her lessons helped me understand perspective, color, contrast and depth.

Gymnastics was the most fun. After exercising vigorously for fifteen minutes we were exposed to real gymnastics such as balancing on a bar, jumping and spinning on a horse and many other activities.

Exams were held quarterly and at the end of the year we wrote a lengthy three-hour paper on every subject we studied. We were supposed to be able to answer any question in full detail on any subject covered during the past year. Joan and I swatted quite hard. We made abbreviated notes and repeated their content to ourselves for weeks. We lay on her bed in the afternoons asking questions and testing each other on every subject we thought they might ask about. I much preferred studying at Joan's house. It was quiet and peaceful. Her mother and father usually sat in their lounge. Her mother knitted beautiful sweaters for Joan, her father listened to the news on the radio puffing on his pipe and Joan's younger brother never came out of his room to bother us.

My house was always chaotic. My three sisters argued and scrapped, they ran in and out of the house slamming doors and using the bathroom, and the dogs barked. Dad told everyone to "pipe down" and Mom talked on the phone to all her Women's Institute friends.

As the number of days left to swat narrowed down, I stayed late at Joan's going over and over everything we thought important. I would fly home at dusk on my bike, eat supper, study some more, go to bed and wake up at five to keep on cramming more information into my brain. When exam day finally arrived, I thought I had prepared as best I could but felt unable to control the nervousness and fear. The class marched into the large hall with individual desks spaced two feet apart and took their seats. Just the hollow echo of the high brick walls all around us scared me.

A strange teacher I had never seen before walked stealthily around the room with an expressionless face handing out the exam questions and blank sheets of paper.

She gave out the instructions and rang a bell. She tapped her watch and pointed at the clock overhead that showed nine o'clock. "The bell will ring at exactly twelve o'clock and you must put your pens down and stop writing."

The first paper was History. I poured over question number one. I'd never even looked at that part of the History book. It seemed so unimportant. I didn't have a clue what to write. Well, leave that 'til later I thought. Next question. Oh good, we had studied this section well. I thought I knew the answer so scribbled furiously because there were fifty questions and I only had three hours.

I started to sweat. The hot December day was getting to me. I looked about the room to see everybody writing. No one stared at their paper as if they couldn't remember the cause of the French Revolution or explain the Napoleonic Wars. My brain seemed to have gone completely blank, while everyone else's looked like they worked just fine.

When the bell rang, we had to stop even if we were in mid-sentence. No leeway at all. This same ordeal carried on for a week as we only wrote one exam a day. We couldn't enjoy the short day though because we had swat for the next exam. Joan and I met Millie outside and compared our reactions to the questions. Millie usually thought it was a breeze. Joan thought it was O.K. And I kept my mouth shut.

In order to play hockey we were required to run around the sports field to get fit. As I ran I felt my bosoms bobbing up and down, very uncomfortably. I didn't say anything to any other girls but I could tell Joan wore a bra. One afternoon as we lay panting on the grass after running a few laps I asked Millie if she had a bra. "Good heavens no. I haven't got anything to put in one. I'm as flat as a pancake. Besides I don't think I could ever ask my mother, we just don't talk about those things."

I thought about asking my mother for a bra but didn't have the courage to bring up the subject to her any more than Millie did. Many an evening I hovered about, talking school and hockey, wishing Mom would notice I needed a bra, but there was always something more important going on in our house. The dog was sick, we couldn't find the cat, Sheila had a flat tire on her bike, Trisha cut her finger and it was bleeding all over the kitchen.

Then one morning I woke up and found blood in my bed. I looked with horror. I was so scared I didn't know what to do and went to the bathroom. Oh God, more blood. Am I bleeding to death? I mopped and wiped but it didn't help. "Doff, hurry up and get out of the bathroom," Dad shouted, "You can't spend all day in there." I stuck some paper in my pants and sidled out past Dad, hoping he wouldn't notice my panic. I had to tell Mommy, how could I go to school? I might die on the way. "Mommy," I crept up behind her and whispered so my sisters couldn't hear, "I'm bleeding all over the place."

Mommy took me in her arms and held me tight. "Oh don't be so upset, you are just growing up and this is part of nature." She sat down on the bed patting a spot next to her with a comforting smile. "Come here, I should have realized this was going to happen soon. I'll explain what it's all about." I got my first lesson in womanhood and with it came the chance to ask if I could have a bra since I was growing up. "You poor child, I don't know why I didn't notice, what a bally fool I am." The next afternoon Mom met me in town and bought me a nice white cotton bra at Ross's. It was stiff with circles sewn round and round the cone shape to keep it firm. I felt so much more secure going off to school the following morning with my bosoms firmly housed in their new support.

Getting my period, as Mom called it, created a whole new anxiety. Maybe everyone could see that big lump in my bloomers. I had to sneak about changing, hiding from my sisters. I sure hoped Dad didn't notice. No one talked about periods at school, but I saw the box with a lid in the bathroom at school and peeked inside. There were a whole lot of those horrid things we had to wear thrown in there. What a relief when it dried up after a few days and I could feel normal again. I didn't like having this recurring disease. Just when I forgot about it, it came back.

In spite of my new ailment I fell into a comfortable routine, biking, studying, marching from class to class and playing sports in the afternoons. One sultry day with no sports to go to, Joan, Millie and I were idling lazily in the school library pretending to study. Our books were open, but Joan was writing a funny poem and I was drawing something to go with it when another girl poked her head around the door and asked if we wanted to talk to our dead relatives.

"How do you do that?" we chimed, all bouncing off our chairs to find out what she could be talking about.

"Come with me, we're having a séance in the prefects' lunch room, there's no one there."

"Won't we get in trouble?"

"Na, they've all gone home. Are you coming?" She turned to leave, her ponytail flouncing. We followed eagerly. I couldn't imagine what we were going to do. How daring to go into the prefects' room. I had never been in their room before. There were three other girls from our class kneeling on chairs. They leaned over a glass-topped table with their index fingers resting on a glass in the middle. The window blind was drawn low. A single dim lamp hung from the ceiling over the table so we could see the alphabet had been printed in a big circle with a black pen. A couple of soft comfy chairs sat under the window, but other than that there was only a table and six chairs. I peeked out of the room and looked up and down the corridor but there didn't seem to be anyone about. I was most anxious to find out what a séance was.

A picture of Miss Grundy, our headmistress and another one of the head prefect hung ominously on the wall. I decided not to look at them but concentrate on the action taking place at the table. Colleen, the short pretty girl with the ponytail who had invited us, put her finger to her lips, lowered her eyes and whispered. "Shsh. We must be quiet or the spirits won't come. Everyone put your finger lightly on the glass, don't press hard, just wait and I'll ask a question." I placed my finger gingerly amongst all the others and waited. All I could hear was the soft breathing of everyone in the room.

"Aunt Lilly, are you there?" asked Colleen in a low husky voice. We waited in silence. Suddenly the glass screeched as it slid across the table to the Y, then the E then the S. "She's there," Colleen hissed. "Are you with Grandma Van Royen?"

The glass slid across the table again spelling YES. We stared at each other in amazement,

"Who's pushing the glass?" Joan whispered.

"I'm not," we all chimed together.

"I bet Colleen is pushing it," guessed another girl.

"No I'm not. I'll take my finger off and you see what happens?"

We placed our fingers cautiously back on the glass.

"Am I going to pass the Math exam?" Joan asked. I felt the glass slide away. I knew I wasn't helping it. It flew across the table. NO it spelled. We gasped. Joan wasn't good at Math, how did it know?

"Is my Mom going to have a baby?" The glass slid again SOON, it spelled. Pat, a tall, flat chested thin girl with almost as many pimples as me, screeched, "I never told anyone here my Mom was having a baby, how could it know?"

"Is my Grandpa going to die?" one of the other girls asked in a soft whisper. Her round face looked sad and anxious as the glass moved slowly across the table, IN A WEEK it spelled. We stared at her as tears welled up in her eyes.

"Is someone moving this glass?" Ruth looked around the room at each one of us with her dark piercing eyes. Her thick lips pressed together. She frowned suspiciously. I could tell she didn't believe it was coming from the spirits.

"I swear I'm not, I'm hardly touching it and it just moves." I said defensively. It felt very real to me. It seemed to be moving by itself and everyone in the room denied pushing the glass.

"It's the spirits." Colleen said, "Only certain people can do this. There must be a medium amongst us."

"Well we all know when Colleen is here the spirits answer us, but she didn't have her finger on the glass all the time." Ruth gave us an accusing look. "Let's test it with you three who came in last."

"Dorothy and Joan take your fingers off."

They asked a question and it moved again. Colleen took her fingers off and the glass still responded. "Millie and Colleen take your fingers off," Ruth ordered. The others placed their fingers on the glass. No movement. I wasn't sure if I was pushing too hard. I relaxed my finger and the glass didn't budge.

"Millie's a medium!" Ruth screeched.

"I swear I'm not," Millie said, but when she had her finger on the glass it spelled out the answers.

"We better not do this any more today, we might get caught. We'll meet again tomorrow if I give the word." Colleen ended the session and we snuck out of the prefects' room one by one. As we peddled our bikes home up the last hill we talked over the scary afternoon events.

"Are you sure you didn't push that glass Mil?"

"I know I didn't," she said emphatically. "And you better not tell my Mom about this. She will kill me if she finds out what we have been doing." We promised not to tell. "Cross your heart and hope to die?" Joan, Millie and I ran our fingers across our chests then rode away towards home. We could hardly wait for the next day to try it all again.

I couldn't stop thinking about the séance! I didn't tell Mom though as I thought she might not like the idea we were talking to the spirits. During the night I dreamed of the questions I would ask the next day. I peddled my bike up to Joan's house early in the morning. We couldn't wait to get to school and find out if we were going to meet again. I found it difficult to concentrate in class. Miss Banks was interpreting a poem by Milton written in old-fashioned English I did not understand. I wondered if Milton might answer one of our questions about the test we were going to have on his poetry.

During the History lesson that day, one of my favorite teachers, Mrs. Gordon, lectured on the French Revolution. As she scratched the order of events on the blackboard, I studied her light brown wavy hair finished in a sausage shaped curl across her neck, combed neatly and tucked into a hairnet. The seam on her thick beige stockings was crooked and she wore brown lace up shoes with a practical heal. When she turned around to face the class, she caught me passing a little scrap of folded paper to Joan. Her high forehead wrinkled with a severe frown, her bulging round eyes seemed to pop out of her head. "What are you up to Dorothy Greenland? Give me that note right now." I handed it to her, thinking with relief that I had not written too much. She grabbed it from me and opened it.

"See you after school," she read.

"Well you can stay after school right here and write, 'I will not pass notes' one hundred times before you see any of your friends today." Her eyes boggled as she groused at me.

"Yes Mrs. Gordon." Thank goodness she didn't know what we were really going to do. When I finished writing my punishment, I left Mrs. Gordon marking papers and ducked up the back stairs towards the prefects' room. I tapped softly on the door, hoping my friends were in there. I felt a bit nervous a prefect might greet me. No one answered. The prefects must be gone. I peeked in to see all the girls leaning over the table once again, the glass making a squeaky scratching sound as it slid from letter to letter.

"We're asking who is going to marry Diana?" Diana was a rather fat, pretty faced girl who hated sports and gym. The glass slid around and spelled out MANGO, some pimply youth she had told us about who fancied her.

"Ooh disgusting!" she yelled. "I hate him."

"Let's ask what poetry Miss Banks is going to question us about on the next test?" I asked, hoping for the answer. Fingers pressed and the glass slid to an N, an O, a T and then TELLING. By now I expected real answers. The questions continued. We became so absorbed, voices got louder and no one was paying any attention to anything except the excitement in the room. The tension continued to build as we asked more and more out-rageous questions. Suddenly the door burst open.

"What are you girls doing?" Mrs. Gordon stood at the door as we hastily jumped off the chairs and put our fingers behind out backs. No one said a word. Her face turned red with fury, her stiff wavy hair seemed to be jumping about as she glared at us and her eyes bugged out all the more. "How dare you play Ouija Board on school property, and in the prefects' room too?" We stood frozen with terror as she admonished us for toying with the spirits. How dare we try to speak to God?

How dare we tinker with the occult? "Playing with the devil," she admonished, "that's what you're doing!"

Colleen wiped the letters off the table slowly and we all left the room in silence. The next day a bulletin went out to all the teachers about girls playing with the unknown. There was to be no such activity ever again in this school. GHS was an upstanding place dedicated to the education of fine young ladies. No ladies here would play with the devil.

❖

I settled in happily at Girls' High but one day it dawned on me that Mom was visiting Granny a lot more during the day than she usually did. "She's in the sanitarium again," I heard her telling Dad. "What's wrong with Granny, Mom?" I realized we hadn't seen her for a while and I missed visiting her. Being the eldest, I had a special exclusive relationship with her. I knew Granny better than my sisters.

So many times I stayed at her house and lay on the bed with her, sliding my fingers over her gold eiderdown with its frilly edges. How many times had I played with her bed doll? A doll with a beautiful china face, pink puckered lips and golden wavy hair. She had long china arms, delicate hands with painted nails and beautiful slender china legs attached to her rag body. She wore a rose colored taffeta dress and every morning after Granny's native girl made the bed, the doll was laid on the pillows with her dress spread out as if she was dancing.

Once when on a visit, I poked through Granny's drawers in her bathroom. She had left early that morning with her chauffeur to go to her office. Her drawers were filled with beautiful things, broaches and pretty necklaces, perfumes and powders. I sniffed and soaked up the magic of it all. I opened a delicate little gold box with *Blue Grass* printed in blue on the outside. Inside a glass bottle of perfume lay on a blue velvet bed. I lifted it carefully out of the box and held it up to the sunlight streaming through the bathroom window. I saw a tiny blue horse attached to the bottom of the bottle. I shook it up and down. The horse stood fixed on its hind legs twinkling in the sunlight when the bottle slipped from my hands. I picked up the bottle hastily. Thankfully it hadn't broken. But the little horse was floating about in the pale yellow perfume. I looked around anxiously to see if anyone was coming and stuffed it back in the box, closed the lid and placed it as far back in the drawer as I could. No one had seen me. I heaved a sigh of relief, quickly left the room and wandered casually into the kitchen to eat some breakfast. I never told Granny or Mommy, or anyone else. My guilt rose to the surface. Granny sick in bed, should I say sorry? Should I tell her?

"Your Gran wants to see you all," Mom announced a few days later. "So we're all going to Durban on Saturday." I woke very early, excited to visit Granny. The sun shone brightly. We dressed in shorts and light tops. "Maybe we'll go to the beach afterwards," Mom said, "you know how your Dad loves a swim in the sea."

We loaded beach towels into the boot. We four girls piled into the back seat of our old Vauxhall tight as sausages in a tin and with Dad at the wheel we took off for Durban. The road wound up and down, in and out of the Valley of a Thousand Hills. I always wondered how they knew there were a thousand hills but I could never count them. Halfway there we stopped at the side of the road for a drink of tea. Mom always brought a thermos with her because one of us usually got carsick and the tea break would save the day. Cresting the last hill into Durban I could see the ocean spread out for miles, skyscrapers all along the beachfront and the big city before us. It stirred such excitement in me every time we arrived. The streets heading towards the sanitarium were lined with vibrant flamboyant trees covered in red flowers. Dad found a shady spot under one and parked the car.

We crossed the road together, in line like a family of skunks. We stepped into the entrance of the large hospital buildings sprawling amongst the colorful trees. The smell of Dettol and polish filled our nostrils. Nurses in stiff starched uniforms bustled about. Mom led the way down a long wide hall lined with doors on either side. Highly polished dark plank floors spread before us. We walked along the grass mat down the middle, which stretched the length of the hallway, to soften our clomping footsteps. I peeked into the rooms as we passed. A sickly old man gasping and wheezing, an old lady trying to get out of bed, a thin small child crying softly with his Mom trying to comfort him. I had never been in a big hospital before and the entire scene fascinated me. At the end of the hall we walked out onto a wide red verandah overlooking the breathtaking view of the city and the sea.

We followed behind Mom. "Granny has one of the best rooms, it's just here along the verandah." Mom looked back over her shoulder, then turned towards a large pair of white french doors open to the fresh morning air. Inside, a thin old lady lay in a white bed with shiny silver wheels, the back wound up high and the blankets smoothed tightly over her. Mommy reached down and kissed her. "We're all here to see you Mom."

Everyone stood around the bedside and stared at Granny. We barely recognized her. Her white hair waved across her lined forehead and dark blue circles surrounded her sunken eyes. Her thin lips forced a smile through the yellow pale skin while we girls stood there fidgeting. No one said a word. Slowly she reached out her thin hand to me and I saw that lovely smile in her wan pale face. "Dorothy, come and give me a hug, I've missed you so." I burst forward and grabbed her tight. I could feel her bony shoulders, but she was warm and smelled of powder and perfume just like I remembered. She pulled herself up in the bed. Her fluffy, ostrich feather bed jacket tied with a thin, pink ribbon at the neck framed her skeleton-like face.

What's happened to Granny? I wanted to say. What's wrong with her? She had always been so beautiful, her eyes so bright and blue. But I just stood there looking around the room as everyone jumped onto her bed chattering. Flowers filled every table. A white wooden commode stood next to the bed and a large easy chair was tucked in the corner. A thin, severe looking nurse in her starched uniform marched into the room. She wore a triangular veil pinned to her head with hairclips on either side.

"Now, now. Why don't you children go and play outside in the garden while your mother visits with Mrs. Lewis?"

"We just got here." I complained. Mom gave me the look. I knew what that meant so reluctantly we went out the french doors to the polished verandah and jumped onto the mowed lawn. An old native clipped the hedge and nodded his head in greeting. After an hour of fiddling in the garden, poking shongalolas and disturbing anthills, Mom shouted for us to come back in and visit with Granny again. We stood in line hugging her bony body one by one, kissing her thin lips and telling her how much we missed her. She promised to get better and come visit us soon. I hugged her tight, hating to leave. We marched back down the passage and across the road. "Well kids, how about a swim in the waves before we go home?" We piled into the back seat and Dad started the car, backed out from under the tree, red flowers blowing off the hood as we buzzed down the hill towards the beach.

Mom continued to visit Granny. "She's still in the san," I would overhear her talking to her sister, our Aunty Dorothy. Then Mom began to stay overnight with her and Dad was put in charge. He'd wake us up and I'd get breakfast for everyone and we'd go off to school. One morning as I walked outside to get my bike, our neighbor leaned on the fence.

"I'm so sorry to hear about your Granny."

"What's wrong with my Granny?"

Mrs. King's eyes bugged out of her round face and her forehead wrinkled with a pained look. "Oh, you poor child, I am so sorry, I thought you knew." Tears welled up in her eyes. She turned and walked slowly into her house. I threw my bike down on the ground and ran inside.

"What's happened to Granny?" I screamed. Dad didn't know what to say but the look on his face told me something was terribly wrong.

"I didn't want to tell you until after school. Your Granny died last night."

Dad was standing by the stove stirring the pot of handkerchiefs Mom had insisted he boil. He took me into his arms and as he held me tight I looked at the bubbling hankies, small things Mom made us do while Granny was dying. Who cared about those silly hankies? I thought I might faint. I'd never see my Granny again, never smell her hair or see her in her flowered dresses, with her squirrel's foot pinned to her chest. How I loved to stroke it when she visited. I'd never sit beside her in the back seat of her big car as she drove me to the train to go to camp.

We sat down on the back steps, Dad and I, wiping our tears. I smelled something burning and found the hankies were boiling over. Dad rushed to the stove. "We'd better clean this mess up. We can't upset your Mother, she's been through enough," he said.

"Don't tell your sisters yet. Mom will be home this afternoon and we'll all talk about this together. Now you've got to go to school."

I slowly picked up my bike, heaved my satchel onto my back and rode down the driveway up the hill to Joan's house. I rang my bell and blew my nose hard, wiping my tears away. Joan looked at me.

"What's the matter with you?"

"My Granny died," I stuttered, tears gushing again.

We peddled slowly along the road to Millie's house. The sun went behind the clouds and it looked like rain. My heart was heavy and I could not control my crying. I just wanted to cry and cry and cry. Granny was my best friend. I could tell her things, or most things. I worried about the horse in the bottle, maybe she would be able to see it now she was in heaven. I should have said sorry and prayed God wouldn't let her find out.

"You don't have to cry all the way to school," Joan said. What did she know? Her Granny was still alive. She could still visit. She had time. I didn't. I hadn't realized Granny was so sick, Mom should have told me. Oh God how can I live through this day? I'll never see her again I kept thinking.

❖

After I got over the loss of my Granny, the days were happy and carefree for the most part once again. Joan, Millie and I had become stalwart friends. We followed the same boring routine every morning. The girls lined up outside their classroom in order of height. I always stood last in line. When the second bell rang, all classes marched towards the gym hall where we lined up for morning prayers, a hymn and announcements for the day. Then we filed out, went back into our classrooms and

Sheila and I

stood at attention by our desk until the teacher, nicknamed Breezy, entered.

"Good morning Miss Bradshaw," we sang in unison.

"You may be seated," she replied. The room echoed with the loud shuffling of students and desks, then silence as we looked at Breezy in anticipation of what the day would bring. Even though we opened all the windows in the summer, the room soon became humid and sultry. During the winter months we wore navy gym tunics, long black stockings, long sleeve shirts and a tie. We bundled up in wooly sweaters with our blazers on top as we had no heating in the classrooms. Some days when we got on our bikes to ride to school, the frost was heavy and white on the lawns. Our wooly gloves did little to keep our hands from freezing and as soon as we got to school we huddled around an old heater in the locker room drying our gloves and warming our shoes.

Our days were filled with lectures and note taking. We carried around two black hard cover books for each class, one in which we kept profuse notes hastily scribbled while teachers rambled on, the other for homework and exercises, practicing what we had learned. We moved from class to class at the ring of the bell with a load of books in our arms while the teachers stayed in their rooms.

Clever Millie took subjects like Latin and Science. She never seemed to study hard for tests and exams and was always top of the class. Joan and I loved Biology, a combination of Zoology and Botany. We went from studying the amoeba, a

Eating lunch with Joan

pathetic single cell, through earthworms and their simple asexual division, to the grasshopper, the frog, snakes and rabbits. We became most interested in reproduction and began to realize that all forms of life had interesting behaviors in order to reproduce.

At church, we attended confirmation classes. During one of the classes we reviewed the Ten Commandments. We didn't know what, "Thou shalt not commit adultery," meant. The parson brushed over it. "No sexual intercourse with someone outside of marriage," he explained quickly and then rushed on to the next commandment. Later on I asked Joan what sexual intercourse was. We decided to look it up in the dictionary. When we looked up "sexual" it said interaction between the sexes. Then we looked up "intercourse" and the dictionary said a conversation between two people. So we determined adultery meant conversation between the sexes. Much later I learned the true meaning.

Back in the classroom we continued our fascination with dissection and particularly reproduction. One afternoon we were to dissect a green grasshopper. The class split into pairs. Each pair took a fresh grasshopper from a jar of hopping, struggling insects all scrambling to try and get up the sides and out of their prison. We screwed the lid tight onto the jar so they passed out slowly and died while Miss Clarkson talked about what we were going to do. Joan and I gently took out our victim and followed instructions to pin him to a thick piece of cardboard. We avoided the touch of his prickly legs as we stretched his wings on the board. We examined his eyes and his proboscis, the three parts of his body and then slit his belly open to study the simple digestive system. Green fluid ran out and we pushed his guts around with a sharp pointed tool studying his reproductive organ with the magnifying glass.

Another afternoon, Miss Clarkson beamed as we walked in. "Well girls," she announced in her squeaky voice, "I've been able to get some nice frogs for dissection today, so we can study their anatomy. Get your partners and we'll get started right away." She produced a cardboard box filled with hopping frogs. "Now girls we are going to chloroform these frogs. One partner hold the frog gently, the other girl take a gauze pad, dip it into this jar and place it over the frogs face. Like this." Miss Clarkson demonstrated and the little frog went off to sleep in her hand, his legs relaxed and his front feet drooped. She laid the frog gently on the dissecting board.

Joan wouldn't grab a frog. She said she couldn't touch one. I reached into the box and captured the fattest one, his bulging eyes staring up at me as Joan placed the cloth over his face and he slowly passed out. "Now girls, I want you to lay him on his back and stretch his legs out like this." Miss Clarkson demonstrated and we followed along trying to be biological and not squeamish. Our frog lay passively as we pinned his feet out, with his slimy pink belly exposed for the next step. Nobody wanted to move. Everyone squirmed with anxiety. Ruth, the teacher's pet, handed out a scalpel to each partner and we stood looking at Miss Clarkson, knowing what we had to do next, but not wanting to face it.

"Just take the scalpel like this," she waved it in the air. "And gently insert it under his chin and pull down neatly to the bottom of his stomach. Don't dig too deep. Then stop. I will demonstrate step by step how we can observe each organ starting with his lungs."

I shivered. Joan covered her eyes while I stuck the scalpel in and pulled. I looked away and took a deep breath, but it was done and it didn't look all that bad after all.

One little frog had a heart that wouldn't stop beating. Even when it was right out lying on the table it kept beating. "Just a nerve," Miss Clarkson assured us. We all gathered round and screamed as we watched the tiny heart beat away. It was still going when the bell rang and we had to clean up and dash off to the next class.

In my last year at Girls' High, we did the final dissection on a little white rabbit, the only mammal. By this time we were quite hardened when it came to studying the inner workings and once we made the incision, it was all science and matter of fact. We analyzed bunny's lungs, digestive system and most interesting of all, the reproductive organs.

Our days were always full and busy with school and studying, sports and gymnastics, singing in the choir, trying out for plays and reading Shakespeare. I got to read the part of Sir Andrew Aguecheek from *Twelfth Night,* a silly man but comedic. It suited me just fine.

In the summer season we played tennis and took swimming classes. Our school swimming bath was crystal clear and blue, not like the brackish water in the Greytown pool. We took life-saving classes, learning how to rescue a drowning swimmer for which we were awarded a bronze medal. I never could swim very fast so I began to play the fool and pretend I was a clown jumping off the high diving board. That distracted Miss Basson from the serious business of competing in butterfly or breaststroke. She had to laugh and I relished in the attention developing my skill at pretending to be a serious diver and then botching it up.

Playing the fool

In the winter months we played field hockey as well as tennis after school. I loved field hockey. I always got a stich in my side when we had to run around the field before the game. But as soon as we started playing I forgot all about the pain and ran up and down wildly trying to get the ball and run away with it. I played left half, ready to pass whenever I got the ball.

Not everyone thought I was such a great player. It always seemed they passed the ball to the right, but I tried my best and was never wanting for enthusiastic effort. In my senior year we had four teams. I never got higher than the third team except when someone was injured and they called me to sub. I would give it my absolute all, hoping I would be spotted and move up to the second team.

Most days I rode my bike over to Joan's house after school and sports had finished so we could do our homework on their highly polished dining room table and help each other. I preferred the quiet of Joan's house. I liked their kitchen, tidy and sparkling white, a clean dishtowel neatly folded ready if needed. Her Mother always kept homemade biscuits in neat Christmas cake tins. At our house I had to suffer endless fights amongst my three sisters who ate everything in sight. Our afternoon snack usually consisted of a big hunk of bread smothered in apricot jam.

Sunday was family day in our house. Dad always woke us up early to get ready for church. He hated to be late and Mom had a well-established history of never being on time. Dad insisted we must have our hair in braids, not hanging loose around our shoulders, but there was no time to wash hair on Sunday mornings.

"You're not going to church looking like a bunch of hussies," he'd say.

"What's a hussy Dad?"

"Never mind just get your hair done, hurry up or we'll be late again. Help your mother, Dorothy."

We didn't eat before church because we were Church of England and we had to fast to take communion. Dad took up the collection plate and because Mom was the treasurer she counted the money in the vestry after church while we waited outside. Dad usually chatted with other men and we poked around the churchyard waiting for Mom to finish counting.

The church service seemed long and boring, but I loved to sing the hymns and bellowed them out with enthusiasm. I knew the "Our Father" by heart and when the priest reached a certain part of the service, the words set off the alarm in my head, it's almost over. While they were praying I'd look at the back of the lady in front of me or study the wrinkles on the neck of some old man. Sometimes I could see a big blackhead or some shaving cream on the back of his ear. I would stare at it as my mind wandered in all directions, picturing squeezing the blackhead or the old guy smearing shaving cream everywhere. I'd be lost in thought when suddenly the church shook as the organist pounced again on his keyboard and roared out a great throbbing chord beginning the next hymn. Everybody stood up and I fumbled about hastily looking for the page number so I could join in the singing.

After church we'd drive home. Mom generally made a big lunch, sometimes a roast chicken and vegetables, mostly pumpkin. It had grown abundantly on the farm and we had plenty in our garden in Maritzburg. When we were still living on the farm, Granny used to ship large boxes of tinned foods to us every other month. Mom hoarded them in the pantry and would only open a tin of peaches or apricots on a special Sunday. Our church routine stayed the same as when we lived on the farm, but we didn't have to drive so far so we could lie in bed a bit longer.

Mom bought a new brown suit to replace the old one, shiny from ironing it all the time. It didn't look that different to me, but she seemed very pleased with it. She chose a new green hat with feathers that looked like they had been dyed green. Mom thought she looked really posh.

On Sunday afternoons we would either take a drive out into the country or go to our Aunt Dolly's for tea. We only took the drives occasionally as Dad would have to buy us all tea and scones. Tea gardens were our favorite place to stop.

"Please Dad, can't we stop just this one time? We promise to sit nicely and be good."

"Oh ok," he'd give in with a sigh. We'd sit around an old metal table covered with a flowered tablecloth under an umbrella and study the small menu. Ducks quacked and floated in the pond next to the garden. "Can we have a jam tart with our tea please, please, we won't make a mess?" Dad would give in to everything and the Indian waiter in his starched white coat and black pants would take our order. We could hardly wait for him to return, padding across the lawn in his bare feet, carrying the tray filled with an enormous enamel teapot, a jug of milk covered with a crocheted doily, a small bowl of sugar lumps, cups and saucers, bright red jam tarts, scones for Mom and a bun for Dad. We spread out the cups and saucers. Mom poured and dished out one sugar lump in each cup with the silver tongs.

On the way home Dad usually stopped at Oxenhams Bakery. The aroma of hot bread drifted through the air as we drove up and waited for the first batch to be taken from the oven. The smell of fresh hot bread would fill the car and I wanted desperately to bite into the loaf. Once home we'd eat every last crumb with Mom's leftovers and veggie soup and go off to bed warm and satisfied.

On Sundays when Dad didn't have any spare change, we would go to Aunt Dolly's. I loved going there. She lived in a railway house. Row upon row of houses all the same, but each one took on its own character as the years went by. Gardens flourished and verandahs were added. Uncle Don loved his garden and it was easy to find his house surrounded by enormous blue hydrangeas in the summer and bright red azaleas in the winter.

The house was small and crowded with enormous Chinese carved camphor boxes and dining furniture. I had spent many an hour tracing over the dragons carved on the sides and the Chinese houses and trees on the top. They had a big shed out back piled high with the best comic collection I have ever seen. We could sit for hours reading *Captain Marvel*, *Superman*, *Desperate Dan* and *Crime Does Not Pay*. Even the classics were there. I first read *Wuthering Heights* in the comics and it was in that shed I got my first glimpse of America. Crime fighting cops, beautiful women in skyscraper office buildings, Superman and Lois Lane. America seemed like an exciting place!

One Sunday my cousin Pete showed off his new chemistry set. He lit his Bunsen burner and mixed various chemicals in test tubes, wiggling them back and forth over the flame. Green smelly muck bubbled over as he explained the experiment. The mixture turned a rancid smelling brown as it bubbled and belched, unexpectedly exploding the test tube. The brown goo flew everywhere. Aunt Dolly must have heard me scream in fright. "What are you damn kids doing out there, trying to blow the place up?" Uncle Don came rushing out shirtless as usual, in his boxer shorts and bare feet. He never dressed on Sundays.

"We aren't doing anything, just following the directions," Pete fibbed.

"Well clean up this mess and put it all away right now," he bellowed. That was the last time I ever saw the chemistry set. Dad said Uncle Don was a very strange bod. Most of the time he worked in his garden, even when Mom and Dad visited.

Another Sunday when I was about sixteen, my older cousin Dave and Pete were out so I wandered into the back bedroom of Aunt Dolly's house and looked around for something to read. Mom and Dad were chatting away in the lounge, Aunt Dolly was in her small kitchen making tea and my younger sisters were out back reading the comics. I spotted a fat blue book called *The Kinsey Report* lying on the floor covered with some newspapers. Dave had borrowed it from the library. I had no idea about the book so I opened it up and looked at the index. Some of the titles got my attention, such as Male Sexuality and

Oral Sex. So far I only knew what Mommy had told me, which wasn't much. I thought I would like to know more since I had been feeling sort of interested in boys. I had no idea where to find that kind of stuff but there right in my Aunt Dolly's house was a book.

I opened it carefully listening for voices in the front room. They were all busy talking about some old lady at the church so I read on. I was completely taken in by the candidness of the book, they actually wrote real stuff about sex. That afternoon I read as much as I could, flipping from chapter to chapter, gleaning all sorts of interesting information about men and women and what they like. I was shocked and excited too. Abruptly Dad's loud voice pulled me out of the world of sex. "Come on kids, time to go home, lets get a move on, so we don't miss the hot bread." I shut the book and hid it next to the bed under the newspapers where I had found it.

As we drove home, stopping for the hot bread on the way, I sat thinking about what I read. How could people do that? I buried it in the back of my mind, dormant but not forgotten. I fell back into my mundane life of school and sports, and going to rugby games at the boys' high school with my friend who knew some cute guys.

❖

For almost four years I trudged back and forth on my bike to Girls' High. I had grown to love its staid brick buildings, beautiful grounds and the fish pond where we used to study with tall dark pine trees shading it. Slimy green grey moss and lichen had grown on the nearby stonewall for a long time. Millie, Joan and I spent many hours out there by the pond. We'd lean over the edge, giggling and tossing clumps of dirt into the murky water watching the little fish dart in and out of the water lilies. As we peered at our reflections in the water we'd argue history facts back and forth. We reviewed the Greek Empire, the Roman Empire and imagined ourselves living in the Dark Ages. We studied through the Renaissance, the French Revolution and the Napoleonic Wars. When we finally picked up our bikes and rode off home, the sun was setting. We'd ride as fast as we could to get home by dark, curfew hour for all of us.

I loved my gym and sports teacher Miss Basson. She never gave up on my efforts to be a great hockey player, tennis player or gymnast. I wanted to be the best, but try as I did, I never quite made it. As the final exams of my school days drew nearer, we realized how soon it would be before we all went different ways. "I swear we will be friends forever," Joan and I vowed.

The final exams loomed ahead. Biology, three years of Botany and Zoology, and all those plants we'd cultured in varying forms of light: osmosis, chlorophyll, oxygen intake and carbon dioxide output. Would I ever get it all right? The amoeba, the earthworm, insects, spiders, cold-blooded animals, frogs and mammals? That poor bunny, I actually enjoyed dissecting his tiny body. I could picture it in my mind when faced with a difficult question. That's how I would remember all those facts for the three-hour exams.

We were supposed to know in detail the content of three Shakespeare plays and Thomas Hardy's *Far from the Madding Crowd*, as well as interpret a lot of poems Breezy had read to us. She used to read the Thomas Hardy book out loud, droning on and on. Sometimes I could hardly keep my eyes open with the room so hot and the story so boring.

As for Afrikaans, I hated it, mostly because I wasn't very good at it. The part I liked best was *Mondeling*. Once a month you had to stand in front of the class and tell Miss Marais a story in Afrikaans. I discovered that if I told her a funny story, she actually laughed and I got better marks. Since my life was quite hectic and I had a funny family, I would tell her something we had done and exaggerate a bit to make her laugh. This had always seemed to work but how would it work when I had to write something in an exam. It wouldn't be quite the same. Once you passed all of the three-hour exams you matriculated and received a certificate, which entitled you to go to any university in the world. That's what Breezy emphasized.

As Joan and I poured over piles of books and notes, the magnitude of it all slowly sank in.

"I don't know how they expect us to remember all this stuff," I moaned to Mommy.

"Don't you worry. They are only going to ask you the really important things. You have most of that in your head, you'll be fine." Mom didn't seem too worried at all.

About a week before the finals were due to begin I had a pain in my belly button. I rubbed and scratched it and dabbed it with Mercurochrome, but it didn't improve. I looked into the bathroom mirror and could see a big lump in my belly button that bulged out like a frog's eye peeking at me. I didn't tell Mom, I just hoped it would go away. A couple of days later the bulge looked like a big marble and I could hardly move for the pain. I finally decided to show Mom. "Good God Dorothy! Why didn't you show me this earlier? When did it get like this? Dave, come here and look at this thing in Dorothy's belly button."

Mom and Dad made me lie down on the bed while they poked and examined the bulge. Mom swabbed it out with one of her potions. She had a potion for almost every ailment. No matter what, she had a remedy. This time she wet a lump of bread and wrapped it in a cloth, poured boiling water over it and placed it on the lump. "This bread poultice should draw the poison out," she said. I lay still while the poultice worked. When it cooled Mom removed it. "Well, now we've cleaned out around this, we'll see how it looks in the morning." I hardly slept all night. If I turned over it hurt so much I couldn't move, let alone study. I was so miserable.

The next morning the whole family had to examine the lump in my belly button, now bigger than ever. I couldn't pull my underwear up properly or do up my belt. All my sisters wanted to see the "eye" as they called it. "It looks like one of those big jaw breakers you get out of the machine," one of them exclaimed. Mom finally decided I had better go to the doctor. Meanwhile I had developed two red spots on my bottom that looked scary and hurt like mad too. The doctor laid me down on his table and spread white cloths all around my lump. He put on his magnifying glasses and bent close to examine the lump. Tall and important in his starched white coat, he straightened up and looked at me, his face kind but severe.

"You poor child why didn't you come to me days ago?"

"I thought some sort of terrible disease was growing in me. I didn't tell Mom and Dad as I'd been trying to fix it myself. I thought they might be mad at me so I was too scared to tell them. "My schoolgirl imagination had made me terrified but I realized then it was silly.

"Well I don't think it's all that bad. It looks like a boil and I am going to have to lance it, so you must be brave. This will clean it out and you'll be better in no time."

"What's a boil?" I had never heard of such a thing.

"It's an infection. You probably had a bit of dirt there and broke the skin scratching and then it got infected."

I thought about how I had sometimes picked fluff out of my belly button that had been there for days and it looked a bit off. I supposed I didn't clean it out often enough. No one had ever mentioned making sure your belly button was clean. I thought about how I wanted to be a nurse so I decided here was my chance to be brave and see if I could stand this ordeal.

"Can I watch?"

"Well I don't think it will be very pleasant but if you want to, I see no reason why not."

I sat up half way and leaned on my elbows so my belly stayed flat and he could work on the boil. The nurse brought a tray covered in a white cloth. She held out a pair of rubber gloves and they snapped over his clean washed hands. He picked up a scalpel with a tiny thin blade at the end and bent over me. I couldn't see what he was doing but strangely enough I did not feel the lance at all. Suddenly an enormous squirt of yellow muck spurted out all over the place.

"Good heavens, there must be a good cup of puss in this thing." He pressed down on my stomach and out it poured, oodles of it. "This thing was damn deep," he said. He pressed once more. "There, the core came out so you are going to feel much better." No wonder I couldn't sleep at night for the pain. Almost immediately I felt relief.

"You'll be a lot better after this." He cleaned me up and stuck a large Band-Aid over the boil. I didn't mention the two spots on my bottom. Maybe they were only pimples.

A week later as the days for exams grew close, I felt the pimples on my bottom and strained to look at them in the bathroom mirror. They looked very large and red. One was almost between my cheeks and hurt quite a bit. This time I showed them to Mom. "Good God, I think you've got more boils."

The doctor said they weren't ready to lance, so Mom rented me a rubber ring. I had to ask for permission to take it into the hall where we wrote the exams as I had boils.

"What's a boil?" my friends wanted to know, so I tried to explain leaving out the most disgusting details. During the following week I developed more boils on my face. My cheek stuck out as if I was holding a big donut in my mouth. When

I peered into the mirror in the mornings I looked so ugly, yet I had to go to school and face the other girls. I also had to sit on the rubber ring and try to think on top of it all. I overheard Dad talking to Mom one night. "It's just nerves. That poor kid is staying up every night swatting and worrying. No wonder she's got all those boils."

Somehow I managed to get through all the exams by sitting on the ring. In the end I passed all but Afrikaans. I never was any good at that language anyway. I had to rewrite it in the spring and managed to scrape through on the second try.

Our career guidance councilor helped us apply to University, Teacher's Training College, or to any place you chose to make a future. I decided on Grey's Hospital. By this time I had no doubts that I wanted to be a nurse.

After the final day of exams, I walked in the front door, threw my heavy satchel down on the lounge floor and glared at myself in Granny's old gold mirror. At last the boils were subsiding. I made an ugly face at myself. Yuck. "I wish I could be like those popular girls that never have zits or boils or anything on their face and always look pretty," I said to the face in the mirror. Just then Mom burst into the lounge waving an envelope. "Look Doff, something from the hospital for you. Open it and lets see if you've been accepted."

I tore it open, flung the envelope on the floor and unfolded the official letter.

Dear Miss Greenland, You have been accepted as a student nurse at Grey's Hospital and your initiation date will be in January. A long list of things followed that I had to do before then.

"I can't believe I am actually going at last!" I yelled. "I can hardly wait." Mommy hugged me and we laughed with happiness. But I was sixteen years old and would have to wait a whole year. Not until next January? What am I going to do until then? School will be out and I'll still have so long before I start."

We all sat around the dinner table that evening and talked about what I could do. Dad decided he'd call his friend at the bank to see if he could get me a job. About a week later, he came home with the news that the bank would give me a job. I had to go and talk to his friend.

I poked through all my dresses trying to find one that made me look grown up. Since I made all my own they were mostly flouncy, full circle skirts. I usually wore two or three full circle net petticoats under them, the fashion being to flounce about with your skirt bobbing and swinging. The petticoats never stayed stiff so we would wear two or three to get the desired effect. I decided not to wear the flouncy look and chose a straight skirt, wide belted frock I had recently made in white fabric with big black spots all over. I thought I looked quite sophisticated. I spun around happily showing it off to Mom and Dad.

"Hell Doff you look great, but by God you've got a bum like the back of a bus."

"Dave!" Mom screeched. "How could you say that when she's worked so hard to make that lovely dress?"

237

"Sorry Doff! You know I didn't mean anything, it just popped out. Sometimes I don't think. You look really great," he spluttered apologetically.

I really didn't worry too much about Dad's remarks. I was used to him and he always said what he thought.

On the day of the interview I washed and ironed the spotted dress, did my hair, put on some pale lipstick and caught the bus into town. I had never been interviewed before. The large old Victorian building with tall columns that flanked the stairs on either side wasn't far from the bus station. As I ran up the stairs in my new patent leather high heels an old man walked out of the bank counting his money. I imagined myself counting pound notes at great speed just like I'd seen the tellers do, their rubber finger cover deftly handling thousands.

A lady stood near the front door offering assistance. She pointed to a highly polished wooden door on the right when I asked where I could find Mr. Taylor.

I knocked softly. "Come in," said a voice from inside. I pushed the door open and peeked in. Dad's friend sat behind a big desk. He jumped up, came over and gave me a hug like Dad's friends always did. I relaxed a bit. It didn't seem that bad, even though the office was paneled just like I imagined a bank would look. The overhead fan squeaked, as it turned slowly high above our heads. "Take a seat Doff." I sat on the edge of the chair, my toes hurting in my new shoes. I crinkled them up to relieve the pressure. "Your Dad tells me you're going nursing at Grey's next year, so you need something to do in the mean time. I think we can fit you in somewhere. Would you be willing to do anything we needed?" I nodded eagerly. "Well why don't you come in next Monday at 8 a.m. I will introduce you to the staff and you can get started. Maybe you'll like the banking business."

I felt so excited as I pranced out of the bank down the steps, forgetting all about my pinching high heels. I had a real job. I'd have money for the first time without asking for it. That night we sat around the dinner table as Dad bragged to everyone. I studied the big chunk of pumpkin on my plate while he went on about how his friend had decided to give me a job. We often had pumpkin for dinner, roasted, mashed, boiled and spiced. Dad grew them in the back garden and they got enormous very quickly.

"Let's hope Doff doesn't muck up and get fired." He chuckled away at the thought. "She'll be able to help out with the money at home, maybe give half her earnings to Mom and have all the rest to spend on whatever she likes." I sat quietly thinking that over as I chewed another big mouthful of roasted pumpkin. I had expected to help but not that much. The bank would be paying me fifteen pounds a month and I had to give Mom half. I would only have seven pounds ten shillings left and I knew the coat I had been eyeing in Ross's shop window cost four pounds. That sure didn't leave much. I realized my newfound wealth was not going to go very far. I didn't actually have any money yet. This was all in the future. I thought about arguing when Dad changed the subject.

"So when is Prize Giving, Doff? I'll have to take the afternoon off."

"It's Friday. I can't believe it will be my last day at school and I will start a real job on Monday."

Prize Giving, (December 1954) was the final important thing we did before school broke up. That day everyone dressed in a simple white dress, no low-cut necklines please, black sheer stockings and a panama hat with the green and white band to finish off the look. I made up my mind my home-made dress didn't look too bad next to some of the really smart bought ones.

All morning we exchanged addresses and phone numbers and promised to stay in touch. I could not imagine my life without Girls' High. Breezy handed out the school magazine, a small book containing the best writings from students produced during the year. Joan submitted a poem entitled "Dissection" and I did a drawing of the bunny splayed out on the board with nails in its paws and innards belching out the belly. I had been asked about a week before to modify my drawing and not make it so gory. In the final publication, Joan's poem described the details in rhyme and my corrected drawing barely demonstrated the true gore of dissecting a bunny in biology.

Joan, Millie and I sat with all our close friends and ate our final lunch together on the gym box under the eucalyptus tree where we had first met over three years ago. We didn't giggle and laugh about our teachers like we usually did, instead we talked about how we'd miss them.

"Yeah, old Molly Bea, with her baggy jerseys always pushing poetry on us."

"And Mrs. Gordon, with her round buggy eyes and wavy curls, perfectly combed close to her head."

"Remember when she put that sign up on the bulletin board? Wanted, One Monkey Costume." We laughed hilariously all over again imagining how much fun we'd had picturing her in a monkey costume.

"Things will never be the same. These have been the happiest days of my life." We laughed and cried all at once.

"Not for me, I can't wait to be out of here forever," Millie said emphatically. She hated school and the rigors of it all. She was simply too clever for all the discipline and order and the slow thorough learning process they expected of us.

12th Grade, December 1954, age 16
4th from left 2nd row back

The traditions of Prize Giving were followed with elaborate detail. We marched into the school hall in order of class, the seniors first, as Miss McDonough banged "Land of Hope and Glory" on the old school piano. You couldn't help stepping in time. I choked with emotion as we entered the hall for the last time.

Once every girl was in their place the whole school sang "God Save the Queen" with great enthusiasm. The sound filled the big hall. I swallowed back the urge to cry as tears welled up in my eyes.

Miss Grundy, the headmistress gave her traditional report on the state of the school while we fidgeted, bored with the details. She ended with the usual advice and well wishes for our future, wherever we may go.

After the speech the teachers handed out the prizes. A nice book for the best Literature student, a Science book for the scientific, a boring book for the Arithmetic prize. I never received a prize in all those years. Joan got one once for English. The finale always involved the same question. Who would be the Valedictorian? With great flourish and a description of her many academic achievements, Miss Grundy announced Millie's name. "Heck, can you believe old Mil got the prize? She never seemed to open a book, yet she got top marks for everything!" She received a beautiful leather bound collection of Shakespeare's plays.

After Prize Giving, everybody marched out of the hall into the quadrangle where they served tea and cakes to the parents.

I looked sadly around my beloved brick buildings and the long arched verandahs. The bell monitor rang the bell again for the last time.

❖ 12 ❖

Nursing Days
1956

One of my homemade dresses

With school over I only had one weekend to prepare for my new job. On Sunday I looked through all my dresses trying to decide what to wear for my first day. I had never been in a bank for more than ten minutes in my life and at sixteen and a half I was scared stiff. The interview had only lasted about fifteen minutes. Now they would have to put up with me for a year. I'd better look grown up so they don't think I'm an idiot, I whispered to myself as I picked through my handmade dresses.

Monday morning I woke very early and dressed carefully in my spotted dress with the tight skirt. I brushed my hair and looked at myself in the mirror. Not too many zits. Mom suggested I cover them with calamine and then smooth her powder over my face. I looked pale and pasty.

"I can't go like this, I look dead!"

"Rub a bit of this rouge on your cheeks," Mom said, "that'll perk you up."

I dabbed carefully and rubbed Mom's tatty worn rouge applicator on my cheeks, painted my lips bright red and smiled into the mirror.

I caught the bus into town, crowded with people off to work. I began to sweat with worry. I sat on the stained green leather seat squashed against a fat old man and stared out the window. The bus smelled of aftershave, perfume and sweat. The conductor walked down the aisle collecting money and handed me a yellow ticket. I read the number on one side and turned it over. *Ride At Your Own Risk*, it said on the back. I fiddled with the ticket all the way into town. I jumped off the bus, chucked it into the rubbish bin and took the short walk to the bank. I tried to relax, breathing in and out deeply as I marched up the steps. I dashed across the marble floor right up to the lady at the information desk.

"It's my first day, can you tell Mr. Taylor I am here?"

"Don't worry," she smiled, "we all have to go through this." Off she went to find Mr. Taylor while I stood there sheepishly trying to look like I knew exactly what to do.

Mr. Taylor came out of his office and escorted me into another room where two men and two women stood around chatting and smoking. They all looked very grown up. When they saw him they slipped behind their desks and attempted to look busy.

"Good morning staff." Mr. Taylor smiled. "I want you to meet Dorothy. She'll be handling the bills for collection. Ruth, you can spend a couple of days teaching her until she's got the hang of it."

I began the assignment of writing down bills for collection. The collecting bank in column one, the debtor in the second and the amount owed in the third. It sounded simple enough.

"Be careful with the amounts you write down," Ruth warned, "when he brings them back you have to enter them again, and when the two columns are added they must balance."

The bills were delivered every day by an old man on a bicycle. After I wrote them on a sheet of lined paper, he copied them into a little book and tucked it into a leather pouch with a zipper. A sweet old man with a baldhead and weather-beaten face, he wore wire-rimmed glasses, a jacket and tie. His navy blue slacks were clasped around the ankle with bike clips. His breath reeked of garlic and I thought I'd choke from the smell. "Keeps the colds away love," he said, "eat a clove of garlic everyday and you'll never get sick." When he returned I had to check in the bills that had been accepted, enter them on my sheet and go into the Bank Manager's office to file them alphabetically. Scared to death to go into the Manager's office, I greeted him stiffly without smiling, conscious of my lowly position. "Good morning sir." I shuffled silently through the files, slipping each bill into its slot, sometimes dumfounded at the amount of money promised. I handled thousands and millions and presumed that was why they were filed in his office. He rarely spoke to me other than our greeting, but one morning he cleared his throat. "I hear you are going nursing." I looked up at him as if God had just spoken to me.

"Yes, in January," I replied.

"Well, well my daughter is starting the same time as you, I expect you'll be working together."

From that day on I relaxed and we spoke to each other often just like normal people. He didn't seem nearly so superior as I had first imagined. Sometimes a very handsome man would come into the bank and talk to one of the girls in my area. After he left, they would go and look up his account to see if he was rich, and laugh and joke about whether he was worth chasing.

Another lowly male employee once asked me to go to the bio to see a movie with him. "Stick around, I'll make you famous," he said constantly. He thought he was funny, but I couldn't stand the way he said it so I made excuses until he finally gave up. I did have a crush on a teller a lot older than me. I would rush outside after work hoping he would offer me a ride home in his cute little MG sports car or want to take me for coffee, but he never bit.

The year at the bank passed quickly. I made friends and spent every penny I made after giving Mom her half. I made myself a few sleek dresses, slinky and sophisticated. I bought a russet brown pair of high heel pumps and thought I looked

Joan and I, Durban Beach

really hot. I wished the bank teller would notice. I told one of the girls how my Dad had said I had a bum like the back of a bus. "Don't you worry kid," she laughed, "big bums are great. Men love 'em!" I laughed with her and gave up worrying about the size of my bum. The bank helped to prepare me for real life. I felt grown up and ready for the world of nursing.

A short time before I began nurse's training, a young man I had met briefly when traveling on the train with one of my friends, phoned me. He said he was going to be in Maritzburg for a week and would I like to go out with him. I agreed, so we went to the bioscope one evening and out to dinner another. Since neither of us had a car, he rode the bus home with me and then caught another bus back into town to his hotel. A very tall good-looking young man, Keith was quite shy. I had never been on a date before so we made small talk. We were both very awkward. I asked him what he did and told him about my plans to begin nurse's training in the New Year. I did not feel a great attraction to him, but I decided to see how it developed. He lived sixty miles away in Durban so the only way we would be able to continue to see each other was on weekends. I often took the train to Durban because I loved to go to the beach. I would have to stay with my aunt who considered herself a great advisor and chaperone. The first date he arranged in Durban, he asked me if I would like to go to the Athlone Hotel for dinner and dancing. Aunt Vida gave me instructions on manners and how much to trust men, while I put on a frilly full skirted blue dress that I had made for the sixth form school dance the year before. I pulled on my only pair of high heels trying to look sophisticated.

The Athlone Hotel was known for its sprung dance floor and fine dining. I had never been to a posh hotel with a man before so Aunt Vida told me how to act at the table too. "Don't cut your roll, always break it open, put your butter on the side of the plate, then spread it. Use the utensils from the outside in. If you have soup, tip your bowl away from you as you scoop up the last dregs," she instructed. By the time he arrived to pick me up I was pretty nervous about how I could manage to get through the evening. Waiting for his arrival, I worried about my manners and how I looked. Then I heard a motorbike pull into the driveway and stop. I peeked out of the living room window as he climbed off the bike and propped it up. He pulled some metal clips off the bottom of his pants, shook himself out and walked up to the front door.

I didn't know we were going on a motorbike! I opened the door. "I'm sorry we have to go on my bike," he said, "I hope its O.K.?" He kept apologizing for the transportation, but naturally I assured him I could handle it just fine. I introduced him to Aunt Vida. He looked so nervous I expected Aunt Vida to tell him I couldn't go but she didn't. We went outside and I looked at the bike, not a great big Harley like Dad's. I approached the motorbike with extreme trepidation.

"Just sit sideways behind me, put both feet on this pedal and hold onto my waist. You'll be fine."

"I hope so, I've only ever be in my Dad's side car and this doesn't look quite that easy."

I wrapped my dress around my legs and plonked my bottom on the seat, sitting sidesaddle clinging tight to his middle. I stuffed my full skirt between my legs so it wouldn't blow up over my face and tucked my high heels firmly over the pedal. Not too far to the Athlone Hotel. He pulled up right in front and I climbed off the bike. Thankful we had made it, I tried to smooth my hair and my clothes so I didn't look as disheveled as I felt. The evening began awkwardly. I fiddled with the roll and broke it as instructed. A butter dish was filled with little balls of butter as hard as rocks that wouldn't spread on the roll. The Athlone served a four-course meal, first soup then a little toast square with something strange spread on top. I watched Keith to see which utensil he used for each course and made it through the meal.

"Would you like a Port and lemon?" he asked,

"What is that?"

"It's Port wine mixed with lemonade, it's quite nice and you won't get drunk."

I took a chance and sipped it politely. It was a warm night and I could have guzzled it down but I remembered Aunt Vida's lecture. "Don't trust men, they'll take advantage of you if they can."

In the corner of the dining room four elderly men in black tuxedos played old fashioned music and Keith asked me if I would like to dance. I had taken about four dancing lessons during school days so I got up nervously. "I'm not very good," he said, "but I'll try." He couldn't dance very well at all. He stepped on my toes, pushed me about, his hands sweaty and hot. I could feel the dampness through the back of my dress. "Shall we just forget this?" he asked. I was only too happy to give up on the dancing.

When we left the Athlone I climbed onto the back of the bike again, tucked my dress in and held on tight as we went down the hill.

"Let's go along the beach and have a coffee before I take you home," he suggested.

"Ok, but you know I have to be home by eleven."

We sat on the metal chairs at the coffee shop sipping for a while, then he tried to start the bike. He kicked and kicked. It sputtered a few times but would not start. A quarter to eleven! Dressed in my fluffy blue party dress, I began to panic. There were no busses running that late at night so finally Keith asked the man behind the counter if he could please phone for a taxi. When the taxi came he pushed me in and gave the man some money.

"Aren't you coming?"

"No I have to stay hear with my bike." So off I went by myself with a stranger in a taxi. The next day he telephoned to say he had pushed the bike all the way home about four miles and it still wouldn't start. A couple of months later he told me he traded the bike for a fiberglass fishing rod and ten pounds, so he didn't know when he would see me again.

I didn't think about Keith very much but once or twice a month he caught the train to Maritzburg for a visit. I never had enough time to go to Durban so although pleasant, our dating was sporadic. In June he phoned and told me that he was preparing for his Accounting finals and he would not be able to see me for three months, as he had to study. I couldn't imagine giving someone up for exam studies but I said it was fine. He told me he'd be in touch as soon as he had written them.

Meanwhile I received the notice I must come into the hospital for the medical check-up. I found I was one of twenty-six young women in the waiting room, all hoping we could pass the physical. A stern faced middle-aged nurse wearing the triangular veil of a senior Sister summoned us into a long bare room with an X-ray machine at the far end. "Strip to your underpants," she commanded. We self-consciously took our clothes off. "Yes, bra's off too, you all look the same. Might as well get used to it." One by one we were prodded for reflexes and instruments poked into our mouths and ears. Each girl had a chest x-ray, a tetanus shot and immunization against diphtheria and smallpox. "You will be receiving confirmation of your acceptance in the mail shortly," the stern faced Sister told us.

At last that acceptance letter arrived. It was hard to get through that last month at the bank but I was glad I didn't have to be a banker. I made mistakes with the numbers constantly even though I tried very hard not to. Too many naughts (zeroes) or one left off, made for a tiresome end to the day. When the two columns didn't match, a couple of other girls had to stay and help me find my error.

We were ordered to appear at Grey's Hospital at 6 a.m. on January 3rd to receive our instructions. I didn't know what to pack. I put in my underwear and my only other bra, two dresses and a pair of sandals. I'd bought a cool pair of seersucker pajamas but I didn't have a robe or any slippers because I had never needed them. Mom peeked into the suitcase lying open on the bed. "No one cares what you have. You'll be wearing a uniform most of the time so just take the few things you really like."

We only lived about five miles from the hospital but it felt like I was going half way across the world. At five thirty in the morning Mom hugged me hard and kissed me. We clung to each other tightly for a few minutes before I left. "Don't worry Doff, you're starting out on your new life. I can't wait to hear how it's working out so phone me as soon as you can." She stood by the front door biting her lips as I waved. Dad drove me to the hospital. He pulled up in front and I hugged him goodbye too. I climbed out of the car with my small suitcase in hand. "Good luck Doff. I know you'll be happy. Don't forget to give us a ring now." I stood on the pavement watching the car as Dad disappeared. I turned around and marched into the front lobby, smelling of disinfectant and soap. I took a deep breath. I sniffed the bunch of flowers on the entry table. They reminded me of Mom.

As I walked along the long narrow entry, I realized it was the oldest part of the hospital. The building seemed quite small, a bit like an old house. The shiny wood floors and flowers at the entrance made it look inviting. A woman in a nurse's uniform stepped out of the first office and pointed towards a larger room down the hall. Dressed in ordinary clothes and carrying a suitcase, she could tell it was my first day. "All new nurses go to the second room on your right please." I walked into the small room where several other young ladies stood waiting with their suitcases. I smiled pathetically. We didn't know what to say so we stared at each other awkwardly, summing each other up. No one spoke.

As I finished counting all twenty-six girls, a matronly nurse marched into the room. "Good morning girls, I'm Sister Hart. Welcome." She smiled and scrutinized each one of us slowly. She had a chubby round face, blue eyes and bright red cheeks. Her long sleeved white uniform covered her buxom frame and was pinched in with a wide white belt. Several badges pinned to her heaving chest indicated her many accomplishments. Maroon epaulettes topped off her shoulders. "I am going to get you checked in," she announced, "show you around and take you to get uniforms. For the next three and a half years you will follow the routine of the hospital, live here, eat here and learn all you will need to know to go out into the world of nursing. Its hard work and rewarding and if you obey the rules you will get through without a hitch." She glared around the room. "You will be known as Group 1/56" (the date of our entrance January 1956). Nobody said a word. Sister Hart was quite daunting. "Every morning there will be roll call at 6:30 a.m. You will report to the school for your initial training after breakfast Monday through Friday and you will work in the hospital wards on either Saturday or Sunday, with one day off. I will be handing out the work schedules later. Any questions?"

The room was silent except for the nervous fidgeting sounds as we listened to the details of our future. "Now everybody go across the road to the Nurses Home where Sister van der Vet will be waiting for you. She will be fitting you for uniforms and allocating your rooms." We headed off across the road packed in a group. A big redheaded girl with lots of freckles broke the silence with a couple of jokes and laughed. "Boy what did you think of that old Sergeant Major?" she said in a hearty gruff way. We were all too scared to say what we thought. She turned to me. "I'm Bobsy Morkel, are you from around here?" She led the way as we followed like a herd of sheep.

Sister van der Vet was standing at the top of the red polished steps of the Nurses Home with her arms folded over her chest. The large, three story, brick building had verandahs all the way around. I could see a couple of girls looking over the edge watching the new bunch arrive. "Good morning girls, I am Sister van der Vet, Sister Hart's assistant. I'll be helping you get your uniforms and everything you need to begin your career in nursing." I looked her over. Her face was round and chubby with blue eyes and bright red cheeks. She looked like she had been cooking over a hot stove. Like Sister Hart she had a buxom frame and wore the same straight white uniform, long sleeves, buttoned down the front with several badges pinned on her chest. Her shoulders were topped with similar maroon epaulettes and brass buttons. "Once you've got your uniforms I will be assigning rooms so come over to me when you're ready." We followed her into a stark green room, lined with shelves piled full of white uniforms, belts and caps. Navy blue capes lined in red hung on hangers in one corner of the room. "You know your size, it's clearly marked. Choose the one you think fits and try it on."

We wandered around the room looking for our size and then stood self-consciously in the center of the room, hopping from one foot to the other as we slipped into one of the stiff white uniforms to see if it fit. Straight cut and too long, with my height they hit me at mid-calf, but I had to get the one that fit around my bottom. Some of the uniforms went almost to the floor on the shorter girls. As we studied each other, most of us looked so funny it broke the tension. We laughed and made comments to each other. With the four uniforms, three stiff white belts three inches wide, four caps and a navy blue cape tucked under my arms, I filed out into the main lobby. I liked the cape immediately; it made me feel like a real nurse.

While we waited in the lobby for everyone to get their uniforms the phone rang loudly. A barefoot Zulu native girl in a green uniform with a green matching doek ran to answer it. All the native staff women we had encountered so far wore the green uniform and covered their hair with the three cornered green doek tied in a knot at the back of their head. "Hello," she bellowed into the phone. She listened for a minute then plonked the receiver down on a ledge by the phone with a bang and marched into the middle of the lobby. "Ness Brown, Ness Brown," she shouted a few times before she reached back into the wooden phone booth. "She's not answer," she continued to shout into the phone, "I take a message." We watched as she scribbled something into a big black book tied to the phone booth with a thick piece of string.

"Mtomba takes messages for the girls during the day," said Sister van der Vet. "Always check the book when you come in."

"Mtomba, meet the new girls and take good care of them for me now."

"Yes Ma'am, I do that for all of them."

She beamed at us all with her toothy white smile and nodded her head up and down enthusiastically. Short, black kinky hair outlined the green doek and her pretty face.

Sister explained that each floor had a furnished lounge in the center and a block of showers and toilets. The lounges were all furnished the same, a couple of brown leather couches, four big comfy chairs and a large coffee table in the center. A bookcase stood on one side filled with old books, nursing books from the thirties, and various raggedy novels which had been read from cover to cover many times over. On the other side, a smaller table pushed against the wall had a neat stack of mugs, a jug and a bowl of sugar on a tray.

Long hallways branched off both sides of the central lobby. There were twenty rooms on each side of the hallways. Every room was identical, neatly furnished with a small single bed, a chest of draws, a four-foot wardrobe, a tiny washbasin and mirror, and a desk with a small chair. The dark stained furniture was not very old. The beds were made up with stiff starched sheets and green coverlets, two pillows and two towels lay on the bed. The room smelled of floor polish. A glass door provided light in the room and led out onto the wide covered verandah. I peeked out and saw that many girls had pulled their beds outside. It was January and the nights were getting very hot. There was no air-conditioning or heat in the building.

Once allocated to my room, I unpacked my few things, hung my new cape in the wardrobe, put away my toothbrush and paste and the few face things I had. We had been instructed to put on our uniform and cap and come down to the dining room for breakfast. I dressed and looked at myself in the mirror. The uniform looked much too long but I would have to hem it up later. I rubbed some lipstick on my lips, stood it on the glass shelf, pulled the belt tight around my waist, put on a new pair of nylons we had been told to bring, and my new brown lace-up shoes. Ready for the world, I wandered out into the hall to see if there were any other new girls around. I spotted the loud red head, already commenting on the fit of the uniforms. "Come on," she shouted at me, "lets go check out the grub in this place."

We had been instructed to go back across the road to the dining hall. Sister Hart showed us which tables our group would be sitting at. The dining room was empty except for the new girls, since breakfast was served at 6.30 a.m. every morning and nurses were on duty by seven. "Roll call is at 6.30 a.m. girls, tardiness will result in you losing night out privileges." We didn't yet appreciate what that meant but we'd soon find out. "Now be seated and enjoy your first breakfast." Black waiters in white coats rushed around offering bowls of oatmeal porridge, brown sugar and milk. A stack of both white and brown toast sat piled on a plate in the middle of each table, two large pots of butter and marmalade placed at each end. After the waiters scooped up the porridge bowls, they brought in platters of bacon, sausage and fried eggs, which we passed around the table. All of us were taken by surprise. The food seemed too good to be true. After we finished eating we were escorted outside and down the road. We followed Sister Hart like school children to the Nursing College where we were about to spend the first two months of our nursing lives.

Sister Hart marched up the steps of an old Victorian house into a large, high-ceilinged room with rows of desks in the middle. It had been the main lounge long ago. Several cabinets with glass doors filled with bottled specimens lined the room. A grey looking heart, lungs, diseased lungs, kidneys and a brain that must have been there for years caught my eye. A skeleton hung in the corner. Two rubbery blowup dolls hung beside it. You could tell they had been manhandled over years. Cupboards were filled with splints, bandages, beakers and jars. A sour, potent smell permeated the air and made my eyes water.

An older nurse stepped into the room wearing the standard triangular starched veil of an RN, her qualifying emblem pinned just below her collar. Several other badges were pinned to her top pocket. None of us knew what they represented but we were soon to find out she was extremely well qualified to teach and train us. Her shoulders were adorned with the usual maroon epaulettes. She had soft fine hair around her face poking out from under her veil. Although fairly old, she looked pretty with her pink cheeks, shiny pink lipstick, and nicely made-up face.

Sister Hart stood next to her and faced all of us as we piled into the room.

"This is Sister Moyer, she will be teaching you for the next two months, preparing you for your hospital training so pay attention to her. You'll need to learn all you can from her," Sister Hart said. "There will be a lunch break at 1 p.m. Classes will finish at 4." She marched out of the old building and left us gawking at Sister Moyer. "Be seated girls, take any desk and let's get on with the program." Let's start off by going around the room and introducing yourselves." At last we were to learn each other's names.

Sister Moyer surveyed the room slowly looking us over. "I am going to be your teacher for the next two months. I will prepare you to be let loose amongst the patients and give you all the knowledge you need, so you don't kill anyone on your first day out there, or on any other day thereafter. You have this week to learn some basics before you go on duty in the wards this coming Saturday or Sunday. All the staff will know who you are because you will not be wearing a button on your collar. Once you qualify from the two months with me you will be issued a green button. After your first year you will receive a red button. In your third year of training, you receive a dark blue button and finally a light blue button when you are in your final year. That way everyone knows what you know and don't know."

We began our day learning how to make a hospital bed with straight envelope corners. The classroom was hot and muggy, so we rolled up our long sleeves and stood around the bed as Sister Moyer demonstrated how to flip up the corner of the mattress, fold the sheet, flick it under and drop it down again. "And don't try to fudge on this job because when Matron inspects the wards you had better have perfect envelope corners." We practiced the corners two at a time, one girl on either side as Sister Moyer watched over us. When we fumbled with the mattress and the sheet, she would push us aside and show us once again, deftly flipping and folding. I could feel the perspiration running down my back. "You'd better practice on your own bed every day until you get the hang of it." It took the whole morning for everyone to make a perfect envelope corner.

After our first lunch, a large bowl of thick potato soup, brown bread and salad we trooped back down the road to the Nursing College for our next adventure. When we walked into the classroom Sister Moyer was standing in the middle of the room with a shiny stainless steel bedpan and a urinal on her table.

"Now girls you are going to learn how to administer these utensils to the patient, and how to clean them up and make them comfortable afterwards. If a patient rings the bell for a bedpan what do you do? What if they are sick or have a broken back or pelvis? You can't just hand it to them. You have to know how to get it under their bum. You, Pat, that's your name right? Get into this bed." Pat lay down on top. "Get under the sheets you fool, not on top. The patient is sick in bed."

We all looked at each other with trepidation. Obviously Sister Moyer wasn't going to let us get away with anything. "I am now going to demonstrate how to lift the patient onto the bedpan." She rolled Pat over on her side and pushed the stainless bedpan up against her bottom, then gripped her arm and heaved her up onto it. "If it's a big fat patient you get another nurse to help you. I'll now show you how two nurses put the bedpan under the patient." She called me up and together we heaved Pat onto the pan, Pat trying hard to be limp and useless. "And don't take a cold bedpan in the middle of winter, warm it up under the hot tap first. But be careful not to make it so hot it burns them," she added as we practiced lifting poor Pat. "Then you ask the patient if they would like to be left alone. Don't go off and forget them and leave them sitting on the pan for hours cutting off the blood supply to their legs." How the heck am I going to remember all this? I thought.

"The next step is to learn how to wipe the patient when they are finished." Sister Moyer picked up a roll of toilet paper, held up three fingers and slowly rolled paper round and round her three fingers, demonstrating how it's done. She then turned to the blowup doll lying on another table and showed us how to wipe. "Always from front to back," she emphasized. I couldn't even imagine myself wiping a complete stranger's bottom. Everyone practiced rolling paper around three fingers. Then we took turns wiping the blowup doll's bottom from front to back.

"Next you learn to give a man a urinal. Almost all the time they can handle that on their own, but when they are finished don't leave it sitting by the bed for hours. Always check if it must be measured. If so write down the quantity on the chart before you chuck it out. It's too late when you watch it go down the toilet and remember that you should have measured it." She waved the chart and empty urinal at us. During our first week we learned how to measure urine samples, how to test them for sugar, blood and pus, and the basics of simple patient care.

Hot and muggy, there was not a breath of air blowing into the rooms even though the windows were wide open. Some afternoons when we were given lectures on general nursing I felt so sleepy I could hardly keep my eyes open.

On the third day, the weekend schedules were posted and I found I would be spending my first day in B Ward, Men's Surgical. Three of us were assigned there but we had different hours. You either worked the seven to five, or the seven to nine schedule with three hours off during the morning or afternoon. I got the seven to five shift my first Saturday.

On Friday night, I hemmed up my uniform so it just covered my knees and looked much better. I lay in my bed outside on the verandah and gazing up at the stars anticipating my first day in the hospital with excitement. I fell asleep exhausted from the week of instruction.

On Saturday morning, I hopped out of bed very early so I could shower first. I dressed in my starched uniform and stiff cap. When I saw myself in the mirror I looked like a real nurse. At 6:25 a.m. I marched across the road for 6:30 a.m. roll call. We stood in a line as Sister Hart called our names, thirteen of us terrified in anticipation of our first day in a real ward with live patients. After breakfast the three of us assigned to B Ward walked briskly to Men's Surgical. We had been instructed that since we were at the lowest level we must respect all staff and stand aside so anyone senior could pass.

The many, single story, brick hospital buildings spread out over several acres of grounds were connected by cement pathways. Sister Moyer had explained the pecking order and the whole place ran as rigidly as the army. It took us ten minutes to walk five hundred yards. We were stepping off the path every few seconds to make way for more senior staff or doctors.

Finally we three found B Ward. The head night nurse greeted us and told us to step into the duty room and listen while she read the night report. We would be assigned to a green button who would show us what to do. There were about thirty beds in long rows, some with curtains around, on either side of the ward. Some men slept and others moaned. The strange sour smell, like formaldehyde, permeated the room.

The report was a running commentary on the goings on throughout the night. Patients who couldn't sleep, wanted to get up, wounds bleeding, emergency surgery admissions and a mixture of other minor or mundane happenings, all documented in the report book. I sniffed the hospital smells and listened to the stories of the night with fascination. Once dismissed, we followed Nurse King, a green button, into the sluice room. "Your first duty will be to wash all these bedpans with Dettol in hot water so they start out sterilized and clean for the day," she instructed. Thirty bedpans sat neatly stacked in rows on the shelves.

Already hot and muggy, I rolled up my sleeves and began to work. The sluice room had an automatic bedpan washer. You popped bedpans into a bracket one at a time, poured in a squirt of Dettol, pushed it shut and waited while a great whooshing noise carried on for a few minutes and steam belched out of all sides. It didn't take me long to get through the bedpans, but by the time I finished I was a bedraggled lot. My hair hung in wet strings and my stiff uniform looked a mess.

Next we were instructed to help with bed making. We knew how to do that. Nurse King wheeled a trolley into the middle of the ward piled high with sheets and pillowcases. "We are going to change every patient's sheets and we must be finished by 10 a.m." Some patients were still picking at their breakfast and some were sitting on bedpans or waiting for a nurse to help them get up. "The way we handle this," she said, "we pick the easy ones first, the one's who can lift their bum or sit in a chair." On my first attempt, I smiled at the patient trying to pretend I knew what I was doing. He smiled. He knew the pecking order. "You're a new one, aren't you? I'll try and make it easy on you." I was glad he didn't realize it was my very first day.

The next patient asked me for a bedpan. I panicked. I just couldn't do it and I ran to the green button.

"He asked for a bedpan, what should I do?"

"Well get him one, you've got to start sometime!"

I warmed it, dried it and walked towards the patient terrified. The green button came over to help.

"This is Nurse Greenland," she laughed to the patient, "she's new and she's never done this before."

"Well, she may as well get started with me," he offered. His leg was in a cast up all the way up to his groin. He pulled on a chain hanging over his bed and hauled himself up. The green button and I slid the warm bedpan neatly under his bottom and he lowered himself down onto it. "Easy," he said. "Hey nurse, now give me a bit of peace and I'll ring the bell when I'm finished." When I returned to do the wipe he rolled sideways knowing the routine. He hated it just as much as I did. I never did get used to the undignified act of wiping bottoms.

The next procedure, a bed bath, was easy compared to the bedpan. Sister Moyer's vivid instructions on the blowup doll paid off. I did everything just like she had instructed us. The patient didn't seem to want such a detailed going over but I insisted on washing every nook and cranny the way we had been taught. Facecloth neatly rolled around four fingers, dipped into the warm soapy water, rinse and dry. "Start with the face," she said, "and work your way down the whole body, except for the genitalia. You don't want your cloth near those things until you've done the whole body," she emphasized. "Then hand over the facecloth and tell him to do his or her own." My first patient obliged perfectly.

On weekends Matron rarely came around to inspect the wards, but we were fully instructed on how to prepare for her onslaught. "You never know what time she's coming," said the green button. So by ten in the morning all the patients were shiny clean, their beds made neatly. The stainless steel locker tops were polished and glistening in the morning sun and all their belongings neatly stashed in the drawer. No urinals were to be left lying about, especially not full ones. The patients lay in their beds with the sheets absolutely straight across their chest, their pillows square and neat. If a recovering patient complained they were hot under the covers, they were allowed to lie on top of the white bedspread, but were not allowed to mess the straight sheets folded over the top edge of the bedspread. Most patients soon learned the routine for Matron's inspection. Occasionally a spy, one of the patients allowed out of bed, warned us of Matron's approach.

The first time I saw Matron I knew why everyone was scared of her. She marched into the ward with the Head Sister hovering beside. She folded her hands behind her back as her eyes scanned the room for dust, crooked beds and anything out of place. Tall and big bosomed, she was an imposing woman impeccably dressed in her white uniform. She wore a pleated cap, designed for matrons exclusively, her maroon epaulettes adorned with badges and buttons. She wore polished brown lace up shoes and the seams were dead straight on her thick beige stockings.

We stood at attention as she walked through, "Good morning Matron," we mumbled as she passed. I crossed my fingers hoping I had not left something out. She inspected the sluice rooms, the nurse's duty room and the instrument rooms before leaving. If Matron spotted something she didn't like, then the Head Sister reamed us all after she was gone.

Sister Moyer spoke with a gruff Afrikaans accent. She did not tolerate stupidity and expected us to catch on quickly. One of the junior duties we were taught was how to give an enema. A patient could not go home if they did not have a bowel movement. So the day they were to be discharged they had to be given an enema if they hadn't done anything. The day of the enema lesson, Sister Moyer stood in front of us with a trolley loaded with the kit. "You have a one pint beaker," she waved it in front of us, "a catheter, a jug of soapy water, gauze wipes, gloves, vaseline and a bedpan." She demonstrated the mixing of soap and water. "Be sure it is warm but not too hot." She picked up a red rubber catheter and attached it, sliding the thick end over a nozzle at the bottom of the beaker.

"Put on your gloves, take a gauze square and wipe some Vaseline onto the end of the catheter. Pour the soapy mixture into the beaker." She hung it onto the hook on the wheeled trolley and approached the blowup doll. She took the catheter in her gloved hand. "Insert it slowly into the anus, don't just shove it in, consider the patient," she said. "Hold the beaker up. But don't hold it too high so the mixtures pours into his bum too fast." She raised the beaker up, then lowered it down so we could judge the flow into the blowup doll's fake anus. All day we practiced giving enemas. Fortunately the blowup doll lay on a draining table and was able to tolerate as many as we could administer without complaining.

We were told the importance of having a bedpan close by. One day I forgot. The poor patient screamed anxiously as I ran to get one. We barely made it. Over the next two months I became quite adept at giving enemas. I would load my trolley with multiple beakers, catheters, gauze squares and a big jar of Vaseline. When I wheeled it into the ward the patients would laugh and say, "Here comes the enema queen. Who is she going after today?" I felt quite important, as I knew how to do the procedure. I was on my way to becoming a real nurse. We had a lot of fun the first sixty days under Sister Moyer's instruction. She taught more by describing what not to do, than how to do it.

Even though I was already seventeen, having grown up with three sisters, I realized how ignorant I was about men and their stuff. One day a patient asked to go to the toilet. The ward had a wheel chair with a toilet seat instead of a regular seat so a bedridden patient could be helped onto the wheel chair seat and easily wheeled over the toilet, a pleasant alternative to a bedpan. I had seen this gadget in the corner but never actually used it. So I brought it over to the patient's bedside.

He wore a hospital gown open down the back. Together we loaded him onto the wheel chair with the toilet seat. As I pushed him over the toilet he screamed. I didn't have any idea why, so I backed up and pushed him forward again. He gave out another terrible yowl and yelled at me to back off. "What? What's the matter?" He pointed desperately towards his lower front. He didn't want to say, but it suddenly dawned on me what I had done. His genitalia were dangling down between his legs and he had nothing on underneath the gown. I was squashing them between the fake seat and the real seat! "Oh my gosh! I'm so sorry," I blurted out, blushing and flustered. He pulled everything up with his gown covering it all up. Neither of us actually said what had happened, we both knew. For a few days after that whenever I walked into the ward the patients would laugh and tease me. "No nurse, we don't want any help to the toilet today."

I grew up a lot on B Ward during the hottest months of the year. We rolled up our sleeves as soon as we entered the ward and only rolled them down for the fifteen minutes while Matron did inspection. The daily routine of washing patients, making beds, emptying bedpans and urinals, assisting with serving breakfast, lunch and dinner, made the time fly. Before I knew it I had earned my green button.

On hot afternoons we could roll the patients' beds out onto the verandah where they might get slight relief from the gentle breeze blowing off the Umzinduzi River at the bottom of the hospital garden. They usually appreciated the pretty surroundings and the twitter of birds flitting from tree to tree. Patients who were physically well except for their broken bones mending often slept outside all night.

With the addition of the green button I moved up in my duties. The head nurse decided it was time I learned how to give a shot. Made of glass, all the syringes were sterilized on the stove in a large steel pot so they could be used over and over again. Every morning one of the junior duties consisted of packing stainless steel drums. A native picked the drums up on a large trolley and took them to the autoclave where they were sterilized in hot steam for several hours before being returned to the ward. Each drum was filled with folded white cloths for draping the patient during a procedure, basic instruments, scissors, scalpel, carefully folded squares of gauze and various tweezers. Some drums were packed for a special task such as removing stitches or doing a cut down. The list of contents was posted on a wall. Woe betide if you packed it wrong. You'd be relegated to scrubbing bedpans and cleaning the sluice room.

The first time I was to give a patient a shot, a recovering young man volunteered to be the guinea pig. He smiled at me with a tea stained toothy grin, pulled up his sleeve and stuck out him arm. "Go ahead nurse, you can't hurt me." He was to receive 50cc of penicillin. The red button nurse carried a tray covered with a sterile white cloth. She lifted one corner and pulled out a three-inch long syringe with a two-inch needle filled with thick white penicillin. She held it up to the light and slowly squeezed the white stuff through the needle, a small drop running down the side of the syringe. "You always make sure you squeeze the air out, you don't want to inject a bubble of air into the patient and kill him," she cautioned. "It might go straight to his heart and block an artery." I looked from patient to nurse and back, picturing a bubble rushing through his veins to his heart.

"Now just toss the needle gently into his arm after wiping the area to be injected and then squeeze the solution into him. That's all there is to it. Go ahead and try."

"Go on nurse I'm ready," the patient said bravely.

I held the syringe in my three fingers as shown, thrusting back and forth in the air trying to get the feel, and some courage. I plunged it into his arm as hard as I could, terrified it might bounce off his skin. It shot right in, nice and deep and hit the bone. I drew back and squeezed. I pulled it out only to see the needle bent almost in half as I heaved a sigh of relief.

"You damn fool, you're not supposed to shove it in so far you hit the bone. You're not playing darts. Just look what you've done to this needle?" The patient laughed good-naturedly.

"Ag nurse, I didn't really feel a thing. She did a pretty good job."

"Well next time don't throw it so hard into the arm, be a bit more gentle," the red button groused and marched to the next patient. I followed behind dreading the next shot.

One day when things were a bit quiet the head nurse told me to clean all the patients' false teeth. I had been moved to Men's Medical Ward, a place filled with older men not requiring surgery. Many of these men stayed in the hospital for months, some never had any visitors and their only friends were the nurses. They knew the routine, did as they were told and we gave them our basic training care. About twenty patients had false teeth. I knew because I saw their teeth fizzing in a tin cup as their hollow empty cheeks gave me a toothless grin when I brought their breakfast. They would swish them about and pop them into their mouth, give me a new toothy smile and tuck into the meal.

Being a young budding nurse I always did everything with enthusiasm to the best of my ability. So I marched into the ward with a large white enamel bowl and collected the teeth from my patients. I took them to the bathroom and scrubbed each pair with a new toothbrush and lots of Ajax. I surveyed my work. Boy did those revolting old teeth look a whole lot better. I rinsed them thoroughly in bleach, swished them about in boiling water and finally went back into the ward feeling quite pleased with myself. When I walked in holding the bowl of teeth in my hand I looked around and suddenly realized that I didn't have a clue which set of teeth, belonged to which patient! I could feel my face going beet red. I looked around anxiously for Sister. Thank goodness she was nowhere to be seen so I quickly went up to each patient to see if they knew their own teeth. To my amazement everybody seemed to recognize theirs. I heaved a sigh of relief as the last set was reclaimed. The patients laughed and promised not to tell on me.

Men's Medical had two private rooms at the end of each ward. Rich patients whose families could afford to pay extra occupied these rooms. One old man had had a stroke so he couldn't do much but he was still very handsome and charming. Whenever I had to help him with his bed bath he would reach around with his good arm and pinch my bottom. I soon found out he did that to all the nurses no matter what they were doing for him. Staff Nurse said just laugh it off, he is a frustrated old gentleman who is really harmless. So we'd laugh and make jokes and he'd joke back with his slurred speech. He must have been a very attractive man in his younger days and his condition distressed him a great deal.

❖

In the winter of our first year of nursing Sister Hart organized a dance for all the nurses. If you didn't have a boyfriend they invited young men from Cedara Agricultural College, an all men's school, to come to the dance. I donned the blue party dress again and put on my new makeup. Pat curled my hair and tied it up on the top of my head so I felt really glamorous.

We unattached nurses sat around the tables making small talk and the Cedara College boys stood in groups talking amongst themselves checking us out. Sister Hart did her best to make an enchanting atmosphere and this particular evening she placed Chianti bottles on the tables with candles burning in the neck, dripping down the sides. She really tried to make things pleasant for her girls but she couldn't match everyone up and take away the tension. One by one some of the boys asked girls to dance and eventually a nice young man, a bit shorter, asked me to dance. He was better than Keith but not too polished. I wasn't very good anyway but we shuffled around the floor as he clutched me tight burying his face in my neck and pressing me closer to him. I felt all stiff and nervous but he came over and sat with our crowd after that dance.

Later that week I found a message in the phone book from Randall, the Cedara College chap. Should I call him back? I telephoned Cedara and left him a message. Eventually we spoke and I went on a few dates with him. He managed a farm while he attended college and he invited me to come out for a weekend so we could go horseback riding. He tried to hug and kiss me after our few dates. Although scared, I went along with it reluctantly. I liked his manner and his love of farms so I continued to date him. But he didn't give me the butterfly feelings I imagined I should have on a date.

In October I told him I was going off on holiday to the berg and he said he would call me when I got back. While I was at the berg he wrote me a letter telling me how much he missed me and how much he liked me! The first day back at Grey's there was a message in the book from Randall.

Time passed quickly and the days at Grey's were full and exhausting. I became accustomed to the routine and lay in bed a few minutes extra so that I had to run across the road from the Nurses Home to the hospital, just in time to stand panting at attention as roll call began. I loved the hearty breakfasts.

The dining room smelled of hot bacon and sausage, and toast. Selections of jam and marmalade and a variety of eggs were always ready for us. Sister Hart made sure there was a big pot of tea on the table so by the time we hit the hospital wards we were well fortified for the busy day ahead. Twelve girls sat at each table. Things were pretty quiet in the mornings, but when we hit the lunch table everyone had a tale or adventure to talk about.

The large airy dining room overlooked the Umzinduzi River and the tennis courts. Mid-day meals consisted of soup, enormous bowls of assorted salads, platters of cold meats and wonderful hot rolls. "Baked in our own kitchens," Sister Hart proudly emphasized. When the dinner bell rang at night hearty beef stews, roast beef and roasted chicken filled our tired bellies. Big bowls of vegetables were passed around the table and a delicious pudding concocted by Sister Hart finished things off. She believed in feeding her girls. Never married, she had worked at Grey's Hospital for twenty-five years, doing her training just like us. She worked her way through the system until she found her love, the Nursing Home kitchen.

Speaking fluent Zulu, Sister Hart ruled the roost, making daily menus, bossing the chefs and the enormous kitchen staff. Almost all the staff was black and they worked hard together to keep us well filled and strong for our busy student days. The seating arrangement in the dining room depended on the established pecking order. Matron sat at a head table nearest the door with other senior sisters. Senior staff nurses sat at the next tables, then senior student nurses, blue buttons, red buttons and finally the green buttons at the very back of the dining room farthest from the door.

Our waiters were Zulu males, assigned to the same tables most days so we grew to know them by name. Sister Hart would pace the dining room, her eyes darting from one corner to another, missing nothing. The waiters spoiled us rotten thanks to Sister's vigilance.

One Sunday we were served a roasted banana floating in a bowl of yellow custard. Most tasty, it was smothered in brown sugar and baked a nice rich brown. I lapped mine up, but someone didn't like the look of it and wrote *Specimen for Lab*, on a piece of paper and left it in the bowl! All hell broke loose the next morning at breakfast. Sister Hart stormed into the dining room carrying the suspicious bowl with the note waving it in the air. Custard dripped as she narrowed her eyes and bellowed. "*Specimen for Lab*, is it? Who wrote this?" She glared around the room, her large bosom heaving with anger. "How dare you insult my chefs? There will be no lunch served today except sliced bread until the person who did this owns up. There will be no dinner tonight until I know who did this." She waved the soggy note again. "You have until midnight tonight to come to my office and own up. That's all. You are dismissed." She turned and stormed out of the dining room back into her corner office. The room was abuzz with murmurings and giggles. We thought it was terribly funny and daring. I looked around our table, everyone shrugging their shoulders with "it wasn't me" looks. Thank heaven the perpetrator of the deed had the decency to own up before we all starved to death.

To round out our dining room experience, Sister Hart never let us down with her afternoon teas. Cake and endless varieties of biscuits were served every day at tea break. In the evening, the last waiter on duty brought a pot of hot chocolate to each floor in the Nurses Home around ten o'clock without fail. We worked very hard but were well fed and enjoyed almost every minute of our long days. We fell into bed exhausted around eleven every night. In the summer months when we slept outside on the verandahs, I would fall asleep listening to the last gory story of the day.

When we arrived in the ward at 7 a.m. the night staff read the report of the night events followed by a note about each patient before we took over. Mr. Brown slept well without sedatives, Mr. Smith rang his bell most of the night complaining about pain, the intern gave him a shot of morphine and he fell asleep at 5 a.m.

As a junior I had to head into the wards to complete the baths the night staff had not finished. Bathing began at 5 a.m. so that all patients would be clean and washed by 8.30 a.m. Quite a feat with about forty to forty-five patients in each ward. Most of them did bed baths. We handed them a basin of hot water, a face cloth and a towel. If we were lucky they washed themselves down and we just had to make the bed around, under and over them. Some days it was difficult to finish with so many very sick patients who had to be washed by us. We followed

Sister Moyer's procedure to the letter and never cheated just because we had too many patients. The Staff Nurse ran a well-disciplined ward and you could not be caught cutting corners with the bed baths.

After bed baths each patient was handed a bed tray, set with white cloth, napkin and cutlery. A Zulu staff member from the main kitchen wheeled a large stainless steel trolley into the middle of the ward. Deep troughs were filled with the day's breakfast: porridge of the day, bacon and sausage, egg of the day and lots of dried toast made in the enormous automatic kitchen toaster. Staff Nurse or a senior would preside over the trolley, offering each patient a choice. She'd dish it onto a plate and we handed it to the patient. Special diet patients had signs posted on the end of their bed if they couldn't have the trolley food. Often it smelled so good wheeling through the ward they would beg us for a little tidbit.

"Ag please nurse, just give us a bit of mash and gravy? I hate this salt free muck."

"No, you know I can't. You want me to get into big trouble and be sent to Matron?" The patients feared Matron almost as much as we did.

We cleared the breakfast trays away and got the beds straightened perfectly, the top sheets folded neatly over the white bedspread ready for Matron's morning inspection. "Don't leave your urinal on top of the locker, next to your drinking water," we'd say, "you must ring the bell when you are finished so we can clean up." We carried patients' flowers back into the ward from the verandah and placed them neatly on a long table down the middle of the ward. During the morning, doctors, often two or three, came to visit. We'd make them a cup of tea while they sat chatting in the duty room.

When I worked in Women's Surgical, one day, just after lunch a nurse came rushing from the ward kitchen to the duty room as I was looking over a patient's notes.

"Has anyone seen that jug of mother's milk I had covered with a doily in the fridge?" I looked up.

"The only milk I saw I served to the doctors with their tea this morning."

"Oh God, you fool," she screamed, "It took ages for the mother to pump that milk. I was supposed to deliver it to the baby's ward after lunch!"

"Are you sure it's not there? The doctors drank their tea and never complained."

"God," she burst out laughing, "You served breast milk to the doctors! What sweet revenge for all the bull they dish out to us. This time you are forgiven."

With that she marched off to get more milk from the mother. She never told me what she said to her.

After a long day, I walked across the road to the Nurses Home and checked the message book. Nothing for me, so I poured myself a nice cup of tea that Josephina, our house native girl, had just made and wandered out to the verandah on the third floor. The sun was setting behind the hills of Maritzburg. The dark silhouette of the hospital outlined by the bright orange sky made me reflect on all the things I had experienced the past month in Women's Surgical.

Coming in contact with so many different women, very young and very old, gave me a new perspective. In the women's ward, smells of powder and perfume covered up the disinfectant smells of hospital life. Before visiting hours they put on makeup and we combed their hair. They leaned back against their pillows, dressed in frilly nighties, some with soft, fluffy, pale pink ostrich feathers outlining their pretty faces, waiting for their man or mother or boyfriend. Some did their make up for themselves, even though no one came to visit.

I felt particularly upset about a thirteen-year-old girl who spoke only Afrikaans. I had nursed her for three days after she had an abortion. I didn't know much about abortions other than the cold hard facts in my textbook. This young girl placed the reality in front of me. On her chart just plain harsh words, "D and C, an incest victim." When she woke from her surgery she whimpered and cried and hid her face in the pillow. I had no clue about the depth of her shame so I tried to comfort her with my limited Afrikaans language skills. She reminded me of my younger sisters. I wiped her tears and patted her hand. She simply sunk lower into her bed and hid her face in the blanket. She wore the wrinkled, ill-fitting hospital gown during her stay. There were no pretty pajamas in her locker, just a small bundle of simple clothes she had arrived with. No one came to visit her. We young training nurses shared her pain in an abstract way but did not know how to deal with it any better. Later

Staff Nurse told me she was from a very poor family of six children. Her brother had made her pregnant. Three children slept in one bed while the parents slept in another bed in the same room.

Miscarriages were common in Women's Surgical. One young woman cried when her husband came to visit. They held hands as he tried to comfort her. Tears rolled down her cheeks and he wiped them gently away but he couldn't wipe away the loss of their baby. When the visitors left, I brought around my cheery trolley of tea and biscuits and tried to make them smile and laugh. At the young innocent age of eighteen I thought my silly jokes and quips could wash way their heartbreak.

The first time I helped dress a mastectomy wound I had a very difficult time hiding the horror I experienced as the dressings were removed. The poor woman had her breast removed and the incision went all the way from behind her armpit, across her chest and up the middle of her rib cage. The stitches were dark, black and stringy, each tied with a knot. The skin between the stitches puckered and protruded like a sea anemone waving its greedy lips. We swabbed the dried blood and yellow discharge oozing from the wound as she lay there. She couldn't lift her arm or turn her body by herself. They had taken out her lymph nodes so the skin lay tight across her ribs and beside this horrible mess drooped one saggy breast. Later on when she tried to dress in her own pretty nightie she stood in front of the mirror studying her mutilated body. I could not think of anything to say as I swallowed my own shock at the sight. She turned away sobbing and got back into bed. We were not taught anything about the emotional stress of such devastating surgeries. Young and helpless, we offered the best comfort we could, but it was almost as traumatizing to me as it was to them.

In Women's Surgical I experienced a variety of duties. Every day I learned something new and how to cope better. I became stronger at curbing my personal emotions. Some new mothers had a C-Section to deliver their first baby, recuperating and pumping their breasts for baby's next feeding. They were only allowed to visit their babies in the afternoons.

Hysterectomies and D and C's were the most common surgeries performed. After a D and C (Dilation and Curettage) junior nurses were given the job of positioning a heat lamp on the patient's genital area. I had no idea what the benefits were but I recalled the class instructions from Sister Moyer. "First you make the patient comfortable, pull the curtains around the bed. You don't want to expose their fanny to the whole world, then you cover them above and open their legs with their knees bent up like this. Nurse, get up on the table and demonstrate. No you don't have to take your clothes off, you're just going to demonstrate the position. Now you place the heat lamp on the bed and face it towards their you know what, not too close, you don't want to burn the patient. Don't leave it too long, about five to ten minutes will do. Always use a timer. It will save you a lot of trouble later." So I drew the curtains and told the patient what I was going to do. It was easy to get them in position as their surgery was internal and their only pain was inside their hearts.

"What good is this nurse?" one particular patient asked.

"Staff Nurse told me it will make you heal quicker and you'll feel better." I didn't know why we did it but I always referred to Staff Nurse if I didn't have an answer. The patient didn't complain. I drew the curtains around the bed and made sure the blankets were neatly folded back, as she was completely exposed. I had to plug the lamp into an extension cord, which reached across the ward to the nearest outlet. I pointed the lamp in the direction of her fanny and a warm glow radiated out. I set the timer for seven minutes and left to attend to another patient. Some minutes later the bell rang. As I rushed to the patient's side, I tripped over the cord and the lamp came crashing to the floor. "Nurse, nurse, I smell something burning." I had shaved her thoroughly, it couldn't be her fanny hairs. I looked around frantically and saw pale, white smoke wafting up out of her dainty, silk robe hanging by the bed. I grabbed it, rolled it in a ball and dunked it in the hand-washing basin. I must have placed the lamp so it faced the robe.

"Oh my gosh, I'm so sorry, I think I have ruined your dressing gown." Sheepishly I gathered up the cord and the lamp, covered her up and tucked her into bed.

"Never mind nurse," she said. It was an old thing, we'll just forget about it shall we? Why don't you put it into my locker and I'll take it home?"

I knew I had narrowly escaped causing an awful fire or doing some terrible damage. It was a harsh lesson for me and I promised myself I would not be so careless ever again. I could just imagine what Staff would have said to me. I did not dare to report the incident when it was time to make reports. I resolved to become a better nurse as I reflected on how close I had come to disaster.

I sipped my cup of tea watching the sun sink below the horizon and the hospital light up twinkling in the dark. I had learned so much and come such a long way from my first nursing days. I shuddered in anticipation of the discoveries that lay ahead of me.

Our rooms in the Nurses Home provided a respite from the daily hard work in the wards. Surrounded by sickness, injury, bad news and occasionally death, I had to learn to cope with it all. The first time I saw a major stab wound the curtains were already pulled around the bed. I almost vomited. I had to turn my head away and swallow before I could look at the patient again. A handsome young man, gaunt and pale, his terrified eyes blinking rapidly as he groaned in pain. Staff Nurse lifted the sterile cloth draped over the wound and instructed me to clean it. We had practiced cleaning a wound over and over on the blowup doll, swabbing away from the opening. "Don't drag all the sweat and dirt from the patient right into the cut," instructed Sister Moyer. I uncovered the sterile kit and draped the cloths around just like we'd been shown. It made the wound look a bit less personal. As I picked up a swab with the forceps, I took a deep breath. I looked at the dried blood all over his belly and dabbed away from the middle outwards, checking for Staff Nurse's approval.

"Don't just pat it, give it a thoroughly good wipe," she admonished.

"What if I hurt him?" I whispered. I didn't want him to hear me.

"Don't be silly, he's all doped up with morphine, he won't remember a thing."

I picked up another swab, dipped it in the alcohol and swooped it firmly across the wound. "There you go that's much better. When you have finished let me know. He is going to have to be shaved for surgery as he has internal injuries." When I finished, I trotted into the nurses' duty room feeling quite pleased with myself, to report to Staff Nurse.

"Well now you've done that you're going to get another new experience in your repertoire. There's no male orderly on duty today and the patient has to be shaved so you can go and do it." I looked at her with horror.

"I have never shaved a man before, I just can't!"

"Everybody is too busy, it's not a big deal. Prepare a shaving kit as if you had to shave a beard and then just go to it. They all look the same you know, it's not going to bite you."

I got out the shaving brush, some soap and a razor. I covered it with a cloth, sidled up to the patient and said I had to shave him. "Ag sorry nurse, but don't worry I won't look." He turned his head to the side on his pillow. He's all doped up with morphine I thought, so get going. I pulled back the sheet and looked at his thing lying there in all the hair I had to shave. I had never seen one close up. I didn't know how to go about it. I couldn't look at the patient. We were both beet red in the face. So I grabbed a bit of skin on the side and held it so I could dab soap all over with the shaving brush. I made it all nice and foamy and really concentrated on the job at hand. I picked up the razor, still hanging onto the piece of skin and started scooping the foam and the hair around it. The next thing I knew it started growing and growing. I didn't have to hang onto the piece of skin. I had never seen anything like that before. The patient turned his head away, "Hell man, nurse I'm so sorry, I can't help it." I didn't say a word. I just shaved furiously and wiped everything up. I covered it with the cloth, pulled the sheet up and dashed to the duty room.

"You won't believe what happened to me when I shaved him?" I told Staff. "God I've never seen that before, it scared the heck out of me!" Everyone shrieked with laughter.

"You're such a greenhorn Greenland. You mean you've never seen a hard on?" I blushed beet red again. One of the senior nurses laughed loudly.

"Man," she said, "You should just *sommer* hit it with a pencil and you'll have no trouble at all."

That night we new girls sat around on our beds on the verandah, talking shop.

I sipped my hot chocolate as I thought about the day and told my embarrassing story. Everyone shrieked with laughter. It was quite revealing to me, the difference between what we all knew about men.

I had been training for four months when assigned to Children's Ward, the most touching and heart wrenching place to work. On our first day the Staff Nurse walked new nurses around the ward and introduced us to our patients. Although Children's was housed in a similar brick building to the other hospital wards, that's where the similarity ended. We walked from child to child listening to Staff Nurse's comments. Right away the sounds bothered me. A little laughter, but loud cries and soft whimpering permeated the wards.

"Morning Joey, how you feeling this morning, any better?" Nurse looked back at us with her hand covering her mouth. "Early stage Leukemia," she whispered, "getting blood transfusions. Not much we can do for this poor little kid."

He sat in the middle of an iron cot and looked up at me with his big brown eyes sunken in his head, which looked like a soccer ball perched on his small thin body. "I'm going to beat you at tic–tac-toe today nurse." He smiled sweetly. "I've been practicing with the night girls." We bent over and told him our names. I wondered if he was sick of different nurses all the time.

We met all the patients this way, from small babies on IV's to a twelve-year-old boy with two broken legs suspended in casts. The walls were painted a cheerful green and parents pinned lots of cards and drawings all around the kid's beds. I tried to be warm and friendly but I realized these kids were very sick and quite shy. Parents were only allowed to spend time with their children during normal visiting hours. Sometimes we'd let them stay a bit longer and pretend we didn't notice. I hated to see the children crying when their mothers and fathers left, but there was no easy way. Only the kids who had got used to the rigid system handled it without so much pain. The sick children didn't let us into their hearts easily. It took time and patience to build their trust. Slowly I would interact with a child, try to give him or her a little treat or take time to play a game. Eventually he or she would ask for me and decide I was the only one who could give shots. Most of them did not know their prognosis and no one told them.

Our job as juniors was to make them comfortable and clean, be kind and loving. I found it very difficult. Some of the older kids opened up, made jokes with us and helped with lunches and afternoon teas. I'd let them push the dinner trolley around the ward, hand out plates and offer bread. They looked happy for a bit. Thin young bodies, in washed out hospital nightgowns, their skinny pale arms holding trays and passing out food.

Working in Children's Ward proved to be one of the most difficult months of my nurse's training. I became involved emotionally, talking to parents and trying to give them encouragement when there really was very little hope. This experience gave me a greater insight and appreciation of the role of a parent.

❖ 13 ❖

Meeting Boris
October 1956

Boris and I with Pat, Cathedral Peak Hotel

In October, after nine months of learning and adjusting to nursing life at Grey's Hospital we were given one month's vacation. Two of my new friends had the same time off so we planned to go for a holiday in the mountains for two weeks. We decided on the famous Cathedral Peak Hotel. Known for its scenery, hiking trails, horseback riding and great food, it also fit our very limited budget. Lots of young people took holidays there.

Allison's boyfriend Paul had an old Citroen, so he agreed to drive. We piled into his jalopy like sardines in a can and drove through some of the most beautiful countryside. Soon after we left town we found ourselves on a rough dirt road winding in and out of the foothills, which were bright green from the new spring grasses. We left the farming country behind as we drove through Zululand, past many grass huts built in clusters. *Umfaan*s tended skinny cattle along the roadside. Many Zulu women wearing colorful doeks, their breasts wrapped in bright fabric, carried babies on their backs. Zulus walked along the side of the road for miles and miles. Some balanced heavy loads of wood or fifty-pound sacks of flour on their heads. I had tried to do that so many times when I was a child but could never balance a basket or a bag without holding on. As the road wound higher we passed streams and rushing water cascading over the rocks. Zulu women were doing their washing in the river, their young kids naked, playing in the water and throwing stones. They waved and shouted as we passed. The rain-washed dirt roads were full of rifts and potholes making the journey slow and tedious as we neared the hotel. Finally we rounded a bend and the full majesty of the Drakensberg range of mountains spread across the sky like a wide smile, the teeth formed by rivulets carving deep gullies down the mountainside.

Cathedral Peak Hotel sits nestled below its namesake, the tallest of the rugged peaks creating a stunning backdrop. It was late in the day so the mountains took on a purple hue. The main building with its dark thatched roof and wide front verandah looked warm and inviting. Guests were enjoying their afternoon tea, lounging about waiting for the sun to set, as we drove up in front. Down below the verandah, a fountain bubbled and I saw a dragon fly settle on a lily pad, the lush lawn spread out in front.

Left to Right, Allison, Paul and I, with Pat, Dawn and Ferdie

Paul went off to park his car and we checked into the lobby. Wide and open, the high thatched ceiling enabled us to see the Cathedral Peak through the window. The thick stonewalls and floors polished to a high gloss made the place nice and cool. An old. fat Zulu woman greeted us with a cold glass of spring water while we waited for our room numbers. There were no keys to the rooms. Two Zulus balanced our suitcases on their heads and led us outside across the lawn to a long row of thatched rooms. They were small and square, with two twin beds, a chest of drawers and a washstand with a bright colored jug and basin under the window. A towel and facecloth hung on a rack on each side of the washstand. The beds were neatly made and covered in white matelassé bedspreads with two pillows each. She showed us the common bathrooms. Each building had six rooms and one central bathroom, a separate toilet and a room with a large footed tub and a washbasin with two worn brass taps. They had been well polished over the years.

In the mornings I could lie in bed, look out of my window and watch the sunrise. The deep orange color of the mountains gradually changed to luscious green as the sun rose higher and higher in the sky. On our first morning we ate a delicious breakfast and rushed outside to explore the beautiful surroundings. We found the swimming pool and tennis courts quite near the hotel. About thirty young women were vacationing at the hotel at the same time as us. We only counted about ten, single young men that night at dinner. The rest of the guests were families. The first day we signed up for hikes and horse back riding and any activity that looked like the young men would want to do. Within a couple of days both my friends had met someone they fancied and our group grew in size.

A German with a rugged square jaw, bright ocean blue eyes and lots of wavy hair, who wore lederhosen, long socks and European suede walking shoes, had been chasing me. I was somewhat wary when he showed a slight interest in me. My friends told me to watch out he looked like he might be too experienced. I wasn't sure what that meant, but when Ferdie sidled up to me in the evening as we were dancing and suggested we go to my room, I got a bit nervous.

"No thanks, we don't take men to our rooms."

"Come on man, let's have some fun. All the German girls do, they aren't full of inhibitions," he begged. I remembered *The Kinsey Report*. I didn't know what Ferdie wanted but I didn't take any chances.

"No, I think we should just stay here with everyone else, besides the lights go out at ten and you won't be able to find your room." Ferdie did not consider that a problem, but lucky for me he must have decided it would be easier to go after a more experienced girl.

On Sunday morning when we needed a fourth for tennis I saw two young men sitting on a bench outside the bar. "Do either of you play tennis?" I asked cheerfully, swinging my racquet and bouncing a ball. One flaunted a thick Elvis Presley quaff of wavy hair, a bit greasy looking for my taste, but he smiled and spoke first with a thick London accent.

"I don't, but me mate here probably does, he's more athletic than me." He grinned and pointed to the tall chap sitting next to him. I looked him over. His eyes twinkled with a mischievous look and he smiled broadly revealing two crooked front teeth.

"I'm Boris. I do play but haven't had much of a chance lately, what do you need?"

His sweater hung sloppily on his thin body, but he was clean-shaven and slightly tanned. I studied him quickly, khaki shorts, nice legs, not too bad looking, seemed friendly. I decided to take a chance.

"We need a fourth player so if you'd like to join us that would be nice."

"Ah! We were only waiting for the bar to open anyway," he said," I'm sure my pal won't mind if I go and play tennis for a bit." He turned to his friend.

"O.K. Doug, I'll see you later, I'll get my racquet and meet you at the courts."

"You go off and get all sweaty, I'll be cooling off with a nice cold beer." Doug laughed. He dashed off at a run to fetch his tennis racquet. I waited, chatting to Doug and found out they had only arrived the day before. Since I had been there for a week, I felt comfortable in the surroundings and had already formed casual friendships with some of the other guests.

Boris reappeared, racquet in hand, and we wandered down to the tennis courts. He seemed like a pleasant young man. Glad to see my friends warming up and feeling a bit shy and awkward, I introduced myself and he told me his name was Boris Karloff!

"Gee that name sounds familiar," I said but in my head thought, say something intelligent, you darn fool.

The tennis was mediocre, but he hopped about, chased every ball, sliced and bashed, laughed and made funny jokes so I

Doug Green and Boris

felt myself becoming more and more attracted to him as the game went on. After the game I dared to ask him to join our crowd for a drink. It suddenly dawned on me who Boris Karloff was.

"I suppose you thought I was a real idiot when you told me that movie star name," I said. "I only just realized who you were talking about! What's your real name anyway?"

"Boris Ralphs, I didn't know you didn't realize I was joking." He was quite nice looking really, except for those teeth. I could get used to them.

299

On the steps of Cathedral Peak Hotel
I am front row center, wearing a hat

Everyone had signed up to climb the Cathedral Peak the next day.

"Have you signed up to climb the Peak tomorrow?"

"No we only just got here. What do you think Doug, should we give it a try?"

"Why not?" Doug nodded.

They put their name on the signup sheet and I went to bed that night very excited about the next day's coming adventure.

Climbing a 10,000-foot peak proved to be a very long tiring ordeal. There were fourteen young people on the hike and Boris walked much too fast for me. When I finally arrived at the highest point hoping for an awe-inspiring view, the mountain was shrouded in fog. There he sat on the five-gallon can of water he carried all the way up wearing that same baggy sweater, fog swirling about. He looked well rested and beamed from ear to ear.

"What kept you? I've been waiting half an hour for you to get here." His funny grin revealed his crooked teeth again. Those last several feet to the top were very steep and it was a few minutes before I could catch my breath. Everyone drank water from the can he had carried, grateful for his help. It wouldn't be nearly so heavy to carry down the mountainside.

"I was pretty scared those last few hundred feet clinging to that wire climbing the rocky face. Weren't you a bit nervous carrying the can at the same time?" He didn't have time to answer. Just as I spoke Ferdie reached the top and began chatting to me. I didn't want to seem too friendly. Boris stood up.

"We'd better get going back down now, we don't want to be stuck on this mountain too late." He heaved the five-gallon can onto his shoulder and he and Doug began the descent down the other side of the mountain. I jumped up and tried to follow but they were too quick for me. I never saw them again until we dragged ourselves wearily into the bar, very hot and sweaty, and guzzled a lovely, cold beer. Boris and Doug were sitting at a small round table. I smiled at him thinking I must look a real mess. I don't suppose he'll look at me again, I thought, but he smiled back.

"Want to join us for some dancing tonight?" The toothy grin again.

"Sure, we'll see you after dinner." My friends and I went off to bathe and try to recover from the tiring day. The dining room had assigned everyone to tables so I didn't know if we would bump into each other at dinner. I spotted him across the room with Doug. I played shy, looking forward to the dancing later. After dinner while everyone else was dancing, Boris suggested we go and apple pie some of my friends' beds. I was only too pleased to go along. We wandered slowly outside. The moon peeked out from behind Cathedral Peak and lit up the grounds just enough for us to find our way around. There were no locks on any of the rooms. He grabbed my hand and pulled me with him as we crept in between the rooms, not wanting to get caught. We folded the sheets short in the beds, tied knots in pajamas and put rocks into the pillowcases. We had such fun together, laughing and giggling as we thought about the reaction of my friends.

There was no regular supply of electricity to the hotel. The pool filled up all day, then the water was pumped through the generator to keep the electricity going until about eleven o'clock in the evening, when there would be a warning dip of the lights and the hotel would plunge into darkness.

Breathless, we plopped down on the verandah steps outside the dining room. The lights had just gone out. People were slowly leaving the dance floor and wandering off to bed. Someone wound up the old gramophone and put on Elvis singing, "Love me Tender". Boris leaned over and put his arm around my shoulder. "Shall we dance?"

He whirled me around and we laughed happily, he leading me with the greatest of ease. It seemed like we had been dancing forever. The shimmering moon gave the mountain an icy glow as we wandered outside in the cool air taking in the breathtaking night scenery.

"We had such fun together tonight," he said. "What shall we do tomorrow?"

"What do you want to do?" I couldn't think of anything I wanted to do more than be near him.

He took my hand in his and closed his fingers tightly, giving me a warm squeeze. I stared up at the moon and wondered what he was feeling. Did he sense the chemistry too? We sat there silent, close and electric for quite a while. Then he pulled me back to reality. It was two o'clock in the morning. "We had better go off to bed. I'll walk you to your room." He held my hand all the way. I stood at the door hesitant, not knowing what to expect. He gave me a gentle kiss on the lips and was gone.

Pat was fast asleep, so I slowly undressed and lay on the bed staring up at the thatched ceiling. Moonlight streamed through the windows as I lay dreaming of our next day together.

Next morning bright and early, I could barely eat my breakfast. Boris wolfed down eggs, bacon, potatoes and toast and asked if I wanted to go for a walk. "Lets go and check the stables, maybe we could go horse riding later?" We meandered along a narrow dirt pathway, worn deep into the grassland from the hundreds of cattle who had trodden the route back and forth along the foothills of the mountains. I asked him about his English accent.

"I was born in England and came here with my parents when I was fourteen. They've gone off to live in America now. I'm supposed to go there one day but I like it here."

Rene Ralphs (Boris' Mother) with Zulus

"I'm a student nurse at Grey's Hospital in Maritzburg. I've got a couple of years to go before I finish my training." Just as I was telling him about my mundane life he jumped aside.

"Watch out there's a snake on the path!" he yelled looking terrified. Without a second thought I grabbed a big stick lying on the ground close by and bashed the snake repeatedly, squashing its head with gusto.

"Wow, weren't you scared it might strike you? I hate snakes."
He looked at me with admiration. I glanced up breathlessly.

"No, I've shot snakes lots of times, you just have to get their head." I would have killed a lion for him, I thought.

During the rest of the week we played tennis, went horseback riding and hiked beautiful mountain trails along the streams in the foothills. We often encountered baboons scampering across the terrain, barking and chasing each other, some with babies clinging to their bellies. Big old daddy baboons would grunt as they sat around and the younger ones picked fleas off their backs.

We had fun whenever we were together. Every day we talked a little more about our lives and families. He told me he worked as a compositor.

"A what?"

"A compositor, I hand set type. I just completed a five year apprenticeship at Hayne & Gibson in Durban.

❖

I had never been so comfortable with a man, easy to get along with and always fun. The next three days were a whirlwind of excitement. We walked, we rode and we hiked up streams and swam in the icy mountain water. And talked and talked. I loved and laughed at all his jokes, posed for photos and jumped from the highest rocks showing off how tough I was. We danced the evenings away. Boris whirled me around, clutching me tightly. He held me close and pressed us cheek to cheek when the music was slow.

"I've bought you a flower for your hair," he smiled, as he met me outside my room.

"I recognize that flower. I saw it growing down by the pool. You can't fool me, I know you stole it." I laughed as I pinned it into my hair.

"You've got the most beautiful cow eyes. I love to look into them," he said.

"Cow eyes? Is that supposed to be a compliment?" All I could think of was old Molly with her big, round eyes mooing softly. I let it go.

The girl at the front desk, a few years older than me, had a voluptuous figure and it was obvious she took a shine to Boris. Everywhere we went with the crowd she showed up too. Helping with his every need, Zoë hovered around him making little jokes.

"I'll sign you up tomorrow Boris. I'll tell them to get you a nice, large, tame horse. Here are some new tennis balls." Whatever she thought he needed, she offered.

I don't think he even noticed, but I sure did. I got so sick of Zoë hanging around him and worried what would happen when I went home. She had another week to fawn all over him.

On the last day before I was to leave Boris suggested we go hiking alone. We took a picnic lunch packed by the staff and followed the familiar path along a cool stream heading up towards the Peak. He took my hand and helped me over the rocks, then held it when we were on the path. I loved his kind tender touch, a new attention I had not experienced before.

"When I get home next week I'll call you and we can go out if you'd like."

"I'd love that, we've had so much fun together."

If that darn Zoë doesn't get her claws into him after I am gone, I thought. I didn't know how I was going to be able to get through the next week. But I made a plan. We discovered we both lived in small towns about sixty miles apart and I began scheming how I could make it easier for him to get in touch and see me again. "I happen to be going to my aunt's next week to visit. She lives quite near where you live so I'll give you her phone number. I'll be staying there for the rest of my holiday." I hoped Aunt Dorothy would be home the next week and wouldn't object to my sudden visit.

On our last evening, I put on my favorite dress and my new sandals. Dawn squirted perfume on my neck just behind my ears and helped me with my hair. "So when he holds you close he'll faint!" She laughed. Dawn was in love with an older guy but I was afraid he would never call her again once we left. We were all anxious about our holiday romances and whether they would go any further, except Ally, who was looking forward to Paul arriving the next day to take us home. I studied myself in the mirror, swished my ponytail about and smiled, anticipating our evening together.

We sat outside after the lights went out on the verandah steps. The moon had faded away during the week and it was very dark close to the mountain. He hugged me and kissed me gently. So new and exhilarating, it made me feel quite breathless.

We talked for hours sharing our life stories, mine of farming and our family struggles, his of living through the bombing of London as a small boy and coming out to South Africa on a ship as there was no work for his father in England.

He finally escorted me to me to my room. I hated to part with him, "See you in the morning before we leave?" I asked. "I'll be up early." I crept quietly into the room and flopped onto the bed. The crickets outside chirped continually. I could have stayed out all night. I wished that night would never end. I didn't know how I was going to be able to leave the next day. "I'll call you as soon as I get home next Saturday," he promised. I couldn't tell him what I was really feeling. I was hopelessly in love.

When I arrived home bursting with the news of Boris, my young sisters were very excited. Dad was a bit more skeptical.

"He's British and fun and has twenty three shirts, a new car and earns sixty pounds a month!" I bragged.

"He's either a bloody marvel or a bloody liar. Why would he tell you how many shirts he has and what he earns. Probably a typical Pommy full of bull." Since the war, lots of British people had been immigrating to South Africa. Their pale skin turned red in the South African sun so everyone thought they were drips. My British guy wasn't a drip at all and I wanted Dad to be impressed.

"Where would he get a name like Boris?" Dad mocked. I just prayed he would call me next week so Dad could meet him and see that he wasn't just a drippy Pommy. I didn't know how I was going to get through the week waiting for him to call. What if he didn't? The week dragged on slowly. I sewed a new dress. I phoned Aunty Dorothy several times to tell her I was still coming. I caught the bus into town and met Mom for lunch one day and at last Friday arrived. Dad drove me down to Granny's old house, where Aunty Dorothy still lived, and dropped me off.

My favorite Aunt, she seemed delighted to hear all about Boris. She had been very much in love when she met Uncle Edgar many years ago. I always liked the way he put his arm around her waist. She understood how I felt. Most of my friends told me that holiday romances never work out. The fellows promise everything and then you never hear from him again. I sure hoped they were wrong.

Saturday was the longest day of my life. He had a long drive home from the mountains. What if he had lost my phone number? I paced around the house, went for a long walk and paced around some more. Aunt Dorothy tried to make me relax. At last the phone rang about five o'clock. Aunty and I looked at each other.

"Yes, she's here, let me get her for you." Aunty beamed as she handed me the phone. I could hardly speak. My heart pounded in my chest. He's really calling me!

"Hello." I listened while he told me all about the drive as Doug's old car was a bit temperamental. He asked if I would like to go to the movies that night.

"Yes I'd love to."

"Do you mind if my best friend Ronnie comes with us, I want him to meet you?"

"Of course not," I answered, disappointed we would not be spending the evening alone. But he had kept his promise and phoned and now we would be going out together, so I relaxed and tried to be happy. Aunt Dorothy poured her evening gin, squirted a dash of soda water into it and took a big swig.

"Thank God he called, I don't think I could have stood another minute of you fidgeting and pacing."

"We're going to the movies and he's bringing his best friend Ronnie with him. I suppose that's better than nothing."

We saw *The King and I* starring Yul Brynner. I really don't remember it much. Ronnie was a nice fellow. We went for coffee after the movie and Boris asked me if I would like to go to the beach on Sunday. I stayed at Aunt Dorothy's for the next week and we saw each other every evening. He told me he lived with some friends of his parents, Tom and Gwen Finnemore. He rented a bedroom in their house.

I gradually broke it to him that I had a couple of men I was dating. After our wonderful week at Aunty Dorothy's, he told me if we were going to see each other regularly he didn't want me to go out with other men. He promised he would come to Maritzburg every weekend. Mom thought I was nuts to listen to him. But I knew I had fallen in love and I didn't want anything to spoil it. So I had to tell Randall when I got back, I had met someone else and wouldn't be seeing him any more. He was so upset. I had no idea that he had fallen for me so hard. By this time Keith had written exams and he telephoned me to tell me he was available again. So I had to tell Keith.

"You shouldn't tie yourself down," Mom said, "go out with them all and play the field a bit, you're too young to commit to one guy." She lectured me about choices and judging men, but I had already made up my mind.

❖

My life would never be quite the same after my romantic holiday but I soon got back into the routine of nursing. The month after I returned I was assigned to Men's Medical Ward, two long rooms with twenty beds on each side. In the middle we worked from the nurses' duty room and a small kitchen used for making tea and serving special diets. The wards were bright and airy but most of the patients were chronically ill and rather old. Some had been lying there for months. The patient could be given privacy by pulling the curtains that hung from the rail surrounding the bed. I had never worked with so many old men before. They coughed and wheezed and rang their bells constantly. Summer was just around the corner so we opened the windows and french doors wide to let in the fresh air and get rid of the obnoxious hospital smells.

Staff asked me to change all the scrub-up basins in each ward one morning. There were no sinks so we filled basins with some pink liquid and put them on wooden stands at each end of the ward with plenty of clean towels nearby. Nobody ever told me what was in the basin. I sniffed it but couldn't tell what it was. I looked around the sluice room for something pink, nothing there. So I washed out each basin, filled it with clean water and poured in a good dose of mouthwash I had found in the bathroom. The pink color looked about the same so I hoped I had the right thing. About an hour later I heard Staff Nurse.

"Nurse Greenland, come over here right now!" I ran over to her wondering why she sounded so angry.

"What the hell have you put in this water?"

"Well I put that mouthwash concentrate that I found in the bathroom into it. It was the only thing I could find. I didn't know."

"Why didn't you ask someone?" she snapped. "Can you just imagine what the doctor said when he went to wash his hands. Now get out of here and change all those basins before another doctor comes along."

I still didn't know what to put in the water but I was not about to ask her. So I went off and found a red button. "You use this formaldehyde concentrate which sterilizes the basins, bedpans and the sluice rooms, you idiot!"

Another lesson demonstrated to us during our three months of general nurse training was laying out the dead. Sister Moyer had some very definite ideas about this job. We laid the naked blowup doll out on the table. Sister proceeded to tell us each step immediately after the doctor pronounced the patient dead. "You don't go off and do something else and forget about him until he gets so stiff you can't do things respectfully." She straightened out the doll and crossed her arms over her chest. "As if she is praying," Sister instructed, "next you cover the body with a shroud. Be sure you push their jaw shut and close their eyelids gently so they seem to be asleep. Most important of all, press down on their stomach so their bladder empties. You don't want to send the body to the morgue with a full bladder. Don't worry if anything runs out, you'll be cleaning up the bed afterwards. Next you make their legs nice and straight and tie their big toes together so their legs don't fall apart and slip off the trolley on the way to the morgue." We all took turns tying the toes together with a bandage.

In the nine months I had been let loose in the wards, I had never experienced a patient dying. Very early one morning before I came on duty one of the patients died. I had just arrived at the ward and all the staff were hustling around getting the death certificate signed. Chaos reigned. All the family members were crying and kissing the dead patient goodbye.

"Nurse Greenland," Staff Nurse pointed at me, "Mr. van Zyle has just passed away. I want you to go and prepare him so the morgue can pick him up. Do you know what to do?" Sister Moyer's coaching popped into my head.

"Oh yes, I know what to do," I said confidently, racking my brain for the order of things. I was not going to tell her I had never done it. The family stood around the patient uncomfortably, so I offered to make them a cup of tea.

"Perhaps you could come and sit in the duty room while I make it," I said.

"Thank you that would be nice," Mrs. van Zyle wiped her eyes.

I realized we never had any training on what to do with the family. I felt so sorry for her but I didn't have any idea what to say, so I just left them standing there and rushed off to make their tea. It was much easier to get things organized in the kitchen than to actually talk to people I did not know.

"Get a shroud from the linen room," Staff ordered as I headed for the kitchen, "they're on a shelf in the corner." I rushed off and found a pile of them in paper packets. I returned to the family and told them the tea was ready in the duty room to get them away from my job. That seemed to calm them down a bit.

On the way back I decided to get a bowl of water, a face cloth and a clean towel. When I opened up the shroud it was too short for the man who must have been six-foot five inches tall. When I covered his face his feet stuck out the end. I smoothed out his face, wiped it softly and shut his eyes perfectly. Poor Mr. van Zyle, he didn't look dead. He looked as if he was just sleeping except his chest wasn't moving. He was still warm to the touch. Sister Moyer had showed us how to tie a bandage around the head under the jaw to keep the mouth shut so the patient's jaw did not drop. Mr. van Zyle's mouth flopped open a few times so I got a bandage, tied it under his chin and up over his ears around the top of his head with a nice bow. He looked a bit funny but his jaw held firmly in place. He was fairly bald so I didn't have to comb his hair. I focused next on emptying the bladder. I pressed his stomach from the naval downwards. All of a sudden bubbles came out of all orifices. His bladder must have been full so I had an awful mess. I pushed him over gently and rolled up the sheet to remove it and bubbles blew out of his bottom as I turned him. God, I hope this man is really dead, I worried. He flopped back and one eye fell open. I gently closed it again, pressing slightly on the eyelid so it looked sleepy. Satisfied, I pushed his legs straight and pulled his big toes together. I had never really examined old men's toes before. His toenails were greenish, really long and curled over the ends of his gnarly bent toes. I mopped his feet with the facecloth then picked the big toes between two fingers and pulled them together. I hated to touch them but I had to get the bandage between them so I made myself do it. I pulled the shroud over his feet only to see it slip off his face. The shroud was just too short. I left Mr. van Zyle lying there peacefully with the curtains drawn around the bed.

"Is he dead?" one of the patients asked as I emerged.

"Yes." I whispered. We hadn't been told how to deal with that part of the process. A half an hour later Staff told me to shut the curtains around everyone's bed.

"What's up nurse?" some of the patients asked.

"The morgue is coming to pick someone up," I said and quietly closed all the curtains.

I had never seen the morgue cart, a high, rusty old trolley with a stainless steel bed. It was pushed by an enormous Zulu in a heavy khaki army coat with polished brass buttons that closed the front. An army cap balanced on his thick wooly head. The trolley squeaked and rattled as he pushed it down the middle of the ward. Why don't they oil the wheels, I thought? He pulled in beside Mr. van Zyle's bed and he and I slid the body onto the trolley. I pulled the shroud up over his face and his toes popped out again. The Zulu unfolded a big, grey army blanket and covered the body. The last thing I saw as he pushed Mr. van Zyle out of ward headed to the morgue was his big toes sticking out from under the shroud and the blanket.

I came back on duty at five o'clock that day, having had the afternoon off. When I walked into the Duty Room to sign in Staff Nurse called me over.

"Nurse Greenland did you forget anything when you laid out Mr. van Zyle this morning?"

"Not that I can think of. I tried to do everything I had been taught."

"Well not everything." She held out a little box. "Open it nurse." I took the box and opened it slowly wondering what the heck it could be. Inside was a set of false teeth. I blushed and panicked.

"What shall I do now?"

"Well you can just go down to the morgue and put them right into his mouth. Can you imagine what his family would say if his teeth aren't in?" I looked at her then I looked out the window. It was quite dark.

"Now?"

"Yes, right now. He's in a refrigerator and you'd better hurry. You just push them into his mouth so he looks natural."

I pulled my smart nurse's cape around my shoulders, put the little box into my pocket and stepped out into the darkness. The morgue was far down at the bottom of the hospital grounds near the river. I could barely see anything as I felt my way down the path. I heard an owl hoot above me in the trees. Scared stiff I pulled my cape tighter around me and hustled along. The river made an eerie sound as the water rushed over the rocks. I shivered in fear when I knocked on the door of the morgue. The old Zulu opened up. He had been dozing in his tiny front office and looked so surprised to see me. When he held up his flashlight to see who it was, it lit up his brown face and shaggy beard so he looked like a scary monster. I showed him the teeth and he beckoned me to follow him. He didn't say a word. A small light bulb hung in the center of a cold room with things that looked like oven doors all around the walls. He led me over and pulled out the drawer with Mr. van Zyle's body lying in it. His face and mouth were stone cold. I had not tied the jaw closed as tight as I thought and I was able to force the teeth into his mouth. The big native pushed the drawer shut. I didn't wait for a second, I just ran out all the way back to the ward as fast as I could.

❖

On our days off we could sleep in. Sister Hart had breakfast delivered to our room at nine o'clock. I loved that treat. She said nurses worked so hard they deserved to get breakfast in bed and the waiters weren't busy at that time of day. "Blekfast Madame," one of the native waiters would call out in a singsong voice as he knocked on the door. "Nice and hot, wake up now. Wake up." I would roll over and hear him plonk the tray down at the door and his bare feet pad away down the passage. Although we nurses were all white and our waiters were all black Zulu's, we trusted them as if they were our family and knew them all by name. We saw them most days, laughed and joked back and forth in the dining room. "Waiter, waiter Incubator," I'd shout when I needed some extra milk or toast. They always followed along with the banter, but the relationship ended there. It was against the law to socialize with a black person in any way.

Most nights, if we went out we had to be back in the Nurses Home by eleven. Once a week we could stay out until midnight. I usually saved that late night for a weekend when Boris visited. He would drop me off on the dot of twelve and go and stay with my parents. The rule was you signed into an old hard bound book kept in the Emergency Department. Then the native night guard would walk across the road with you, open up the front door, let you in and lock it again. One night we had been out dancing and drove up to the hospital fifteen minutes late. This was considered a serious infraction of the rules and you would lose your next week's privilege. Luckily for me that night one of the doctors who knew my mother was near the sign-in book. The night nurse was giving me hell when he interrupted. "Oh for God's sake nurse, let her sign in. It's only fifteen minutes, don't be so rigid." What could she say? We never argued with the doctors, they were like gods. I thanked him quietly and slunk off with the night guard before she changed her mind.

There were two rooms on the ground floor of the Nurses Home with doors opening onto the front verandah. They were supposed to be locked and the wardrobe was always placed in front of the door, however sometimes we were lucky and a good sport or a greedy nurse would have that room and they would leave the door unlocked. You could just push the wardrobe a little and sneak in, leaving her a couple of shillings for the favor. Sometimes nurses would be sneaking in every night at all hours and they would cut them off after a few weeks, lock the door and say, "Forget it, I never get any sleep. It's over."

One evening after a tough day, six of us were lying around in our PJ's talking shop.

"Why don't we go out to the bio tonight?" Bobsie, the big red head suggested. She always thought of things to do first.

"We're all in our PJ's, I'm too lazy to get dressed again," I said.

"It's a cold night," Bobsie kept on, "let's just put our coats over our pajamas and go. No one will know."

We donned our coats, buttoned them up, pulled on some shoes and took off for the bioscope three blocks down the road. We laughed all the way. We got back just before eleven and rushed up to our rooms thinking we had got away with it. The next day after lunch I was called into Matron's office. She sat behind her desk, looking very stern when I walked in, her round bosom heaving up and down. She tapped the desk with a pencil and looked over her glasses at me.

"You were seen in the town last night wearing pajamas under your coat. How dare you disgrace the hospital reputation behaving like that? Who were the other five girls you were with?"

"We were fully covered up. No one could see them," I stammered.

"Well you didn't do a very good job of it. One of the Staff Nurses going off duty saw you lot. So you may as well own up now."

We never seemed to be able to get away with a thing so I confessed and we had our late privileges taken away for a month. We didn't dare take a chance and use the special door either. It was simply too risky. We could get thrown out of the nurses training program and I couldn't imagine that.

When Boris came to Maritzburg on the weekends I tried to arrange afternoons off. I had to be back on duty at five and finished about eight thirty at night. That worked well most of the time and he stayed with my family while I worked. He played games with my younger sisters, bought them ice cream and sometimes conned them into washing his car. They thought he was very cool. We'd go out dancing or to a bio and stay out late because I could sleep at home. He would drop me off outside the hospital at six thirty in the morning so nobody noticed I didn't come back the night before.

When I had known Boris about three months, I felt in my heart he was the right man for me. He never let me down. He had promised to come up and see me every weekend and he never called and made an excuse or said he couldn't come.

❖ 14 ❖

Another Hailstorm
1957

Portrait of Me
My first Christmas present to Boris!

One afternoon several months later, we were out when it poured with rain. A howling gale blew and the rain turned to enormous hailstones stones that pelted the car. We dashed under a huge tree and parked, preventing the hail from damaging the car. We didn't dare venture out until the storm passed. While we waited, we sat snuggling in the front seat and talked about life and what we both wanted. Cautious, I didn't say too much even though I knew exactly how I felt. He leaned back with his arm across the seat watching the rain. He reached for me and looked sweetly into my face. I could barely hear him for the hail.

"I want to marry you."

"I want to marry you too." I spluttered without hesitation. We sat there, each full of our own thoughts. The storm subsided and left an eerie silence. The sound of the raindrops from the leaves plinking on the car broke the tension. We laughed and held each other tight.

"Did you really mean it?" I said.

"I don't propose marriage every day. Of course I meant it. I love you and I want you to go to America with me one day."

"America! It's so far away, I would have to think about that a lot."

"Well let's go home, and we'll talk about it later. We're having too much fun right now to make any real plans."

So he planted the seed in my head. I didn't say a word to Mom and Dad as we told them all about the hailstorm and the car. Dad then told bigger hailstorm stories and I sat there quietly. How could I ever go away from Mom and Dad, leave my sisters and my Africa and all that I had ever known. It was too much to contemplate that day.

Later on we began talking about where we would go and what we would do.

"We could save a lot of money while we are there," he said, "maybe come back home after a year?"

"I know I can't leave here forever, a year would be enough."

"You'd find a job nursing and I'd still be in printing. I can go anywhere in the world with that trade."

"I don't have any money."

"I do. I've been saving for a while. I just never dreamed I would be going to America with a wife."

"Well, I'll think about it a bit more." We left it at that the first weekend.

❖

On the last Friday of every month the duties for the following month were posted. Anticipation filled the air as we waited to find out where we were going. Because I was tall I could usually read over the heads of the crowd around the bulletin board. Craning my neck I spotted my name under *Diseases Training, Wentworth Hospital, Durban.* I'd been nursing for a year before being assigned to this training. Six of our group were on the list as well as about twenty nurses from different groups. I could hardly wait to telephone Boris that night and tell him I would be in Durban for three months.

On the first day of the month we packed our bags and boarded a small bus, which transported us to Wentworth. A small hospital, Wentworth sat on large grounds on top of a hill just outside Durban overlooking the harbor on one side, the ocean on the other. The single story buildings had been constructed during World War II to treat wounded soldiers coming home from North Africa. Some were built to house tuberculosis patients. Since the hospital was located in a warm sunny part of South Africa the rooms were bright and airy. Large windows and french doors opening into the gardens allowed the patients to benefit from the warm climate.

The nursing staff lived in similar buildings at the far end of the hospital, two to a room. Most of the permanent staff at Wentworth lived off campus. My first friend was a Nurse Small. "Hell, I wouldn't live in this miserable place," she announced, "I have a nice little flat I share with my boyfriend. He's a wild bugger, they wouldn't tolerate him around here with his noisy motor bike."

❖

The hospital was broken up into the TB block, polio block and contagious diseases where whooping cough, scarlet fever, cholera and severe cases of mumps and measles were treated. The first day we crowded into a small classroom to be briefed on the common symptoms and general nursing care of contagious patients. We were given extensive training on how to protect ourselves from catching any of these diseases. There were no disposable plates or utensils so the handling of everything used by the patient was very important. Each patient had their own set of dishes, a bedpan and any other items required for their care. Gloves and masks were available outside every room. There were no long wards full of beds like I was used to, but patients still shared bathrooms with the supervision of the nurse. Strict procedures were enforced when a patient used the common bathroom.

They assigned me to contagious children my first three weeks. The sounds of constant coughing, raspy breathing and crying never stopped. Little kids suddenly isolated from their family, lying in an iron crib, burning up with fever and no mother to comfort them, was a most disturbing experience. I learned for the first time how to comfort kids and understand the agonizing pain of isolation. I'd read them a story and try to make them smile.

Mothers and fathers could only visit for an hour or so each day. They had to put on a white gown, gloves, masks and booties so the child hardly recognized them when the ghostlike figure walked into the room. After the parents left, everything they had touched was thrown into a special basket and taken for sterilization.

Nurse Small, not a registered nurse only an assistant, knew her way around and kept us smiling in spite of the heartbreak around us. In her mid-thirties with shoulder length, smooth blonde hair curled under neatly around her face, her wide grin and naughty smile fascinated us. When the doctors did their rounds she knew all the scandal. "See that dirty bugger?" She'd whisper, pointing at the doctor." He's having a good go with old nurse Engelbrecht over there, has a wife and kids too." Of course I could never look at Nurse Engelbrecht again without thinking about her being unfaithful. Smalley had a tale for everything. I learned more about sex from her, things I could only imagine. "Once we did it up against a wall back of our place, we were so horny we couldn't wait."

Barefoot African women cleaned everything daily. They scrubbed and mopped with Dettol enveloping the rooms with a heady disinfectant smell. I suppose their feet were well sterilized for they left wet footprints down the hallways as they mopped from room to room. If a patient left the hospital they scrubbed every inch of the bed with disinfectant. The mattresses were put outside in the sunshine for the day before being readied for the next patient. One time I was sent to clean up a small

Nursing friends on day off

Off Duty — Wentworth Hospital

child who had vomited all over his bed. The smell overpowered me and I vomited all over the child as I was cleaning him up. I can still see that little face looking up at me, so forlorn and miserable, covered in puke. For him it was just part of another agonizing day.

We learned how to make tents over the crib or bed so the child could be given breathing medications, drops of strong stuff plopped into a bowl of boiling water. Sister showed us how to examine the swollen strawberry red tongue, an early indication of scarlet fever. She taught us how to administer medication to a resistant, small child. Not an easy task, we used a lot of jam and sugar.

We worked two different types of shifts, either 7 a.m. to 5 p.m. or 7 a.m. to 1 p.m. with the afternoon off and then back to work from 5 to 9 p.m. On the days I was given the 7 a.m. to 5 p.m. shift I would let Boris know. It took him about twenty minutes to drive from work to the hospital to pick me up. For the first time we were able to see each other much more regularly. It gave us the chance to get to know each other better and we didn't have the problem of being around my family all the time when I was off duty. He would take me to some of his favorite places to eat. The one I liked best made a curried pickled fish, which we bought often. Wrapped in parchment paper we drove down to the beachfront to eat it. We'd sit outside on a bench enjoying the pounding surf while pigeons surrounded us waiting for the last few tidbits. Many evenings we had nothing to do so we'd drive up to the top of the hill, find a secluded scenic spot and park the car. Durban is a very hot place and in summer evenings the mosquitos reign. They were so annoying, humming and flying around the car. I waved and slapped but couldn't see them so we closed all the windows. Then they fogged up and it was even hotter so I decided on a solution. I bought a few yards of netting from the fabric shop. We opened the windows and stuffed the netting into the cracks so we could get some air without being bitten alive. Those hot, summer, mosquito ridden evenings cemented our love for each other. We talked about everything, our dreams and our plans for our life together. We smooched and hugged and kissed for hours. I had never known such a thrill from so much kissing. Sweet and innocent, I experienced happiness beyond anything I had ever imagined. I learned how to communicate with a man and the new feeling of love and being loved. I also discovered the pain of parting each evening and the thrill of anticipation for the next time we would meet.

❖

The second month at Wentworth, they assigned me to the adult polio ward. Polio is a strange disease and strikes with swift veracity. A headache, maybe some pain in the neck and then paralysis. We would never know what degree of paralysis would occur in a particular patient. A patient could arrive with a high fever and pain in the neck area but still able to move. Paralysis would creep over their body. If they were lucky just one leg would be affected, but with some patients the paralysis crept quickly up to their lungs and chest and they had to be put into an iron lung. The huge tube-like machine, airtight, encased the patient. They were completely trapped. Every part of their body lay on a bed inside the lung except their head while the giant machine heaved and groaned incessantly, breathing in and out for the patient. There were two machines and I was given the job of caring for these patients. While on duty I had to feed and attend to the their every need. I understood so little about the fear or the feeling of paralysis. I stood there helplessly trying to encourage and add some cheerfulness. The first days for a patient were ones of shock. Frightened, they couldn't sleep for the noise of the machine. They were afraid if they went to sleep they would never wake up again. Everyday they hoped they would move again soon. We were told that reducing their fever reduced paralysis, so we bathed them in cold, wet sheets over and over, praying we were doing some good but not really knowing.

One night a handsome man of about fifty was wheeled into the ward and pushed into the iron lung. He had been experiencing extreme difficulty breathing and appeared to be in a state of panic. The machine gave him instant relief and he fell into a deep sleep as we bathed and cooled him. We reached him through holes in the sides of the lung, which had rubber suction surrounds. We could push our gloved hands through these openings to wipe the patient down with the cold cloths.

The next morning I became acquainted with this wonderful intelligent man. Over the next few days I discovered he held a high position in the business world and now he was reduced to a paralyzed body over which he had no control. During that month I cared for him. He could not do anything for himself. The loss of dignity a man experiences with polio is quite overwhelming. A true gentleman, his education and knowledge surprised me every day. "What did you do before you got polio?" I questioned him and learned so much while I fed, washed, shaved and changed him. His family brought him shorts and shirts and we dressed him every day as if he was normal. He talked about life and asked me questions about Boris. He expounded on the relationship between a man and a woman, his mind full and rich with knowledge. I had never talked like that to a grown up stranger before. He loved books and I found a way to prop them overhead so he could read.

"Can you see the pages yet?" I asked as I fiddled with the book holder.

"No, I can't see a darn thing. You need to lie on the floor and see what I see!" I pretended to lie on the floor to make him laugh.

"Oh Mr. Longman, I'm not mechanical. Shall I get you your Vat 69 now, that will cheer you up?"

"Can I have my glasses on please?"

"Where did you put them this time?" I kidded. He had to suffer me putting things down and mislaying them constantly.

"I don't know how your mother has tolerated you all these years. You're a damn disaster on wheels." We joked and laughed a lot. I tried to make him happy in spite of his travesty and sometimes I actually thought I succeeded. He enjoyed his Vat 69 sipping it through a straw. The doctor said he wasn't really sick any more just suffering from the paralyzing after effects of the disease.

Nursing this gentleman every day was a life changing experience for me. I witnessed the heartbreak for his family, the longing to breathe normally again and the frustration and boredom he experienced when his entire normal life was snatched away from him. He forced himself to be patient and remain hopeful. His strength of character proved a huge lesson to me, as I nursed him and witnessed his wonderful qualities and thoughtful behavior in spite of his adversities.

Three weeks after he came into the hospital the therapists began taking him out of the lung. They helped him with a smaller machine to be outside the dreadful tube of a prison. We experienced the joy together as he managed to cope and breathe. I pushed him out into garden and he tried to suck in the smell of flowers and fresh air. Gradually he breathed more easily on his own and he had hope. He would be able to have a life outside the lung.

When I left Wentworth he was sitting up in his wheelchair beginning to think about his business world once more. I visited him often during my last month. On the final day we said goodbye. I kissed his forehead and ran off before he could see the tears in my eyes. I think I fell in love with that man in a strange way. The bus whisked us away back to Grey's Hospital and I never saw him again.

❖

Boris and I became used to seeing each other almost everyday. My time in Durban at Wentworth Hospital completely changed our relationship. Boris didn't have to drive all the way to Pietermaritzburg and he could meet me after work within ten minutes of finishing. Spending so much more time together, we grew closer. Before we knew it the three months were over, and I had to return to my erratic schedule at Grey's

Hospital sixty miles away, and found myself working most weekends. Boris resumed the long drive to Maritzburg every Friday night and then back on Sundays. The road was narrow and winding for a large portion of the way so it usually took about two hours.

We missed seeing each other so much that I found myself feeling quite restless. The telephone no longer filled the gap during the weeks that followed. I decided to try and transfer my training to Addington Hospital in Durban, a fifteen-minute drive for Boris. I didn't see why I couldn't carry on in a different place.

Boris with his car

I spoke to Matron about the change but they said the hospitals did not have cooperating programs in spite of them both being owned by the Natal Provincial Government. There was nothing we could do to alleviate our problem. Boris had his printing world in Durban and I had my nursing career half completed in Maritzburg. On the weekends we saw as much of each other as we could. We stayed out late on Saturdays and I got back to the hospital and Nurses Home by midnight on Sunday.

I worried that one day Boris would call and say he was too tired to come up or too busy. He was getting really sick of the drive, but I didn't know what to do. Such a sweet gentle man, but I could sense his deep frustration with the situation. Our passion intensified. I still had over a year and a half to go before I finished my training and got my RN Degree and I couldn't transfer. He wanted us to get married but that was not allowed while in training, so the situation became more and more tense and difficult. After thinking about it for a long time I decided I would quit nursing. We were going to America anyway, I would probably never nurse there. I pictured myself living in Hollywood bumping into stars everyday. I would just find a new career in the movie business. I rationalized I didn't need the nursing.

As I broached the subject to Boris, I knew it was not the right thing to do, but I wanted to be with him more than I wanted my career. At twenty-four, Boris was more sensible. At nineteen, my world experiences were very limited and my love for him was stronger than anything I had ever experienced.

"What do you think of me quitting nursing so we can get married?"

"Your parents would never allow it, they'd have a fit. I know we are going to America but this is not the solution." He paused for a few minutes and frowned.

"Maybe you could continue your training when we get to America?"

"Yeah I bet I could. I like that idea." Happy to have some sort of solution on the table at all, we immediately began planning to talk to my parents and tell them our great idea.

At about nine o'clock one evening, Dad had finished his dinner and was reading the paper and smoking a cigarette. Mom always told me, "If you want anything from Dad, wait until his tummy is full before you ask him." So we sat down on the sofa together and stared at Dad saying nothing.

"What do you kids want?" He dropped the newspaper down, lowered his glasses on his nose and peered at both of us sitting in front of him like a pair of seals about to do a trick. "You don't usually hang around me this time of night so I know you've got something up your sleeve." Smoke drifted into the air and I watched it curl and vanish.

I looked at Boris, silent, waiting for me. I decided I might as well get it over. It was my career we were talking about anyway.

"Well Dad, I've been thinking."

"Oh, oh. That's usually pretty dangerous Doff, when you start thinking."

I plunged straight in.

"I am thinking about quitting my nursing training and after we are married, when I get to America, I will continue," I said all in one breath. Dad was dead silent. I waited for his usual reaction. I expected him to refuse to consider it and shout at me about how ridiculous I was to think of such a thing. Then I could argue back in defense of my idea. Instead tears filled his eyes. He wiped them with his old cotton handkerchief that he carried in his pocket and slowly put his glasses back on.

"I'm just getting used to the idea of you two going off to America and now you want to give up nursing too. It's just too much for an old guy like me to handle Doff. I'll have to dwell on it for a bit." He picked up the paper and turned a page. It crackled. He was very quiet. We waited, but he ignored us completely. Boris squeezed my hand. He was much more patient, I wanted to talk it over and debate. I didn't want to wait for Dad to think it over.

"Dad. Why don't you answer me?" Engrossed in my own exciting future, I had no comprehension of his pain. My mind went wild imagining all the things that would happen to us traveling to America. When I was thirteen and Queen Elizabeth was crowned, I imagined I would meet her one day and be invited to her annual Garden Party. Now I didn't even care about the Queen, I was going to America. I would be rubbing shoulders with the stars, skiing in the mountains, maybe driving a red Thunderbird convertible. I had seen it all in the movies. Ordinary people did so many different things in America, why shouldn't I?

"Doff, your mother and I love you a lot, we want what's best for you, but, giving up your whole career? You must think this through, don't rush your life away. Think about what you are doing for a few days and then we'll talk again." He let out a big sigh. "I'm going off to bed now. It's late." Dismissed. Dad got up and called the dogs to go outside. There would be no more discussion that night.

Eventually I was assigned to night duty. That meant going on duty at seven in the evening and getting off at seven in the morning. The day I was to begin night duty I didn't sleep at all. I went over to the dining room, ate a hearty dinner and reported in for my first night. The routine began with the reading of the day report, listening to the activities of the day, new patients, preparation for surgeries and the condition of patients who had just had surgery so we had a pretty good idea of what the night might bring.

That first night, things were quiet and just after midnight I was told to go to lunch. I walked along the pathway through the hospital grounds to the dining room. There were no lights showing the path and the breeze rustled through the gum tree leaves creating eerie shadows and sounds. I imagined someone lurking in the dark ready to nab me, so I picked up my step and ran all the way, relieved when I reached the light of the dining room.

Even though it was the middle of the night they served cold meats and salads. "We try to make your night life seem like a normal day," Sister Hart told me. I noticed several nurses flopped out on the lounge couches fast asleep. I slowly enjoyed my meal and ran back to the ward so I wouldn't be late. Around two in the morning everything was quiet. I walked around the ward checking the patients and sat in a chair planning to read a book. All of a sudden it hit me, I couldn't keep my eyes open. I felt so tired it was painful trying to keep my eyelids from dropping shut. I got up and wandered around again, yawning my head off, splashing water on my face. I thought I would fall asleep standing up. From that day onwards I ate my lunch quickly and tried to take a nap for the remaining part of the break. I mastered the art of falling asleep in one minute over the next two months.

At least one qualified nurse headed up the night staff assisted by a dark blue button, a red button and a green button. Occasionally two green buttons. For the first time I found myself amongst a small group of mixed levels. We became close during that month because night nursing brought us together in unexpected emergency situations. With the tension high, we had to work side by side regardless of our level.

On quiet nights, after reading the day report we walked through the ward in a group. The head nurse chatted to each patient briefly so they became comfortable with us.

When we came on night duty the wards were filled with chattering visitors who would leave as soon as we rang the bell at 8 p.m. The red button nurse would go through the charts and make a tray of night meds. She placed the appropriate sleeping or pain pill into little white paper cups with the patient's name on a small label underneath. It was a serious responsibility and she took her time preparing the tray while the other nurses attended to patients' needs.

As a green button and junior nurse, if things were quiet, my first duty was to prepare the evening tea trolley. The cups had been washed and piled high by the native day staff. I'd boil an enormous kettle of water, make the tea and wheel it around offering it to the patients. South Africans consider tea drinking a national pastime so it's an important part of making a patient feel comfortable and at home as best one could in a hospital setting.

I had the tea ready right at eight o'clock. I rang the bell as loud as I could so the visitors knew to leave and pushed the trolley into the ward. Anxious husbands reluctantly kissed their wives goodbye. "Come on love, get going, we'll take good care of her." We were instructed to hustle the visitors out, no dilly-dallying permitted. As each patient looked longingly at their departing spouse I'd ask, "Would you like a nice hot cup of tea before you settle down?" Sometimes I had to help an old lady with her tea in an enamel mug with a spout, holding it to her mouth, careful not to pour it all over her, hoping it wasn't too hot or too cold. As I served her I thought how glad I was not drinking my tea out of a spout.

One night when I arrived for duty, a new patient who had just had surgery was being brought back to the ward. There were no recovery rooms, patients arrived from surgery still anesthetized and it was our job to bring them around and watch over them. This was my first chance to put into practice what Sister Moyer had taught us about caring for a patient post operatively. The blue button reviewed the procedure with me. She seemed satisfied and I assured her I knew what to do. I took the patient's pulse and blood pressure, wrote it down and all was fine. Then I patted her cheek gently and called her name a couple of times. She didn't stir. I remembered that Sister Moyer had demonstrated how to press on the patient's eyebrows to wake them up. So I pressed, but no movement. I pressed again a bit harder, patted her cheeks and called her name. She still did not stir. I thought for a bit then I decided I must have not been pressing hard enough so I pressed her eyebrows all over quite firmly, again and again. At last she stirred and opened her eyes. "Well hello Mrs. Brown, how do you feel, you came through your surgery with flying colors." I picked up the jar next to her bed with her organ floating in solution and wiggled it. "There's your appendix, you can see it was considerably enlarged." I shook it again and she gave me a pathetic smile. The next night when I bounced up to her bedside to see how she was doing, she gave me a pained smile.

"Well I think I am doing okay except for the terrible pain all across my eyebrows and my forehead. I can't imagine what it could be."

"Oh my," I said, "I hope it goes away soon, it can't be anything too serious."

I never said a word to anyone but I never pressed eyebrows again and the patients woke up just fine.

The night nurses slept in a separate building away from the Nurses Home so we missed most of our friends. One week-night a rugby team came to visit from Johannesburg. A friend of ours called the night building to see who was off duty. Pat, my friend and I were the only ones there. She said they were all going out for a bit of fun with the team and they needed a few extra girls to go along and make the evening complete. Since we had nothing to do we decided to go. Four guys picked us up in an old jalopy. They stuffed us into the back seat with two of the fellows. They were all very jovial and I could smell beer on their breath but I didn't think much about it. They sped down the main road with the windows wide open blowing our hair in our eyes. I was most excited when they drove into the parking lot of the Wanderers Club where I had never been allowed to go. "I don't want you going there with all those drunks Doff," Dad always told me, "it's not a suitable place for young girls." At last I thought, now I'll find out why Dad didn't want me to go to this place.

We walked inside to see the whole rugby team waving their beer mugs and singing funny naughty songs. I spotted my friends sitting around a table, with a drink, laughing at every-thing the boys said. I stood and grinned at everyone sheepishly, not knowing what to say, secretly worrying that Dad could walk in at any minute and find me in this forbidden den of iniquity. One of the burly rugby players talking to his friend looked over at us with a grin. "Nothing but a bunch of virgins," he muttered to his friend as he swigged his beer and puffed on his cigarette.

It scared me. Everyone ordered food and kept drinking. I didn't have any money with me so I just pretended my water was a drink and picked at the chips on the table. At last the club announced "last drink" and they all swigged another one down and said they would take us home. They dropped my pal and me off at the night Nurses Home but unbeknownst to me one of the guys followed Pat to her room. In the morning I woke about ten and went over to see if she wanted any breakfast. She was sprawled on the bed naked, her chest and thighs all black and blue. Her torn dress lay on the floor.

"My God what happened?" I screamed when I saw her lying there sobbing.

"That guy followed me to my room. He said he thought I was pretty and he wanted to come in. I told him no men were allowed into the building but he didn't care. He pushed his way in and threw me onto the bed. He started tearing my clothes off. I screamed but no one heard me. He forced me down, ripped my dress and raped me. Then he left as if it was nothing." Pat sobbed and cried. I tried to wipe her bruises and get her some clothes but I didn't know what to say. "Don't tell anyone," she said. I thought she would get pregnant. She walked around in a daze on night duty and every day I asked her how she felt or if she was sick. About ten days later she got her period and for the first time she smiled. We hugged each other with relief. We never told anyone.

❖

My parents went to church every Sunday but this particular time Dad didn't go as he had a lot of lawn mowers to sharpen. He did this most Sundays after early church to make a few extra bob. When Mom came home from church she was usually relaxed, reformed and refreshed. She pulled into the driveway, climbed out of the old Vauxhall, patting the dog on his head as he hovered at the kitchen door and waved to Dad busy repairing lawn mowers in the garage. Boris and I were standing in the kitchen talking about how to broach the subject of marriage to Mom, when she walked in and dumped her things on top of the washing machine.

"Boy it was hot in church today. Doff put the kettle on and lets have a nice cup of tea and sit outside in the garden." Boris and I looked at each other thinking the same thing. What a perfect chance to bring Mom up to date with our plans. I made a big pot of tea and Boris looked into the biscuit tin. "There's still a couple, I'll bring the tin outside."

We sat down under Dad's favorite tree, an old willow that spread its branches wide providing shade. Mom had painted the chipped garden chairs and table over and over. The last time she painted them a dark green. Old white paint showed through the chips where they had been banged against each other for years. I tried to push the table into the shade a bit more but its cement terrazzo top made it heavy. It was difficult to move it over on the grass so we settled for half in and half out of the shade. I poured the tea for Mom.

"We asked Dad if we could get engaged today and he said yes."

"You mean now, today. Good God I can't think about you two getting married yet. It is just too much of a rush. Why didn't you ask me about it first?" We almost always asked Mom first and she didn't like it that we hadn't. She swigged her tea, swallowing with a gulp, her neck wobbling like a turkey, lips pursed, silent, looking very stern.

"How do you expect me to plan for a wedding, I need at least a year?"

"How about six months? That's next April, do you think you could manage with that?" I said cheerfully. Mom sat quietly.

"Explain to me how you are going to get around being married and continue your nurses training?" Mom knew the hospital policy did not allow student nurses to be married. She knew they expected us to work so many hours plus providing our schooling, they simply forbid marriage until after we finished the course.

"Well we thought we wouldn't tell them. Boris works in Durban and I work here in Maritzburg sixty miles away so we would just continue with that arrangement."

"Well let's get through the engagement and then we can talk about your future and set a date, provided you two can work out some important details. I'm not going to worry about all that right now." So Mom gave her blessing reluctantly and we made plans to announce our official engagement.

In October (1957) we bought a small diamond ring from my sister's best friend's Dad who owned a jewelry shop in Maritzburg. He showed us a variety of beautiful, sparkling diamonds and told us half a carat cost fifty pounds. That was all the money we had so we paid and asked for it to be set in a solitaire. I was nineteen when we bought the ring. I showed it off to all my friends, waving my hand around. It seemed like a million carats to me and one of my friends told me I glowed with happiness.

Dad arranged for our family and friends to come to dinner with us at the Plough Hotel to celebrate. One of the oldest hotels in Maritzburg, the dark, wood paneled dining room and subdued lighting looked warm and romantic. The white linen table cloths and the serviettes folded like birds of paradise, placed in the center of each plate, exuded formality and elegance. I had very rarely been in a hotel where people enjoyed fine dining, candles twinkling on the table and cut glass wine goblets sparkling in the dim light. An Indian waiter in a short white coat and bow tie hovered near Dad and Boris asking if we would like champagne. "In order to celebrate the most special occasion of the engagement to Madam."

Boris pulled back chairs for Mom and I to be seated. He beamed and charmed everyone with his crooked toothy grin and sat down next to Dad. We were served a three course dinner: soup, a small delicate salad and the main meal of roast leg of lamb. Dishes of steaming vegetables were served with a silver spoon. It seemed terribly posh to me. The menu was passed around the table. Everyone wrote congratulations and signed it so Mom could put it away for me to keep. A cellist played romantic classics in the corner of the room as I held out my hand and showed off my ring.

Dad made a toast and everyone held up their glasses. Boris grabbed my hand under the table, rubbed his foot against mine and slid it up my leg a little way. I dropped my shoe to the floor so I could slide my toes over his leg. It was sweet and naughty and exciting. We stared into each other's eyes. As we locked arms the bubbles jumped up and tickled our noses. We clinked glasses and sipped the champagne.

❖

The week after the engagement I began to prepare and study for the three-hour paper on Materia Medica and medicine. I thought I was ready but the morning of the exam I got my period. Crippled over with a nagging stomach ache, I was utterly unprepared for the nuisance that day. We filed into roll call as usual but instead of reporting to our ward we had to go to the old hall across the road where tables were specially set up for the nurses writing the exam. Before I checked in, I decided to run over the road to the women's ward and grab some Tampax from storage. I shoved a couple in my pocket and walked quickly back to the exam room thinking back to the first time I had ever used a tampon. I usually used a Kotex pad with a belt, but they were most uncomfortable and I had complained to Bobsie about it.

"Why don't you use a tampon?"

"A tampon! I couldn't, I'd never get it in, and I'm too scared to try."

"Don't be silly," Bobsie laughed, "there's nothing to it. You've got to try sometime." A couple of days later Bobsie produced a tampon. It looked like a white cigar. "Go on, give it a try. Go into the john and I'll stay outside and help with instructions. So I went into the lavatory, shut the door, pulled my pants down and tried to push the tampon in between my legs, somewhere, hoping it would just go. Nothing went anywhere. It hit a solid barrier.

"I can't get it in."

"Push harder," Bobsie said.

"It hurts when I push harder!"

"You've got to bend down and look and find the right hole you idiot." No sympathy from Bobsie.

"What's going on in here?" someone shouted. I pushed again and tried to look but couldn't see anything.

"Dorothy's trying to use her first tampon," Bobsie laughed and another nurse joined the helpful group. Everyone shouted their suggestion on how they got it in the first time. The tampon was getting bent and looking a bit the worse for wear so I gave up and marched out of the lavatory. "Next month girls, I'll give it another try" The next month I tried again, without the help of Bobsie. Finally I succeeded with considerable pain and misery but I had graduated to the big girl's league. I could use a tampon. Not that the darn things helped much, you could never trust them and you always had to have a spare handy. I constantly forgot that. I laughed to myself thinking back on the first fiasco as I crossed over the road into the hall panting like a dog.

"Cutting it a bit fine, aren't you nurse." A stern starched rigid Staff Nurse I had never seen before checked me off her list and handed me the questions. Once we were all checked in she marched to the front of the room. "There will be no talking, no breaks and no moving about the room. You have three hours to complete the questions. When I ring the bell you will put down your pens and hand in your papers to me. You may begin." I grabbed my pen, scribbled my name on the paper and opened it up. Right away I recognized the first question and knew the answer. Each question asked either a prognosis for a disease or the treatment and sometimes the symptoms. Each time I thought about the day I imagined having that disease and talking about the cure, so the paper wasn't too difficult at all. I was feeling quite pleased with myself. But when I got up to walk out of the room a friend behind me whispered, "Greenland, you'd better check out the back of your uniform before you leave here." I strained to see the back. There was an enormous dark red blotch on my white uniform. "Oh no!" My stomach ache reared up again immediately. "How am I going to get back to the hospital?" Luckily several of my friends were still checking out so they bundled around me, escorted me down the street and back into the Nurses Home.

A week later the results of the exams were posted on the bulletin board for all to see. We crowded around pushing and shoving looking for our names, praying we weren't at the bottom of the list. I finally spotted my name about half way down the Passed column and heaved a big sigh of relief.

Once the exams were over we went back to working six days a week in the wards. I was placed in Women's Medical. I hated it there. Most of the women were chronically ill and detested the hospital and complained continuously. Some very ill and too old to help themselves had been there for months with no family visitors. They were just waiting to die. Much too impatient, I did not like feeding old ladies. I would get the next spoonful ready and be waving it in front of their face as they chewed slowly through each mouthful.

"Don't be in such a rush nurse," one mumbled with her mouth full.

"I've got a lot of mouths to feed," I retorted. Most of the time I was a very kind, sympathetic nurse, but the disgusting feeding drove me crazy. Sometimes I really had to control myself when they dripped and drooled, coughed and spat. As a young nurse I found it sad to watch such awful things happening to people.

Days were busy and full. We washed the patients in the mornings, fed breakfasts, changed sheets, handed out medicines, dished out bedpans and tidied up over and over. At lunchtime we worked hard to feed the little old ladies who weren't interested in food. The bells rang constantly. I think some of the woman competed with the neighboring bed for most attention.

"Nurse can you crank my bed up a bit?" I cranked away.

"How's that Mrs. Grogen?"

"Just a bit more upright nurse." Just as I got to another patient their bell would ring again.

"I just left you Mrs. Grogen, what can I do now?"

"I think the bed's too upright, can you wind it down a tad?" I grit my teeth trying to be patient. When I saw her bell light flashing for the umpteenth time, I called her Mrs. Wind-me-up, Wind-me-down in the nurse's station.

Being newly engaged I had taken on a more impatient attitude with my nursing life. I wanted to get on with it and finish so I could get married and get a decent job with decent pay. The slow pace of the medical ward showed me I did not want to go into the field of geriatric nursing. I much preferred the pace of surgery. I really loved making people well quickly and moving on to a new challenge every few days.

The six-day schedule allowed us a lot of flexible time even though we worked very hard when we were on duty. If I was off during the day I loved to meet Mom for lunch. I wanted to make plans as I began thinking seriously about going to America and Mom and I would talk about the million things I had to do.

Meanwhile Boris still drove the long distance to Maritzburg every weekend as my attempt to transfer to a hospital in Durban had been unsuccessful. I had to work most weekends so we began discussing the idea of me quitting nursing. We were so in love and wanted to get married and go to America. I could be a nurse there. We dreaded bringing it up with Dad again.

"Let's not mention it until we've had our vacation," Boris said. "Meanwhile we still haven't asked your Mom and Dad if they will let us go on vacation together this year."

The next weekend we plucked up some courage. We waited for Dad to finish his lunch and have a cool beer. He lay out in the sun relaxing in his lounge chair as we approached him.

"Dad?"

"What do you two want now?"

"Can we go to the berg together and then go to Joburg to visit Tom and Gwen in October?" Dad sat up straight in his chair. He didn't answer right away. We fidgeted about looking all around the garden. Silent.

"Well, I don't see why not. Where are you thinking of going?"

"Drakensberg Gardens," I muttered. I could not believe Dad was so casual.

Boris and I by the car, Ebie and Trish with Dad sunbathing

"Well you might as well go if you can afford it. Boris you had better look after my girl and if anything happens to her, by God I'll bloody well shoot you. And I mean it. Do you understand?"

"Oh yes I do! Thank you sir, thank you!" He was astonished. Dad sure had mellowed. I think he liked Boris. He never said much, but we were so happy and telephoned the berg right away to make our plans.

We often spent time with Ronnie Kelly who I had met on my first date with Boris. A brilliant, funny chap with a pointy nose like the joker, Ronnie was studying at the University of Natal to become a nuclear physicist. He rode a Triumph motorbike and often took me on the back when Boris was at work and I had a day off. One of those days he took me to the university and showed me all about nuclear energy. I didn't really understand much of what he told me, it seemed a very difficult subject. Ronnie lived at home right across the road from Tom and Gwen where Boris stayed.

We spent many hours at the Kelly's house playing LP's. We'd lie around their lounge listening to Louis Armstrong and Sammy Davis Junior, playing them over and over again. Old Mr. Kelly never seemed to finish remodeling their house and everything was covered in dust. Mrs. Kelly never fussed about anything. She loved her boys as she called Ronnie and Boris. One afternoon Boris told her that Tom and Gwen were moving to Johannesburg. "Why don't you come and live here with us?" Mrs. Kelly said to his surprise and gave him a hearty squeeze. "One more won't make any difference. Mr. Kelly is busy adding on another bedroom so it may as well get filled up. No use having a great big house with nobody in it. Besides, it makes me feel young with you lot around." Mrs. Kelly had always been very fond of Boris. He teased and kidded around with her and you could tell she liked it. So with that Boris found somewhere to live and we could carry on with our plans to go to America.

I had done two years of my nurses training and wanted it to be my life's work but I was madly in love. We wanted to be

Ronnie Kelly

together. Boris hated the drive to Maritzburg every weekend. How can we go on this way, I thought.

"Maybe I can quit nursing and we can get married, then I can carry on with my training in America?"

"You just can't, I'd feel guilty for the rest of my life."

"I'm not giving it up. It's just temporary. I'll study in America."

As a sixteen-year old school girl I'd read so many books about Cherry Ames the nurse, I pictured myself as Cherry Ames Special Nurse or Cherry Ames Field Nurse. I imagined bumping into movie stars in Hollywood, probably nursing them when they were sick.

The next weekend we decided to approach Mom and Dad. The sun was warm and Dad sat outside on the lawn in his lounge chair with a book sipping his Sunday beer. He'd pulled his running shoes off and they were lying next to his chair with his shirt. Dad loved to improve his suntan every weekend. He looked so brown and relaxed as we walked over and lay down on the grass near him.

"Dad, we need to talk to you." He put his book down. I looked at the cover, another war story. Dad only read war stories.

"What's up now?" His frown lines deepened.

"Well, we are trying to work out how to get to America." We explained the visa situation. Dad didn't say anything for a minute or two while I picked at the grass, twisting it around my fingers.

"What's the rush? You kids have your whole life ahead of you."

We looked at each other. I couldn't think of a quick answer. Didn't he realize we were in love and couldn't bear to be apart another month, never mind another year?

"Well we've been thinking about going sooner," Boris said timidly, "and Dorothy could continue nursing in America."

"Good God! After all this work, Dorothy just gives up her training. Are you two mad?"

"No. Well I've been thinking about ways to solve the problem and thought maybe I could quit and finish later," I burst out.

"Just give up the career you've dreamt about for years. Just like that, as if it was like changing your pants? Impossible. What on earth has got into your heads?"

"I don't know Dad, we love each other and we want to be together. We miss each other all the time and they won't let me move to Addington or get married so I just thought . . . "

"You just thought? You haven't thought this through at all or you wouldn't be talking like this." Dad's fury showed in his face and eyes, his brows lowered and his smile disappeared.

He sat bolt upright on his chaise lounge and slung his feet over the side. "I don't know Doff. I thought you had more common sense that this." His sad blue eyes began to water. I couldn't look at him. I was too full of my own emotions and didn't even see how much hurt I was creating in his heart. Boris stood up and tried to smile at Dad. "We'll have to think this through more thoroughly. Let's not talk about it any more today." He changed the subject and nobody spoke about it again that day. We stayed for lunch as Mom had made a lovely roast beef and Yorkshire pudding. We marveled at how high it had risen and I said I hoped I could match it one day. I could feel the undercurrent at the table but my young sisters loved having Boris around so they relieved the tension with their silly talk.

The seed had been planted and I couldn't let it go. I became obsessed thinking about how we could do everything, be happy and have it all.

❖

One weekend I had a few days off so I went down to Durban to stay with the Kelly's where Boris lived. I had come to know Mrs. Kelly and became very fond of her. She was older than my Mom, quite round and not very stylishly dressed. She had a sweet face, a pointy nose and a double chin. She spent almost all her days in the kitchen baking, frying something and cooking up another big meal.

I stayed over on Monday and went into town with Boris when he went to work. I looked around the shops waiting to meet him for lunch. He took me down to the Cuban Hat on the beachfront and we had Cuban pineapple hamburgers. When he had to go back to work, I wandered out onto the main road thinking I would take a bus into the center of town. As I stood on the corner of the street waiting for the bus a yellow VW bug pulled up to the corner. The driver asked me if I would like a lift into town. He was wearing a suit and tie and looked friendly and pleasant so I said thanks and hopped into the car. As we drove along the highway he smiled at me.

"Where are you going? It's a beautiful day and you are a beautiful girl. Would you like to go and have some coffee down by the beach?"

"No thank you. I just had lunch a short while ago. I want to go to one of my favorite shops in the center of town. Can you just drop me off near the City Hall please?"

We pulled up to a traffic light and stopped. He put his arm out across my chest and pushed me back against the seat fairly gently.

"My you have a beautiful profile," he said smiling. "You look like the bohemian type. I would like to paint you."

"No I don't think my fiancé would appreciate that." I could feel sweat running down the middle of my back. I didn't trust this guy. What had I got myself into?

"He wouldn't have to know. You could come to my studio for the afternoon and I could drop you off later."

As he drove on down the street, I was silent and nervous. My jaw shook and I could hardly breathe. It dawned on me that I could be with a rapist or a murderer or both. I stared straight ahead, longing for the next light to turn red. It was green and we carried on.

"What's the matter, did I make you nervous. Don't be frightened of me. I am just an ordinary man who knows beauty when he sees it. I didn't mean to startle you."

"Well you did and I want to get out. Now!"

"We aren't far from the City Hall, I can drop you there."

Just then the light turned red and he pulled to a halt. I opened the car door, jumped out and ran down the street as fast as I could. I reached the next corner, breathless and terrified, my heart beating right out of my chest. I looked back and saw the little yellow VW buzz away around the corner.

Later that afternoon I told Boris about the incident. He could not believe I had taken a ride with a stranger. "You just don't ever do that again. You have no idea how dangerous that is, you could have been murdered." I realized it only too well. I sat by a man I did not know, flattering an ordinary, trusting girl like me. I knew I would never be that foolish ever again.

❖

One Sunday night a short time before leaving on our trip to the berg and Johannesburg, we were sitting in the car in an isolated part of the countryside talking about our life to come. I had to go back to the Nurses Home that night and we climbed into the back seat of the car so we could be close. The bucket seats in the front with a gear lever between were most uncomfortable for a smooch. The night was warm so I was only wearing a thin cotton dress, a bra, lace pants and sandals. We clung to each other desperately and he whispered in my ear. "Babe, I love you and want you, it is so hard to leave." I could feel him pressed against me. He held me against his chest and we touched in places we had never touched before. He felt so warm and tender next to me. I nuzzled closer but thought I must not do this because Mom said one thing leads to another. I tried to withdraw and just kiss him, but the thrill opened the door to new sensations and I didn't stop him. We touched in secret places and I loved it and him. "That's enough," I said and we pulled away from each other. "You better take me back to the Nurses Home now." I tried to sit back and relax but we were both breathless and grabbed at each other again. "I'd better go before we do something."

He drove me back and we parted with great difficulty. It was late when I walked into the Nurse's Home and no one was about. I wandered into the ablution area and looked at myself in the long mirror, it wasn't the innocent me any more. I felt like a changed girl, stepping into the world of womanhood. I touched my face where he had caressed it and smiled at myself, so happy. I wondered if anyone would see a change in me. Back in my tiny room I lay down on the bed and stretched out naked, enjoying the slight warm breeze tickle my body all over, thinking of him as I drifted off to sleep.

❖

Boris was an only child. He had never experienced the joy and fun of having brothers and sisters. His parents left him with their friends Tom and Gwen and went off to America when he was only nineteen. They wrote occasionally about the wonders of the country always presuming he would follow them when he finished his five-year apprenticeship to become a journeyman. He had planned to join his parents in America in the near future. The dream changed when I came into the picture. Boris was following his dream.

The more we talked about going to America the more I began to realize. My impression of America was all romantic imagination and what I had learned in high school geography class. But in the real world of anticipation, I was too young to understand the undertaking of leaving home, the country I loved and all it meant to me. While Boris was thinking of how to get me a visa, I was thinking about leaving Mom and Dad, my three sisters, my friends, my career and my whole life. Our thoughts and concerns were at opposite ends of the spectrum. But like two blind birds in love, our hormones pumping, we wanted to be together no matter what.

I knew I was receiving excellent and thorough training but felt trapped. Our family never had money to pay for me to attend university, so the opportunity to attend nurses training free meant a lot to me. But I realized I could not have every-thing. I hadn't expected to fall in love so young and with such intensity, early in my career training.

We found out that in order for me to go to America I had to obtain British Citizenship. The American Consulate told us that the British quota for immigrants was open. The South African quota was only twenty-one per year and the waiting list fifteen years long. In order for me to get British Citizenship we had to get married.

❖ 15 ❖

Wedding Plans
1957-1958

Boris and I

Two more years before I finished my nursing training seemed like such a long time to us. So we went back to the plan to get married. I would quit nursing and get a job until we had enough money to go.

The week after we asked Mom and Dad what they thought of the idea of me continuing my training in America, I decided I would go to Matron and ask her opinion. By this time I had become used to the nursing regimen and wasn't as terrified of Matron as I had been in the early days. I walked over to the main building during my lunch hour and slunk past Matron's office to see if she was in. Sitting at her desk reading some papers, she looked quite calm, so I knocked softly on her door. She looked up and smiled.

"Nurse Greenland, what can I do for you?"

"Oh, I just wanted to ask you something."

"Well come in." I stood rigidly in front of her orderly desk, the shelves behind filled with books on Anatomy, Surgery and Medicine.

"Sit down, I'm not going to bite you. What is it you want to ask me about?" I sat down on one of the straight back wooden chairs in front of her.

"I am engaged and I want to ask you about my nursing career."

"You know you can't get married until you have finished your training. You agreed to that in the beginning." I wanted to run out of her office. I don't know why I thought I could discuss it with her.

"Well actually I want to talk about leaving." My chest felt so tight, I could hardly breathe.

"You want to leave, now? Right in the middle, when you have come so far?"

"Well not really. I don't want to leave but I don't know what to do. My fiancé wants to go to America," I blurted out. We glared at each other. I looked down at the uneven highly polished floorboards, the room heavy with silence.

"Do you have any idea what you are thinking of doing? You are so young. You have a career to think of and all the work you have done. This is just pure foolishness. You should go back to work now and think this through. Then come and see me tomorrow." She picked up the papers she had been reading and gave me a long hard look.

"I'll do that." I hurried out of her office and ran back to the ward. I got back into my working mode, scrubbed, cleaned and tidied patients until they were sick of me.

That night I phoned Boris. I had to wait for over fifteen minutes before the phone was free and I only had about four tickies so I wouldn't be able to talk for long.

"I talked to Matron today, she thinks I am mad to quit." Silence. "I don't have much change, I can't talk very long."

"Why don't you ask her if you can carry on your training in America? Maybe she knows about that? I love you, we'll be very happy together and I know it will all work out." I wasn't so sure. I felt doubt creeping into my heart. What if I left everything behind and couldn't find a job? What if he didn't love me anymore after we got to America? The whole romantic idea seemed to be crumbling in front of me. He was twenty-four, I was only nineteen. I felt quite grown up most of the time, but everyone told me I was too young to decide.

"Please insert another coin," said the automatic voice. I didn't have one.

"I'll call you tomorrow, I love you," I shouted desperately and the line went dead. I walked out of the phone booth into the hallway, girls were laughing and joking happily. I climbed slowly up the stairs to my room. As I inched my way up I decided I wasn't going to be young any more. I had managed to do all sorts of things I had wanted before, why not now? I resolved to see Matron the next day, tell her I wanted to leave and find out how I would do that. Then I would tell Mom and Dad and we could begin to make our plans.

When I went to visit Matron I had made up my mind I would not be dissuaded. "Do you realize you are giving up one of the best careers in the world? You can go anywhere with it but you have to be qualified."

"I'll take it up again in America," I rationalized.

"Have you told your parents?"

"No, I decided to tell you first."

"You made a contract with the hospital. You have studied hard, you have friends here and you're throwing it all away just like that?"

"Matron I have decided this is what I want to do and it's difficult for me to explain how I feel." I couldn't look at her. I stared down at the polished floor waving my feet under the chair, sweaty hands clenched. The humidity in the room intensified and I could feel the perspiration trickling down my armpits.

"Very well,'" she said, "I will prepare the paperwork for you to sign and contact you when it is ready. As long as you are here you will continue working on your regular schedule. You may go." I stood up as Matron turned her chair, picked up a folder and walked outside into the sunshine. I didn't really want to leave nursing. I was torn between giving up my career and the new feelings I had for Boris and my desire to be with him. The severity of my actions did not sink in.

Later I told my best friend Pat my decision. She was devastated. We lay out on the verandah in the dark and cried. "I can't imagine being here without you." We lay on our beds talking about our nursing life for hours, but I had made the decision and would not change my mind.

That weekend we told Mom that Matron had said I could leave and I would get a regular job until it was time to go. I had never seen my Dad so upset. Mom didn't say a word. She put down her knitting and just looked at me for a long time.

"God Doff, are you sure you are making the right decision? Hell man, this is such a big step in your life, you just don't have any idea."

"I do. I know it's going to be hard but I love him. I want to do what he wants and I think it will be an exciting adventure. We are thinking we will only go for one year to see what it's like. I will be back before you know it." I wanted to reassure them and make them be happy for me. Mom forced a thin smile.

"Well Dave, you know we did what we wanted when we got married and now it's their turn. It's just so hard to get used to the idea of them going so far away." Dad looked grim and opened the newspaper. All that evening we talked about our ideas with enthusiasm but it would be a while before they could get over the shock of it all.

We had so much to do what with planning a wedding and filling out paperwork that the day I had to leave Grey's came upon me way too fast. Packing my things and lugging them out to the car amongst a million goodbyes, my friends hugging me and wishing me luck, was one of the saddest days of my life. Leaving all my friends far overshadowed the excitement ahead. I sat next to Boris in the car miserable, sniffing all the way home. When I saw Mom at the back door as we drove up the driveway, I cried like I never had before and jumped out of the car to be with her.

"Well Doff you have made your bed and now you must lie on it." Mom always used her favorite sayings to make a point, but she hugged me and held me tight. I could feel her chest heaving against mine and we stood that way for a long while.

Moving home proved difficult. The house seemed so small. Sheila was away at school so I settled into my old room and my two younger sisters shared the bedroom next door to me. They were noisy and very nosey. They wanted to know everything I did and on weekends when Boris came to visit we never got a minute to ourselves.

Everyday I looked in the newspaper for a job I could handle. I soon realized I didn't know anything except how to wash bedpans and patients and hand out medicines. I couldn't

Mom and Dad on the garden swing

type fifty words a minute or use an adding machine or operate a telephone switchboard. I took chances and went to interviews but no one ever called me back so I decided to teach myself to type. Mom was a good typist and she had a few handwritten pages of instruction on how to practice that she kept from her school days. Boris lent me enough money to rent a typewriter for a week. I sat down and opened the instructions. I laid my fingers gently on the letters in the middle as shown on page one, ASDFG for the left hand and HJKL for the right, then up one finger and back, and the same with the right hand.

Easy. I practiced the lessons for eight hours a day and typed the sentences provided. Mom cut the sides off a shoebox and covered the keyboard so I couldn't look. Over and over my fingers felt their way across and up and down the keyboard. By the end of the week I could type thirty-five words a minute. Of course I did the same sentences all the time, but I decided I was ready to go out into the office world and say I could type.

I applied for all the "typing required" jobs in the Ad. Some asked me to do a typing test but I made so many mistakes they would just say, "Thank you we'll let you know." Finally I got an interview at *McDonalds Seeds and Feed*. A sweet elderly man interviewed me who knew my Dad. "Well," he told me, "we are willing to train someone to use the Burroughs book-keeping machine and I think you will work out fine." I didn't dare tell him I was going to America one day. I needed the money and a job.

I started with a small salary and sat down in front of an enormous machine that whirred and clanked and rattled back and forth. I had to insert a statement and enter the sales slips of that particular customer for the day. Next to me stood a file drawer with statements filed in alphabetical order. I read the name on the sales sheet and pulled the statement. Then I inserted it into a slot, entered the figures on the keyboard and pushed a button. The machine switched back and forth, clicking and clacking. When it was done it popped the statement up. I shoved it back into its slot in the file and went on to the next one.

Once I learned the procedure I had to do this all day on my own with my set of customers from my file. There were four of these machines. The other three girls were old hands. They banged, slapped and grabbed statements in and out, their arms flying back and forth. Their pace astonished me. "You'll get the hang of it in a week, don't worry." They clattered on and on. They could enter numbers and talk at the same time. I had to concentrate and remember each step before pushing the "Enter" button. If I left out one step it fowled up the system and I would have to do it over again. At the end of the day the machine spat out a total figure for all the entries I had made and it had to match the number of the added sales slips.

I held my breath every day when that number came out. At first I was off most of the time but I soon realized that I had better be careful rather than fast. I had to stay late to find my mistakes. When I finally got through one week without an error, everyone cheered and we went out to the local pub for a beer.

We set the date for our wedding, April the 26th. I began to sew my wedding dress and the dresses for my sister Sheila and my old pal Joan from school days who agreed to be bridesmaids. Mrs. Kelly said she would supply the chicken for the wedding dinner and Aunt Vida volunteered to make the wedding cake. She made cakes regularly for her friends so I knew it would be beautiful. Since Mom sang in the church choir, the organist agreed to play for free and the boys' choir would sing and lead us into church. As a very active member of the MOTHS Club, Dad got their hall free. The Indian bar tender at the club loved Dad and his sense of humor. He said he would serve the drinks for free too.

I called Boris.

"Babe, our wedding is going to be practically free, everyone is helping us."

"Man, am I grateful, we'd have to elope if we didn't get all this help." We were saving every penny for the fare to America and worrying about how we could have a wedding at all when Mom and Dad's friends and our family came together to help make it a reality.

We went to a travel agent to find out the cost of going on a ship. She found us a trip all the way to America for fifty-two pounds. We would take a freighter that took passengers to England. Then we would board a Holland America Line ship from England to New York. How exciting it sounded. Three weeks at sea to England, where we would catch a train to Boris's birthplace and meet his family. Two weeks later we would take the eight-day trip to New York. We signed the contract and booked the trip.

I became so involved with my own plans I didn't give a thought to Mom and Dad's anxiety. I whirled around the house rushing from one project to another. The dining room table was covered in sewing. I left it strewn all over the table and the floor, paper patterns blowing about and pins dropping everywhere. Wedding gifts arrived and piled up in the lounge.

Short tempered with my little sisters, I barely shared with them what was going on. I had to make a going away dress for my honeymoon while Mom was trying to sew a dress for herself in between my turmoil.

"What am I going to wear?" my little sisters wanted to know.

"I'll make you each a dress too." I developed bad headaches worrying about all the sewing and the cost.

"It's just stress." Mom said. Kind and helpful as always, she put up with my frantic behavior. I didn't have time to think about the plans for going to America during those months before the wedding. Boris made all the arrangements and contacted the British Consulate to find out how I could become a British Citizen. Since he was born in England they told him I would automatically be a citizen once we were married. All we had to do was send in our marriage license, my birth certificate and money, and it would all be handled.

One of Boris's friends told him we should have a pre-nuptial contract. I had no idea what that meant. He explained it was a contract that said, "What's mine is mine and what's his is his." Since we didn't have anything I couldn't imagine why we needed it but we spent twelve pounds getting the contract drawn up. When the paperwork was ready Boris gave me the twelve pounds to pay the lawyer. I rolled it up tight, put a rubber band around it and put it in my purse. The next day my friends were giving me a bachelorette party and we caught a bus across town to the Wanderers Club to celebrate. It seemed like a coming of age party for me. Somewhere between home, the bus ride and all the laughing and giggling, I lost the twelve pounds.

I searched high and low. I must have emptied my bag out on the table ten times hoping it would magically reappear. I phoned the bus company to see if they had found it. Of course it never turned up. I waited days before I confessed to Boris I had lost the money. I had no idea how I would ever replace it. I learned more about his true decency and good nature through that episode. I expected him to be furious with me and shout and yell like Dad did when we did something idiotic. "Don't worry," he said, "we'll manage, there is no use being so upset about it." He was so kind and sympathetic towards my distress.

The following weekend Boris arrived with brochures about the ships we were going to sail on. *The Oranjefontein*, a cargo ship that carried a hundred passengers looked very small in the picture. They allowed about thirty passengers in first class on the upper deck. The brochure featured attractive staterooms with big picture windows, a blue swimming pool surrounded by a good size deck, a beautifully furnished large dining room and a bar, for the first class passengers only. "Well, that looks nice but what about us? Are there any pictures of the stateroom we will be sleeping in?" We studied the deck drawing carefully. Ours was two decks below first class. I turned the brochure to the back page where it showed a picture of a small dining room and a typical second-class cabin with narrow bunk beds one above the other. We would be sharing the bathroom with the cabin next to us. I didn't really mind the look of the ship but I had such mixed emotions about going off to sea and leaving all my family.

The reality was beginning to sink in. I had made a commitment and there was no turning back. The price we could afford for a cabin on the ship from England to America appeared to be on the lowest level without even a porthole. The *S.S. Ryndam* looked much bigger in the picture, a real cruise ship that sailed back and forth between Southampton and New York. I showed Mom the brochures and the deck plans. "That's nice," she said. "I haven't been on a ship since I was a young girl when we left East Africa. I can't remember much about it except it was very hot in our cabin." So wrapped up with my own plans, I didn't notice her subdued stoicism. Mom hid her true emotions from me then. She wiped her hands on her apron and went back into the kitchen.

Boris and I studied the calendar and calculated the days and months we would need to accomplish all our plans so that we could choose the right dates and make reservations at the right time. *The Oranjefontein* was due to leave Durban on July third. The ship took four days to get to Cape Town and would stay there for four more days loading cargo and then leave for England.

We figured out if we got married in April, we could apply for British Citizenship, go to the American consulate and be ready to leave in July. Neither of us had ever done anything this adventurous on our own before so it was difficult to make a final decision. We lay outside on the grass with the calendar spread out and the brochures open, planning every detail, writing it down and calculating the time required. It was a sweet happy time for us, feeling so close, imagining our futures together. My younger sisters were curious about our plans but I brushed them aside impatiently, "We're working out our trip to America, and you're just too young to understand." They were just kids, what did they know about the big decisions we had to make. It never occurred to me that they might be worrying about me leaving.

Boris went home late Sunday night. I stood in the dark driveway by myself and watched him drive up the road, the car lights shining ahead, as he disappeared around the corner. Soon we wouldn't have to do this anymore. I turned slowly and meandered back into the house filled with longing for this to change and the thrill of being together all the time.

The day of the wedding arrived at last. Our little house was in chaos. I left the mess early to get my hair rolled up in a chignon, which I thought looked really dashing. I had to catch the bus home, but as it was only a short distance I didn't worry about the time. Sheila and I both dressed in our small bedroom we shared. I couldn't pull on the big hoop that fit under my skirt until I got outside so I left it on the front verandah so I wouldn't forget it. Dad's friend Cuppy arrived with his newly polished Opel and parked it in our driveway so Dad could drive me to the church.

The wedding was set for two o'clock that warm Saturday but Dad appeared fully dressed by one. He began looking nervously at his watch and tapping it with his finger every time one of us passed him as he sat rigid in his favorite chair in the lounge. "There's one thing I hate and that is for the bride to be late for her own wedding."

I rushed past him into the bathroom chasing my two young sisters out. Mom powdered her face and rubbed rouge on her cheeks and smothered her lips with Vaseline before applying her lipstick. She rolled her lips as she studied her image in the mirror.

"Come on Con, we haven't got all day and you've got to get to the Church before us." Things were getting tense.

"Shut up Dave, I'm not going to be late. Are you kids almost ready?"

The photographer wanted to take a picture of me sitting in front of the dressing table so I had to inch past the mob in the passage into Mom's room for the pose. At last they all left with Mom and it was just Dad and I and the photographer. I pulled my hoop up under my dress on the front lawn and scrambled into the car. I posed for pictures as I tried to arrange myself so the hoop wasn't sticking up like a clown's in the circus. Dad went to climb into the driver's seat and reached over the back of the seat to take a good look at me. "By God Doff, you look so beautiful." A broad grin wrinkled up his tanned face. We looked into each other's eyes taking a moment to feel the intense emotion of the situation. "Well, we'd better get going, we don't want to be late." He turned around and switched on the engine.

When we drove up to the church my bridesmaids stood waiting. Teddy Hogan's choirboys were all dressed in their

Choirboys with the organist's wife Peggy

black cassocks and tightly pleated white collars ready for the procession. The usher gave the signal and the church filled with organ music. The choirboys proceeded down the aisle followed by my sister and Joan in their azure blue dresses and picture hats. Dad took my arm, "Ready Doff?" We stepped through the grand old wooded doors in time to Wagner's wedding march.

As I walked down the aisle I saw so many of my friends smiling at us, then Mom looking back, her eyes filled with tears, her gloved hands folded at her waist, her handbag dangling on her arm. Finally I saw Boris's beaming smile, standing straight and tall with his hands crossed looking towards me. I clutched Dad's arm as I stepped one foot in front of the other in time with the music. When I reached him, he took my hand from Dad and squeezed it so tight. I could hardly breathe. I turned to face my future husband and we looked into each other's eyes like we never had before, a long lingering look. His eyes were so blue. We came back to the present as the parson bellowed, "Who giveth this woman?" I heard my Dad say, "I do" so softly, his voice quivering with emotion.

We only had one wedding ring and Boris struggled to slide it onto my finger. I never thought about a ring for him. Then the organ burst into song and the guests sang the hymn we had

Wedding Day — April 26th, 1958

chosen, or rather been advised to choose, with gusto. I tried to sing and pushed the hymnbook in front of Boris. "Sing with me," I whispered, but he couldn't make a sound. Then it was all over and we turned happily towards the crowd. We marched down the aisle with Teddy the organist pounding Beethoven's Fifth as we burst out into the sunshine. Showers of paper confetti fell into my hair and my face and everyone cheered.

Our reception was a joyous affair, everyone enjoying Aunt Dolly's chicken sandwiches, Aunt Vida's beautiful wedding cake

Cutting Aunt Vida's Wedding Cake

and lots of dancing. I dashed away to change into my going away dress and pranced back into the reception all dressed with hat and gloves ready to throw my bouquet. Boris took my hand and the crowd formed a long arch with their hands joined as we left the party and trotted happily through it towards the car. When we tried to leave, Boris's friends gathered round and lifted the car off the ground so the wheels spun in the air and we went nowhere. Suddenly they dropped the car and we roared away down the road, strings of tin cans rattling behind us. As soon as we were well out of sight, we stopped, and Boris scrambled under the car to undo the strings. They had done a thorough job of tying them up. About five miles out of town Boris asked me if I had brought the keys to the suitcases. I looked at him and thought for a second. I knew exactly where they were. They were still sitting on my dressing table where I had hidden them so no one could fill my suitcase with confetti. "Oh no! I've left them behind in my room!"

"You what?" He pulled over to the side of the road and stopped. "How could you forget?"

"I didn't mean to. Things were so hectic!" I started to cry.

He turned the car around and began to drive home in silence. It seemed like a big deal at that moment but it turned into the smallest matter of our life as we worked our way through the next couple of months.

❖ 16 ❖

Going to America
July 1958

Last family picnic before leaving

After our two-week honeymoon at The Oyster Box Hotel in Umhlanga Rocks, I applied for British Citizenship. A simple procedure, I just had to show my marriage license, Boris produced his British birth certificate and my application was granted.

Next we visited the American Consulate where we received detailed instructions on what to do to get a resident visa to America. This procedure was much more complicated, but we proceeded slowly getting police clearance, x-rays and medical check ups. I left my job at McDonalds Feeds with more sadness. Mr. Wiley had been so kind and tolerant of my bumbling machine operating skills and me, but I had become a more competent operator so he was sad to see me leave. I began to pack my clothes at home and slowly the realization of what I was about to do began to sink in. I moved to Mrs. Kelly's house sixty miles away from Mom and Dad and my two youngest sisters and missed them all terribly. I called Mom every day with a progress report on the impending visas.

We went up to Maritzburg some weekends to visit and I understood more each day what a big part they played in my life. Boris continued to work so we could save every penny possible for the trip. I busied myself sewing and writing lists of all the things we had to do. I did not drive so when I went into Durban I caught a bus and sometimes I would meet Boris for lunch. We'd go and sit down by the beach where we used to go while I was at Wentworth. Slowly we began to appreciate the many things we loved about South Africa and would miss once we left. Small things like the Zulu rickshaw boys in their traditional feathered dress that would run along the Esplanade and take us back to his workplace, or the thousands of pigeons along the beach front cluttering the pathway so there was nowhere to step. We loved the salty sea air and the sound of the waves crashing ceaselessly onto the beach. How many times had we plunged and jumped over and through them, as they thrashed us into the sand and we sunk underneath the pounding sea thinking we'd never come up again?

Although we lived in a time of great political strife for the different races in South Africa, in our own home we had our dedicated family servants whom we had grown to love. For me, our native girl Pawpaw as we had nicknamed her when we first moved to Maritzburg, was part of our family. She had been around us since I was fourteen. She loved and bantered with my younger sisters everyday. When I told her I was going away to America she became extremely upset. Pawpaw sniffled and wiped her eyes with her old hankie and brushed away the tears running down her lovely brown face. "*How how, Misses, wena hamba.*" For Boris, Mrs. Kelly's native garden boy and her housekeeper were very special. It began to sink in how much we would miss so many different people in our lives.

I could barely talk to Mom about leaving. We'd fall silent as we both choked back our emotions. I'd try to be casual and chat as if it wasn't breaking my heart. As the time got closer to the departure date Mom and I talked every day. I ran all my decisions by her and we talked on the phone endlessly. Before we were married I always wanted to go to Durban for the weekends. It seemed like a complete drag to stay at home with my parents. Now living near Durban, I wanted to go to Maritzburg every weekend and see them. Every minute with Mom and Dad was so precious. I started worrying. I didn't know if I'd ever see them again. "America is so far away," I said to Mom. She reassured me that my place was with my husband now. She acted so stoic and brave and Dad gave us endless useless instructions about travel and coping. He seemed quite convinced we'd never make it to America. I felt completely confident we'd make it quite well on our own. After all I was twenty, grown up and married. I thought I knew everything.

The next few weeks I took the bus in and out of town getting organized. We found a stunning travel trunk in a luggage store but it was much too expensive for our budget so we settled on four large brown, fake leather suitcases. We bought two each for the trip. We lay them open on the floor so we could get an idea of how much stuff we could take. The first thing that came up while discussing what we would have to leave behind was my nursing notebooks. I had taken copious notes in black hardbound books and spent hours carefully drawing every bone on the body and all the insides too. I was very proud of my bone drawings. They were works of art. I sketched every detail in pencil with light and dark shadows, smoothed and rubbed so they were almost three-dimensional.

"Why don't you give them to Helga," Boris suggested, "She's studying nursing. She could use them."

"Who? Helga your old girlfriend? I wouldn't think of giving them to her."

"Well give them to somebody, they're too heavy to take."

What did he know about my books? He's not throwing away his old printing books. Packing began to create resentment and things became tense. We couldn't talk about it because my emotions got the better of me. Leaving my life behind slowly became a reality and everything I touched had meaning and needed to be in my suitcase.

The following week we received a call that our visas had come through. We went to the American Consul and they reviewed all the final paperwork with us. It included a set of lung x-rays, a TB test, a certificate of good health from the Natal Health Department, and a police certificate indicating we had no criminal record. They stamped an official visa into our brand new British passports and stapled the paperwork in the back. Everything was placed in a large brown envelope and sealed up ready to hand to the Immigration Officer when we arrived in America. We went into the travel agent a week before it was time to leave to pick up our tickets for the two ships, The S.S. *Oranjefontein* to London and *The S.S. Ryndam* from Southampton to New York. We were instructed to board the ship at twelve o'clock on Saturday, July the third. The fifty-two pound tickets each represented almost a whole month's salary. As we walked out of the travel agent's office it felt so final. Excitement radiated out of Boris as he took my hand in his, skipping towards our car. I could only think of leaving Mom and Dad and my sisters. I tried not to show my sadness that day as the finality began to sink into my heart.

I phoned Mom the minute I got home. "We got our visas and tickets today." Silence. "It's getting so close to the time to go Mom. Did Dad get the day off to come down to the ship to see us off?"

"You know he did. Everyone is coming to see you off. Aunt Vida and Aunty Dolly, and some of your friends have phoned me to get the details."

"Mom, I'm dreading that day. I can hardly think about it without choking up. I'm trying hard to keep busy. Boris doesn't want me to take all my nursing notebooks I made. He thinks we have too much luggage already."

"Well you know pet you have to be practical." I'll never hear Mom call me her pet again I thought. I didn't want to leave all my stuff behind. Making the decision on what to take and what to leave was the most stressful thing I had ever done.

A few days before our departure date, Boris's friends took us out for our last get together. We had a load of fun, got rather drunk and took a couple of pub beer mugs home with us. Needless to say Boris wanted to pack the beer mugs in amongst

Boris and I with my sisters on the motorcycle
the day before we left for America

our clothes. He thought we'd be so glad to have them to remind us of our last night with our friends.

"What about my nursing books?" I fussed.

"They're far too heavy. These mugs will get stuffed with clothes and they don't weigh anything anyway." His reasoning was so practical. I gave up and left the books with Mrs. Kelly to keep. "For when I come back in a year or so," I said.

The day before we were to leave we packed and repacked. We stuffed some of our wedding presents, silver dishes and little boxes of silver cake forks and teaspoons and everything we could into each and every corner of the suitcases. Finally we closed the lids and I sat on top to squash them down while Boris tried to latch and lock them. They were so heavy we could barely drag them to the front door. We laid out our clothes on a chair and climbed into bed exhausted falling asleep in minutes.

About one o'clock in the morning I awoke startled by a terrifying dream that Mom and Dad were dead. I sat up in bed soaking wet, so relieved to find it wasn't real. I shook Boris. "Wake up. I had a terrible dream about Mom and Dad." He took me in his arms to comfort me and we held hands and talked the rest of the night, finally dropping off to sleep about five in the morning.

We got up at seven and I phoned Mom right away. "Are you ready yet? Come to Mrs. Kelly's house early. It's our last day, I want to spend as much time with you as I can." Mom assured me they'd be leaving soon.

"Your father's been up and down all night."

"Ok," I choked, not wanting Mom to hear my quivering voice.

I pulled on the stylish, navy blue dress I had sewn during the past few weeks. I'd added a white v-shaped inlay down the front and thought it looked very smart. I did my hair up in a French roll and put my makeup on with extra care. I put my new pair of white gloves into my handbag and went downstairs. Mr. Kelly helped Boris load the suitcases into two cars. Boris's long time friend Mike and his new wife Lorraine had agreed to drive us to the ship. Shortly after they loaded the suitcases, Mom, Dad and my three sisters arrived. Mrs. Kelly made us all a cup of tea while we sat around making idle talk.

It was the last time we'd have tea in Mrs. Kelly's funny half-built house. The last time she'd shoo the chickens out of the driveway. I breathed in the smell of bacon. I sniffed the doggy smells and patted them all lolling about in the kitchen near the warmth of the stove. How happy I had been there with Mrs. Kelly as I prepared for the trip. We wandered slowly outside saying goodbye for the tenth time to the garden boy and the housekeeper and climbed into Michael's car. Mr. Kelly hugged us once more. He looked like an untidy old leprechaun, forlorn and sad.

"You understand I can't come to see you off. I just can't do that sort of thing."

"We understand." He waved us out of the driveway as we all set off to *The SS Oranjefontein* tied up in the Durban Harbor.

Driving to the ship with Mike and Lorraine helped relieve my extreme tension. Mike made silly jokes with Boris and put us at ease so I didn't think constantly about leaving or saying goodbye.

"Hell man, I'm going to miss you Boris, you bugger. Who will go down to the Rugby Hotel with me on Friday nights?" Mike's infectious high-pitched laugh filled the car.

"You're not going to the pub every bloody night anymore now," chimed in Lorraine. They had been married about six months and I could tell she was in charge. We laughed light-heartedly about silly things all the way in to town. We loved this couple. Boris had been friends with Mike for years and the four of us had grown very fond of each other since they got married.

Ebie, Dad, Mom, Trish, Boris and I, Sheila
Departure Day

I had not seen the ship before. When we pulled up alongside, the natives ran up to the car to unload our luggage. They laughed and exclaimed in Zulu about the weight as they hauled them onto the ship's loading ramp. I looked up and realized how very small the ship was. At the bottom of the gangway, the purser checked our tickets and our passports. So many of our friends were milling around looking at the ship, it overwhelmed me. They began hugging Boris and me and wishing us well. I looked at how many friends we had, so many people I never thought would come to see us off were there. I never realized we meant so much to so many. All the attention and outpouring of love and friendship began getting the better of me. I didn't want to cry and muck up my makeup but it soon became impossible. I sobbed uncontrollably as we hugged each of them goodbye. Then Boris took my hand and led me up the gangway steps. We stopped half way up and waved and everyone shouted bon voyage and waved some more.

Mom, Dad and my sisters followed us up. They let my aunts, cousins, Michael and Lorraine come aboard to see us off. We found our cabin and everyone trooped down several flights to see it. We were told we should have been on a lower deck but luckily someone had cancelled and we got a cabin one deck above with a porthole. When you peeked out the water line was just below it. The cabin looked very small. There were two bunk beds, one above the other, about two and a half feet wide. At the end of the room under the porthole there was a small dressing table and a washbasin. We had to share a

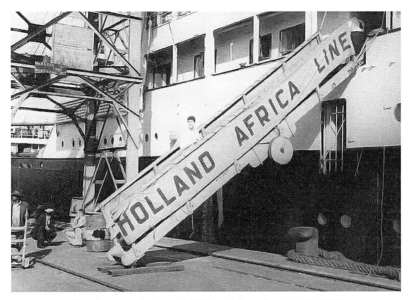

On the gangplank — S.S. Oranjefontein, July 3, 1958

bathroom with the next cabin. Someone sent us an enormous bouquet of flowers and there was a bottle of champagne in an ice bucket filled with melting ice. We didn't see any lounges or dining areas. An announcement came over the loud speaker for guests to return to the upper deck, so everyone hustled back up the narrow stairs into the sunshine. For the next hour or so we wandered around the deck amongst all the other passengers and guests.

I climbed up a ladder on a huge air vent and swung by my gloved hand, laughing with everyone. Lots of pictures were taken, the music blared over the loud speaker and it all seemed very jovial and fun. Then the ships foghorn blasted three short blasts. The captain announced over the loud speaker that all

Wearing my newly sewn dress on the ship

visitors must leave the ship and my heart dropped like a ton of rocks. I looked at Mom and Dad and ran into their arms and they held me ever so tight. Everyone was shouting goodbyes at us one last time.

Michael began taking a movie and we tried to smile into the sun as I blotted the tears from my eyes. I kissed and hugged my Aunt Dolly and Aunt Vida, then some of my friends and my three sisters, one at a time. They were bawling so hard I couldn't hold it back any longer. We stood so still, the four of us girls, clutched together. "Come on kids," Mom said, "it's time to let your Dad and I say goodbye." They held Boris tight and Dad shook his hand. "Be good to my girl hey Boris. Look after her now." He turned to me. "Hell Doff, we're going to miss you kid. Write to us often." His voice shook. I had never seen him that way, his face contorted with sadness as he struggled to control his emotions. "Sorry Doff, you'll understand if I cry won't you?" I couldn't even speak. The lump in my throat was so huge I thought I would choke. Mom put her arms around me and I bawled into her shoulder making her dress all wet. We couldn't say anything.

They walked away reluctant, waving pathetically and I followed them to the gangway. I clutched Boris's hand in mine and squeezed it tight. But it didn't feel very comforting standing there, the two of us, all alone. We stood against the railing and looked down as Mom and Dad stepped off the gangway and the natives began to push it away from the ship. The crew handed out streamers and we threw them down below and the crowd caught them up so we were still connected. Then the PA system blared out "Auf Wiedersehen" (goodbye in German) and the ship began to inch away from the jetty. I waved furiously to Mom and Dad, my sisters and all our friends and they waved back. Slowly the ship left the quay and the streamers broke and fell into the water. We looked over the side at them dangling in the breeze. We waved and everyone looked smaller. We couldn't make them out anymore but we still waved. Everybody kept waving and the music played sadly on. I looked at Boris and buried my face in his sleeve and sobbed. I couldn't see Mom and Dad anymore, only the Durban skyline getting smaller and smaller until it slowly disappeared.

Boris and I — S.S. Oranjefontein to America 1958

❖ POSTSCRIPT ❖

We only make love in the dark now. When we feel our warm bodies together we are young again. I lie with my head against his chest, listening to his heart beat, his arm around me, caressing me softly. There are no wrinkles, just a vital man I have loved and cherished for a long, long time. With a tender kiss, a bit of the old wild passion stirs every now and then.

"I love you Babe," I whisper.

"I love you too." He bites my neck gently.

We make an effort to say it often. I lie still and stare at the ceiling. I can't remember when he wasn't by my side. His gentle snore distracts me and I feel his warmth again, thanking God he is still here beside me. Time is precious. I don't want this to end so I cuddle up close again.

— Dorothy Ralphs, 2016

Drakensberg Mountains, South Africa

❖ GLOSSARY ❖

Coloreds   of mixed blood, lighter skinned than natives

Natives   indigenous black people

Zulu

Baas   Boss

Beshu   covering made from a square of cowhide hanging at the back and fronds in front made of circles of hide threaded onto a strip of leather

Dankie dankie, hamba gashli   Thank you thank you, go carefully or safely

Hamba, hamba mena sabenza   Go away, I'm working

How, Baas, gunjani wena?   Hello Boss, how are you?

How Misses, wena hamba   Oh Misses, you are going away

How, mnigi   a lot or very

Kia   a room at the bottom of the garden for native servants of white South Africans

Knobkerrie   walking stick with a large round knob at one end

Kraal   a windowless round hut with one door made of low mud walls. It has a thatched roof with a hole in the ceiling to allow smoke from the fire to escape.

Legevan   water lizard

Maas   sour milk

Mnige sheesa   very hot

Mooty   medicine

Nkosazanas   young ladies

Numbies   breasts

Put lo lappa   put that there
Putu balls   made from cooked corn meal
Shongalolas   African millipedes
Umfaan   an unmarried black boy
Wena booga mena?   Do you see me?

Zulu Names

Bhekizizwe (Begiswe)   Look after the Nation
Jabulile   She is happy
Sibongile   We are thankful

Afrikaans

Boeties   derogatory term used by English speaking people for Afrikaners
Doek   headscarf
Duiwe   doves
Ek sal jou 'Groenland' naam   I will call you Greenland
Groenland hier is jou plek   Greenland here is your place
Is ye sik?   Are you sick?
Kaffir lovers   a white person who has empathy for blacks
Mondeling   telling a story orally
Nee meneer   No sir
Nie-Blankes   Non-whites
Rooineks   derogatory term for English speaking people
Sit klas   Sit class
Sommer   simply
Wat is jou naam?   What is your name?

Terms / Expressions

A cut down   incision for intravenous drip

Bio or bioscope   the movies

Duty room   nurses' office

Farthing   a quarter of an old penny

Swatting   studying

The berg   Drakensberg Mountains

❖ PHOTOGRAPHS ❖

PHOTOGRAPHS

This book is typeset in Sabon, designed by Jan Tschihold.
Display type is ITC Berranger Hand and Lithos.